The Architecture
of the Glyptotek

THE ARCHITECTURE OF THE GLYPTOTEK

Glyptoteket

Strandberg Publishing

Gertrud Hvidberg-Hansen

THE GLYPTOTEK

An Architectural Oasis in Copenhagen

"I did not want to build an ordinary museum. I wanted to erect a temple to beauty where art could speak to everyone."
—Founder of the Glyptotek Carl Jacobsen's inaugural speech, 1 May 1897

The Glyptotek's buildings are the museum's largest work of art, a monument in the heart of Copenhagen and source of pride and identity for the city and its people. Since its inauguration in 1897 the museum has provided the setting for unique collections from antiquity, 19th-century Danish and French sculpture, and spectacular art exhibitions. All thanks to the museum's founders, Carl Jacobsen (1842–1914) and Ottilia Jacobsen (1854–1903). The brewer Carl Jacobsen's vision was to "erect a temple to beauty where art could speak to everyone". It is this vision that has made the Glyptotek one of Europe's leading art institutions in its field and one of Copenhagen's leading tourist attractions – a living, breathing museum with around half a million annual visitors from Denmark and abroad.

The Glyptotek is first and foremost a sculpture museum. The name Glyptotek is a compound of the Greek word *glyptos* (engraving or carving) and *theke* (storeroom or repository). The word was invented in 1815 for the Glyptothek in Munich to describe a sculpture collection and was the perfect fit for Carl Jacobsen's vision. The Glyptotek has been a collector's museum since its inception, a museum where a collector's passion for sculpture and interest in the aesthetics of its presentation prevailed over the museal and didactic principles guiding many other major public museums created during the 19th and 20th centuries.

A Harmonious Whole
Visitors to the Glyptotek move through the rich multifaceted history of its architecture in a museum that unites the art of building, sculpture, painting and craftmanship. The sensory experience of light, space and colour and their relationship to the works on display have shaped the building, creating a unique aesthetic framework. The goal from the beginning was to create an oasis, a haven in the city that expanded the senses and intellect through sublime art and architecture.

The architecture of the Glyptotek is the perfect example of a museum where form and content unite to create a harmonious whole, and where the art it contains is mirrored in its buildings. Every part of the building, from the complex as a whole to the smallest detail, relates visually and stylistically to the art the buildings were custom-made to house. This is a relationship that goes both ways, because the museum's distinctive architecture also means the individual works of art are experienced in dialogue with their physical surroundings. Seeing a sculpture at the Glyptotek cannot be separated from the colours, light, materials and ornamentation surrounding it. They become part of the artwork. Every dimension of a sculpture – its period, provenance, style, scale, composition, surface, materiality and sensory impact – occurs in a reciprocal relationship with the building that surrounds it. For the Glyptotek is not just a building – a neutral white cube or black box bowing down to works of art indisputably centre stage. On the contrary, it is a rich monumental work of art in its own right, constantly adding new levels and layers of experience and interpretation to the works in the museum's collections.

The Architectural History of the Glyptotek
The buildings at the Glyptotek have a long and fascinating history. From 1897 to 2006 leading Danish architects have designed buildings for the museum. The first building was completed in 1897 and designed by Vilhelm Dahlerup (1836–1907). He also designed the Winter Garden, although this was not built until 1906. His museum building was made to house 19th-century French and Danish sculpture. Works by leading French sculptors such as Henri-Michel-Antoine Chapu (1833–1891), Eugène Delaplanche (1836–1891), Paul Dubois (1829–1905) and Jean Gautherin (1840–1890) and their Danish colleagues Hermann Ernst Freund (1786–1840), Herman Wilhelm Bissen (1798–1868), Jens Adolf Jerichau (1816–1883) and Stephan Sinding (1846–1922) were to be exhibited in the building, where they can still be seen today.

The Glyptotek has been extended several times to accommodate its growing collections and new facilities for visitors and staff. First and foremost, Danish architect Hack Kampmann's (1856–1920) extension for the Antiquities Collection from 1906, then Henning Larsen's (1925–2013) 1996 extension. The latter was built to exhibit the museum's outstanding collection of French painting, most of it acquired after

Relief on the façade of Hack Kampmann's
building representing the founders of
the Glyptotek, Carl and Ottilia Jacobsen,
dressed in ancient robes. Made by Danish
sculptor Carl Aarsleff, 1906.

Galleries 43–44 of Vilhelm Dahlerup's
building with an exhibition of Danish and
French sculpture including bronze sculp-
tures by French sculptor Paul Dubois:
Saint John the Baptist as a Child, 1861 (l)
Florentine Singer, 1865 (r).

1914, when Carl Jacobsen's son Helge Jacobsen (1882–1946) became director of the Glyptotek and chair of the New Carlsberg Foundation. Many parts of the museum stand as they did when first built, but there have also been major renovations and extensions over the years. Most of the historical interior still has its original ornamentation, materials and constructions, all carefully and regularly maintained. Despite changes made to improve the museum's exhibition and visitor facilities, the building remains largely intact. Due to its architectural and cultural-historical significance and its role in its urban surroundings the Glyptotek was classified as a listed building in 1982, and there are now strict rules guiding the museum's restorations and preservation work in order to retain the museum's unique architectural qualities.

A Sense for Art and Architecture

Even though most visitors probably experience the Glyptotek as a single building, its different stages of construction testify to the museum's long architectural history, explored in all its diversity and complexity in this book. The museum complex juxtaposes different styles of architecture from different periods, combining references to the international history of architecture and the period's purpose-built museum architecture. From the outside the museum buildings stand as a single monolithic structure: severe and impenetrable with imposing red brick façades and few points of entry. As such, the museum may seem unwelcoming from the outside, but as soon as you cross the patterned forecourt and step up to the main entrance on Dante's Square it opens its arms and doors to a profusion of art, light and opulent galleries. The Glyptotek comes to life when you cross its threshold: inviting, magical, labyrinthine – full of colour and light. Seductive, some might say. Dahlerup's and Kampmann's buildings are packed with the personality of the museum's founder and benefactor. Virtually every inch of the interior and exterior, every symbol and inscription, express the personal and artistic vision of the brewer Carl Jacobsen. The entire museum has been created with an eye for its overall aesthetic effect and the visual and spatial orchestration of the visitor's experience of art and architecture. Pleasure and enlightenment go hand in hand at the Glyptotek, a monument to new democratic cultural ideals in Denmark at the end of the 19th century with their emphasis on learning through

the senses and understanding through the body. This vision still guides every aspect of life at the museum: our collections, exhibitions, research and how we communicate with visitors and the outside world. Today the Glyptotek operates with a cultural horizon embracing the broad spectrum of the humanities that has shaped it. Based on expertise and research the museum's exhibitions still speak to the senses and intellect in equal measure.

That the Glyptotek was originally purpose-built as an art museum to house a well-defined, high-profile collection is central. The collection had been created over the years since 1874, when Carl Jacobsen purchased his first sculpture, after which it grew apace. In 1882 he built the first of what would become a series of galleries to exhibit the collection as an extension to his and Ottilia Jacobsen's family home. The couple opened their collection to the public, and the galleries, designed by Vilhelm Dahlerup and Hack Kampmann, have gone down in Danish history as the first Glyptotek. Kampmann also designed a villa for Carl and Ottilia Jacobsen connected to the galleries. These buildings laid the seed for the Glyptotek on Dante's Square. There are obvious links between the style and architecture of the first Glyptotek, the architecture at the New Carlsberg brewery site in Valby, and the Glyptotek we know today.

The Atmosphere

A multitude of layers of meaning are one of the things that makes the Glyptotek unique. The museum is famous for its special atmosphere, the immaterial qualities that make the presence of history felt. It is these qualities that make the museum irreplaceable cultural heritage, but also vulnerable cultural heritage. The museum's architecture risks losing its essential qualities if they are not protected, but museum buildings also have to accommodate change. Museums are not static entities; they have to adapt to constantly changing needs in museum life, including exhibitions, public programmes, educational activities and visitor facilities. Over the years many museums, including the Glyptotek, have had to balance the need to develop as modern museums with the need to preserve buildings and the sense of authenticity that generates a museum's atmosphere. Achieving this balance requires in-depth knowledge of the buildings and their history. Which is why the Glyptotek's research on the history of the museum's architecture and buildings is so crucial, as is sharing the knowledge it generates. Knowing more about what can be seen and what is hidden behind the façades of the museum can enhance the way visitors experience its buildings, but an awareness of its unique qualities is equally key when making changes to the buildings. Here, more than 125 years after the first museum building opened to the public, we need to ask what it takes to preserve the atmosphere and spirit of the Glyptotek – the essence of the museum. How to preserve its buildings at the same time as accommodating the new needs and goals that have emerged since it first opened.

Museums today are so much more than displays of rare and beautiful objects for a select audience. The number of people who visit the Glyptotek has multiplied over the years, and they have different needs in terms of communication, educational activities, the café, the museum shop and visitors' facilities. There is also a lot of activity behind the scenes far from public view: maintenance and preservation, storage facilities and exhibition technology, all in a listed historical building. The museum's buildings demand expertise and care, something to which this book and the research on the museum's architectural history behind it – the construction and building techniques, the archives and physical traces – are key. It marks a new chapter in the rich history of the Glyptotek, and the first dedicated to its architecture. It is a chapter that can offer valuable insight into one of the most ambitious museum buildings in Danish history, and an invaluable basis for the future development of the museum.

An Architectural Tour

"Architecture is my greatest passion," as Carl Jacobsen wrote in a letter to the Danish industrial historian Camillus Nyrop in 1894. Carl Jacobsen knew what he wanted with his buildings, and his passionate interest in and knowledge about architecture have been decisive in creating the opulence and quality seen everywhere you look at the Glyptotek.

This book takes the reader on a tour of the 25,000 square metres of a museum complex on several floors, a place many see as a treasure trove looking out onto the world, but also back in time at the art and architecture of different historical periods. The first building designed by Vilhelm Dahlerup is in the style of the Venetian Renaissance but also references iconic museums built during the second half of the 19th

century in cities like Berlin, Vienna, Paris and London. The long flights of stairs and balconies, the lines of perspective and illusionistic effects all help create a theatrical Neo-Baroque setting full of surprises. The Winter Garden forms the pivotal point between the different parts of the museum and its various collections and is both one of the period's most remarkable and technically advanced buildings of glass and steel and a unique green oasis where people can find respite from city life among its plants and winding paths. Visitors to the museum might lose their way among the many floors and galleries of the museum, but they can always find their way back to the Winter Garden. Seen from the outside the glass dome of the Winter Garden is also one of the Glyptotek's most distinctive architectural features, a landmark among the spires and towers of the Copenhagen skyline.

Hack Kampmann's extension marked an entirely new departure for the museum: a building made to house outstanding collections of Egyptian, Greek, Roman, Palmyrene and Etruscan art in simple, symmetrical sequences of daylit galleries inspired by the classical art they contain. Of international repute, the museum's Antiquities Collection is in close dialogue with the building, its combination of Danish Art Nouveau and Nordic National Romanticism underpinning the ornamentation of antiquity.

Henning Larsen's minimalist cubic extension continues the lavish use of marble, daylight and endless staircases of the first architects. As mentioned above, the building was made to exhibit the Glyptotek's French painting collection but is now primarily used for special exhibitions at the museum. At the base of the building a long staircase leads down to a dark tomb-like room of Egyptian grave finds. The building is simple and discrete, its parameters determined by the two buildings that preceded it. It exists entirely within the walls of the museum, invisible from the outside.

A City Catalyst

As Carl Jacobsen said at its opening, the Glyptotek was not to be any "ordinary museum" but a central cultural institution contributing to the benefit of society and the common good as well as the enlightenment of the individual. Architecture and democracy were to go hand in hand. Splendour and opulence were to cultivate a sense of beauty, regardless of any prior knowledge of

Relief in Gallery 44 of Vilhelm Dahlerup's
building representing Carl Jacobsen (l)
and Vilhelm Dahlerup (r). Made by Hans
Carl Christian Lamberg-Petersen in 1897.

Vilhelm Dahlerup's building from 1897 (l)
and Hack Kampmann's building from
1906 (r) seen from Tietgensgade and Tivoli.

the art on display among those who visited. The Glyptotek was and is a vital site of education and aesthetic development, a societal role under-pinned by its location on Dante's Square, where it was a key motor in the development of the area surrounding it. It all began on a remote, swampy building plot on the outskirts of Copenhagen, but with inspiration from other capitals in Europe the area changed rapidly, its large buildings and broad boulevards making it the epitome of turn-of-the-century-modernity. To this day the area's historical public institutions and homes for the bourgeoisie make it one of the most elegant parts of Copenhagen long popular with tourists.

Since its inception the Glyptotek has defined the area of the city that surrounds it. It has two equally monumental main façades: Dahlerup's façade with its sweeping roofs undulating above the long rhythmical building as if mirror-ing the life and movement of the busy street it looks onto, and Kampmann's façade with its steep step pyramid looking onto the museum garden. The garden, which opened in 1908, was designed by Hack Kampmann in collaboration with land-scape architect Edvard Glæsel (1858–1915) and the City of Copenhagen's head gardener Valdemar

Fabricius Hansen (1866–1953). The symmetrical street Stoltenbergsgade forms a clear axis between the garden, the museum and the surrounding city squares and buildings, tracing an invisible line to Christiansborg Palace. The Glyptotek draws the contours of the area around it. The garden and green areas around the museum create a passing distance to the roads on all sides amidst which it stands out as a fertile hothouse for experiencing the beauty of art. As such, the museum and its distinctive architecture symbolised the new ideals for culture, education and urban modernity that emerged at the turn of the century.

Public and private developers and the leading architects of the day shaped the modern capital of Copenhagen with buildings now held to be outstanding examples of the city's histor-ical architecture. The Glyptotek is surrounded by some of the most prominent historicist buildings in the Danish capital, which like the museum itself were built for modern democracy and the common good. These include the Royal Danish Academy of Music, the Royal Danish Academy of Science and Letters, the Palace Hotel, the palatial façade of Tivoli Gardens, the Royal Library, the headquarters of the Royal Mail and Copenhagen

Central Station. Elsewhere in the city this was mirrored in architecture such as the National Gallery of Denmark, the Royal Danish Theatre, the Lake Pavilion and Queen Louise Bridge – all designed by Vilhelm Dahlerup – and just behind the Glyptotek Copenhagen's Neoclassicist police headquarters, of which Hack Kampmann was one of the architects. The many public buildings in the architectural history of Copenhagen are closely linked to the architecture of the Glyptotek, a link rarely made in books or research on Danish architecture. This link is key to understanding the story of the Glyptotek's architecture and its significance in modern urban planning. The story of the museum's buildings is also the story of the Glyptotek as a central Danish institution in the context of broader social developments – a symbol of the modern metropolis, a perspective also explored in this book.

The Glyptotek of the Future

The retrospective focus of the book is key to understanding the significance of the museum and its architecture, but also for the development of the Glyptotek in the future and the challenges it brings. Since opening to the public in 1897 the Glyptotek has been a success story in which new chapters continue to be written. With more than 20 million visitors over the years the museum is inevitably showing signs of wear and tear. Since having 27,000 visitors in 1897 the number of visitors has continued to multiply. From being a museum for Copenhageners, the Glyptotek has become one of Denmark's biggest tourist attractions with steadily increasing visitor numbers.

The Glyptotek's collections have also grown – from a few thousand works at the inauguration in 1897 to circa 10,000 today. The collections are exhibited in the museum's permanent exhibitions, special exhibitions and exhibitions at museums worldwide. They are also a rich source for researchers in many fields. With a collection representative of such valuable cultural heritage the museum faces ever-increasing demands in terms of protection from climate change, theft and fire, as well as conservation. The scope of the Glyptotek's professional and public activities has also grown significantly. In recent years the museum has worked consistently to develop the Glyptotek with special exhibitions, public events and publications for our core audience but also new target groups. In addition to work on the collections and exhibitions, the museum

now has two cafés – in the Winter Garden and on the roof terrace. The number of members of staff has also risen from a handful when the Glyptotek opened in 1897 to around 150 today. All this growth has put increasing pressure on the museum's buildings, which therefore face a much-needed renovation and technical modernisation to ensure that future generations can enjoy it in the same way as those of the past. The new research on the museum's architecture and the history of its buildings represented in this book provides an invaluable basis for the conservation, restoration and technical improvements ahead. All of which are to be done in full knowledge of the rich history of the Glyptotek and the unique qualities the museum is still known for.

Thank You

The Architecture of the Glyptotek has been made possible thanks to the vast number of dedicated people who have made an essential contribution to what will be a key publication on the subject for years to come.

We would like to express our warm thanks to the authors and experts who have contributed essential knowledge and new perspectives on the architecture of the Glyptotek. They are:

Dr Kasper Lægring, art historian, PhD in architecture and holder of a New Carlsberg Foundation scholarship at Aarhus University. As well as his exhaustive article on architecture at the museum, he has also conducted preliminary research on the museum's architectural history; Dr Martin Søberg, art historian, PhD in architecture and senior lecturer at the Royal Danish Academy, and Dr Peter Thule Kristensen, architect, PhD in architecture and professor at the Royal Danish Academy. Their articles explore the subject from the perspective of contemporary international and historicist architecture. We would also like to thank Dr Jakob Ingemann Parby, PhD in history and curator at the Museum of Copenhagen, for his article on turn-of-the-century urban development in Copenhagen in relationship to the Glyptotek.

Several of the articles deal with specific aspects of the museum's architecture. Thanks to architect Birgitte Kleis for her account of the constructions behind the façades of the Glyptotek and the technical breakthroughs they involved, as well as conservators Anne Jonstrup Simonsen and Kristina Lindholdt from Københavns Konservator for their contribution on the museum's original colour scheme. Their article is based on extensive architectural paint research in Dahlerup's and Kampmann's buildings, and the subsequent restoration of the original colours in large parts of Dahlerup's building to mark the 125th anniversary of its inauguration in 2022. Architect Ida Carnera and Vibeke Cristofoli, analyst, dramatist and mosaic graduate of Scuola Mosaicisti del Friuli in Italy, are thanked for their article on the mosaic and terrazzo floors in Kampmann's building and the fascinating story of the links between the mosaic traditions of Friuli and major Copenhagen landmarks. Both authors have a close relationship to the Italian mosaicists who have worked in Denmark for generations.

As well as longer research-based articles, the book also includes a series of shorter texts on experiences of the museum by artists and architects with a close relationship to the Glyptotek. We would like to thank author and architect Eva Tind, architect and professor of architectural cultural heritage at Aarhus School of Architecture Mogens A. Morgen, and visual artists Jesper Christiansen, Sif Itona Westerberg and Sophia Kalkau for their personal and poetic observations and reflections on the museum's buildings. Finally, we would like to express our gratitude to Claus Grønne, archivist at the New Carlsberg Foundation, for his unstinting efforts in sourcing archival material in connection with the museum's research and his illustrated timeline of the origins of the Glyptotek.

None of these contributions would reach an international readership without translation. We would like to thank Jane Rowley for her contribution – editorial and linguistic – to the English edition of the publication.

Anders Sune Berg has photographed all the interiors and exteriors of the Glyptotek for the book, as well as the museum garden. A major assignment demanding sensitivity to the changing seasons to convey the sensory experience of visiting the Glyptotek, a museum bathed in natural light. This skill and sensitivity have been crucial to presenting the architecture of the Glyptotek at its very best in book form.

The book is published in collaboration with Strandberg Publishing and the graphic design is by Cecilie Nellemann and Stefan Thorsteinsson of Studio Atlant. We thank them all for a fine collaboration. Thanks too to the staff at the Danish Art Library for their assistance with illustrations.

This book could not have been realised without the expertise of architectural historian Dr Jannie Rosenberg Bendsen, PhD, and her co-editor Anna Manly, curator at the Glyptotek, whose publication experience and professionalism have been an invaluable contribution to the museum fulfilling its ambitions for a book on the Glyptotek's architecture. Together they have also selected the images in the book, ensuring that the presentation of the monumental buildings and many archival documents behind its creation match the museum itself in aesthetics and quality. They are also the authors of the book's timeline and biographies. Thanks also to Kasper Riisholt, Head of Exhibitions at the Glyptotek, for his contribution to the production of the publication.

Thanks too to architect Agnes Johansson of Rørbæk & Møller Architects, who conducted the extensive archival research that has produced a wealth of information and documentation on the Glyptotek's buildings, providing an essential starting point for any research on their history.

We would also like to thank Arne Høi, Head of Institute at the Royal Academy, who together with architectural historian and contributor to this publication Martin Søberg provided expert advice during the early stages of research on the museum's architecture and invaluable input on the themes of this book.

We are very thankful for the funding we have received to make the publication of this book possible. For many years people have been asking us to make a book on the Glyptotek's architecture. That we have been able to do so, and to make an exhibition on the same theme, is thanks to the generous support of the following foundations:

The Augustinus Foundation
Aage og Johanne Louis-Hansens Fond
The New Carlsberg Foundation
Knud Højgaards Fond
Dreyers Fond

The Glyptotek at the end of the 1800s
without the dome of the Winter Garden
or Hack Kampmann's extension, which
was inaugurated in 1906 to house
the museum's Antiquities Collection.

LABOREMVS · PRO · PATRIA

↙ BILLETTER TICKETS

BILLETTER TICKETS ↘

Claus Grønne

THE ORIGINS OF THE GLYPTOTEK

An Illustrated Timeline

The Glyptotek was founded by Carl Jacobsen and his wife Ottilia Jacobsen. Carl Jacobsen was the owner and director of the New Carlsberg brewery in Valby. In 1902 the couple entrusted New Carlsberg to the Carlsberg Foundation, establishing the New Carlsberg Foundation at the same time. From 1906 Carl Jacobsen was director of the Carlsberg brewery, founded in 1847 by his father, J.C. Jacobsen, and the New Carlsberg brewery. The breweries merged under the name Carlsberg Breweries.[1]

As well as being a successful businessman Carl Jacobsen was highly passionate and knowledgeable about art and architecture. Classical antiquity and contemporary French and Danish art were his main interests. They were at the heart of his prolific collecting and therefore formed the core of the Glyptotek's collections.

Carl and Ottilia Jacobsen initially exhibited part of their collection in a large room accessed directly from their home in the grounds of the brewery in Valby. Even then Carl Jacobsen started calling the art collection he put on display in Valby 'the Glyptotek', a collection the couple opened to the public in 1882.

After a fire at Christiansborg Palace on 3 October 1884, which destroyed almost the entire royal sculpture collection, Carl and Ottilia Jacobsen, inspired by the example of Ludwig I of Bavaria's Glyptothek in Munich, offered to donate their collection to the people of Denmark. The donation was conditional on Copenhagen City Council providing a suitable plot for a museum to house it and the council and government each paying half of the cost of its construction.

In founding the Glyptotek Carl Jacobsen fulfilled his vision of making what he described as "a temple to beauty where art could speak to everyone", a public art collection exhibited in a unique architectural setting where the senses, beauty, knowledge and education could go hand in hand and improve the life of society and the individual alike. The first building of the Glyptotek, designed by Danish architect Vilhelm Dahlerup to house the French and Danish sculpture collection, was inaugurated on 1 May 1897. The Winter Garden Dahlerup also designed and the extension built for the Antiquities Collection designed by Danish architect Hack Kampmann opened on 27 June 1906. This was preceded by the series of events below charting the origins of the Glyptotek up to the opening of Kampmann's building in 1906.[2]

1880

Drawing of Gammel Bakkegård in Valby made after 1885 with bronzes in front and the oldest Glyptotek buildings in the background to the left.[3]

The sculpture to the left is Swedish sculptor Johan Börjeson's *The Swimmer*, which now stands on Langelinie quay in Copenhagen. The sculpture in the middle is a monument to the Danish–German painter Asmus Jacob Carstens by Danish sculptor Theobald Stein, now in the museum garden at the Glyptotek. The one to the right is a bronze copy of the Laocoön Group. Carl Jacobsen bought the property in 1880, and it was his and Ottilia Jacobsen's family home until 1890. The collection started here, with a few select objects to decorate their home. In the late 1870s

Carl Jacobsen's interest in art grew, and from 1879 he started collecting more systematically, creating the foundations for the collections at the Glyptotek.

Gammel Bakkegård was demolished in 1890 after several of Carl and Ottilia Jacobsen's children had died in the old house. In a letter to German archaeologist Wolfgang Helbig dated 24 June 1890, Carl Jacobsen writes that he had the house demolished on the advice of his doctor because it was infected with the scarlet fever that had cost the life of his nine-year-old son Alf.[4] In its place a large villa designed by Hack Kampmann was completed in 1892.

On 5 November 1882 the Jacobsens opened the Glyptotek in Valby to the public. It was open every Sunday, and all income from ticket sales went directly to the local day nursery in Valby.

This photograph from 1884 is the oldest of the old Glyptotek in Valby known to exist.[5] To the far left is the Rayet head from the 6th century BCE, the first Classical Greek sculpture purchased by Carl Jacobsen in 1879. In the middle is the Roman Casali sarcophagus from the 2nd century CE, and to the right of that a Roman grave altar from the same century also purchased from the Casali Collection in Rome in 1884. In front of the sarcophagus is a row of tomb sculptures from the desert city of Palmyra in Syria, and to the far right a copy of *Discobolus* by the Greek sculptor Myron.

1883–1884

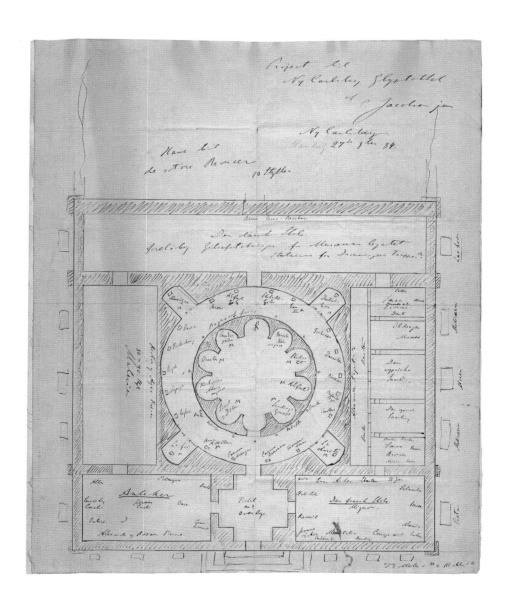

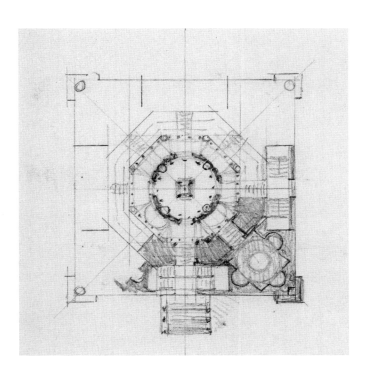

In October 1884 Carl Jacobsen presented his ideas for a Glyptotek in Copenhagen. He had been inspired by the design of architect Vilhelm Dahlerup's proposal for a sepulchral monument to Victor Emmanuel II of Italy in an exhibition at Charlottenborg.[6] To the left Dahlerup's monument proposal and to the right Carl Jacobsen's plan for the Glyptotek.[7]

On 25 November 1884 Carl Jacobsen sent his proposal for a new, larger Glyptotek he wanted to build in Copenhagen to Dahlerup. He asked Dahlerup to develop the sketch, telling him he had informed the Mayor of Copenhagen H.N. Hansen of his plans to donate his collection to the people of Denmark.[8]

1885

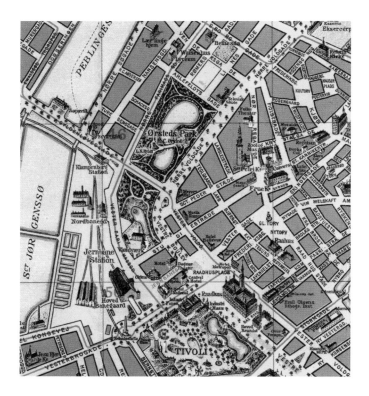

Carl Jacobsen lays out his plans in a letter dated 19 February 1885 to P.V. Grove, editor of the newspaper *Dagbladet*. He describes the nature and scope of the donation he and Ottilia Jacobsen intend to make to the people of Denmark, on condition that Copenhagen City Council provide a suitable building plot and the council and government contribute a million Danish crowns towards building the museum. Carl Jacobsen stresses that the plan is not to be made public before Mayor Hansen has issued an official statement of support.[9]

On 24 February 1885 Mayor Hansen replies to Carl Jacobsen's verbal request to build a Glyptotek in Copenhagen. He suggests locating the museum in Aborre Park.[10]

This section of a map of Copenhagen from 1897 shows Aborre Park below Ørsted Park, separated by Gyldenløvesgade. Aborre Park was established in 1886 but razed again in 1910 to clear a path for railway tracks in the city.

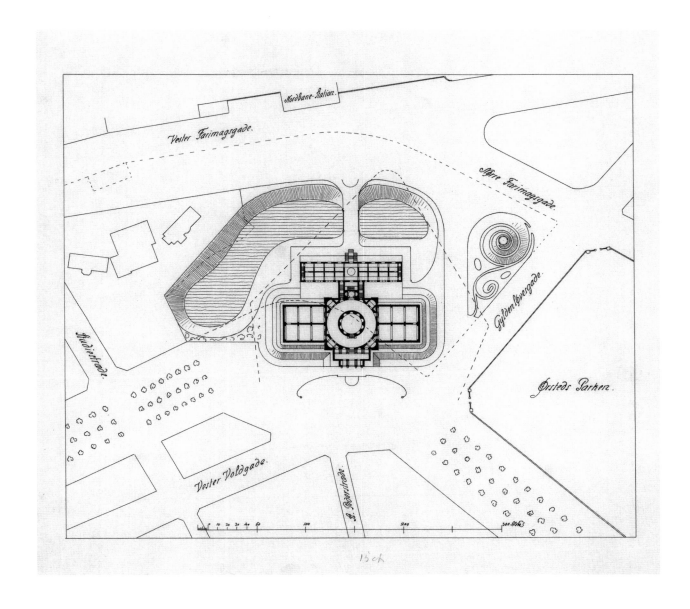

Vilhelm Dahlerup's proposal for the Glyptotek in
Aborre Park, 1888.[11]

We do not know how Carl Jacobsen reacted
to Mayor Hansen's offer of a building plot in the
park. In two letters to Vilhelm Dahlerup from
August and September 1885, however, Carl Jacobsen mentions Dahlerup's proposal for the location
as a project he had never asked him to work on.[12]

In a four-page letter dated 19 May 1885 Carl
Jacobsen writes to the Ministry for Church and
Educational Affairs requesting permission to take
casts of Thorvaldsen's friezes on Copenhagen
Cathedral for the new Glyptotek in Copenhagen
he is negotiating with the city council. The letter
is early evidence of Carl Jacobsen's plans.[13]

1888

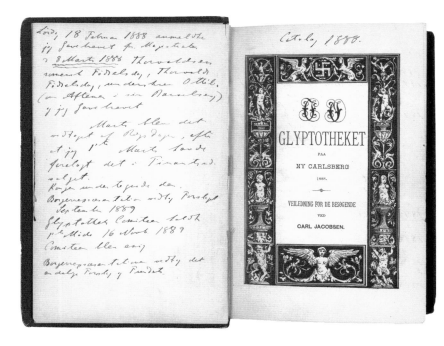

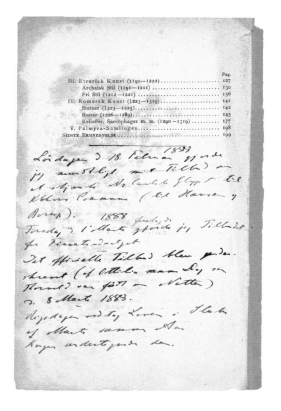

On a page of his own copy of the 1889 catalogue of his collection Carl Jacobsen wrote
that on 18 February 1888 he presented his plans
to the Copenhagen mayors H.N. Hansen and
L.C. Borup. On Thursday, 1 March he presented
his offer to the Committee of Public Accounts.
The deed of gift was signed on 8 March by Carl
and Ottilia Jacobsen, who had given birth to their
son Thorvald in the early hours of that morning.
The baby was named after the Danish sculptor
Bertel Thorvaldsen, who arrived in Rome on 8
March 1797 and subsequently celebrated the date
as his 'Roman birthday'. At the bottom of the page
Carl Jacobsen notes that parliament passed a law
at the end of March 1888 approving a state grant
to build the museum and the deed of gift, after
which it was signed by the king.[14]

Carl Jacobsen recorded key events of 1888 inside
the cover of his own personal copy of the catalogue of the Glyptotek's collection. On 18 February
he notified the City Council Executive, after which
he and Ottilia Jacobsen signed the deed of gift
itself. On the following pages he added architect
Osvald Rosendahl Langballe's timeline from the
beginning of construction on 7 July 1888 to the
opening in 1897. Langballe was the Glyptotek's
on-site architect during the construction of
Dahlerup's building and the museum's architectural advisor after Dahlerup's death in 1907.[15]

Lov

Nr. 63.
5te
April.

om

et Tilſkud af Statskaſſen til Opførelſe af en Bygning for Ny Carlsberg
Glyptothek*).

Vi Chriſtian den Niende, af Guds Naade Konge til Danmark,
de Venders og Gothers, Hertug til Slesvig, Holſten, Stormarn, Ditmarſken,
Lauenborg og Oldenborg,

Gjøre vitterligt: Rigsdagen har vedtaget og Vi ved Vort Samtykke ſtadfæſtet følgende Lov:

§ 1.

Til Opførelſe af en Bygning for Ny Carlsberg Glyptothek, der af Brygger Carl
Jacobſen og Huſtru Ottilie Jacobſen er tilbudt ſom Gave til Staten og Kjøbenhavns
Kommune i Forening, kan af Statskaſſen anvendes et Beløb paa 500,000 Kr., at ud-
betale i Løbet af 5 Aar, under Forudſætning af, at Kommunen tilſkyder en Sum af
ſamme Størrelſe ſamt yder den til Bygningen fornødne Grund.

§ 2.

Ny Carlsberg Glyptothek oprettes ſom en ſelvſtændig Stiftelſe; Miniſteriet for
Kirke- og Underviisningsvæſenet bemyndiges til paa Statens Vegne efter Forhandling
med Kjøbenhavns Kommunalbeſtyrelſe at træffe den nærmere Ordning angaaende Byg-
ningens Opførelſe og Glyptotheksbeſtyrelſens Sammenſætning i Overensſtemmelſe med de
af Giverne herom trufne Beſtemmelſer.

Hvorefter alle Vedkommende ſig have at rette.

Givet paa Amalienborg, den 5te April 1888.

Under Vor Kongelige Haand og Segl.

Christian R.

(L. S.)

J. F. Scavenius.

*) Udfærdiget gjennem Miniſteriet for Kirke- og Underviisningsvæſenet. Se Rigsdagstidenden for
1887—88: Folketh. Tid. Sp. 4890—91, 5019—20, 5061—64, 5100; Landſth. Tid. Sp.
; Till. A. Sp. 3029; Till. C. Sp. 793—94.
Nr. 63. Lov af 5. April om Tilſk. af Statsk. til Opf. af en Bygn for Ny Carlsb. Glyptothek.

GAVEBREV AF 8. MARTS 1888 FRA BRYGGER CARL JACOBSEN OG HUTSRU OTTILIA JACOBSEN

Efterat det af os for lidt over fem Aar siden stiftede »Ny Carlsberg Glyptotek«
har udviklet sig til at blive et af Europas betydeligste Sculpturmuseer, er det af
Vigtighed, at det bevares som Heelhed og ikke er udsat for de Omskiftelser, som
ere private Samlingers hyppige Lod, at splittes eller ødelægges ved Vanrøgt, Brand-
skade eller anden Molest.

Heller ikke bør Adgangen være afhængig af en privat Eiermands Forgodtbefin-
dende, ligesom ogsaa Samlingen bør være lettere tilgjængelig end den ifølge Ny
Carlsbergs Beliggenhed nu er.

Da Glyptoteket netop indeholder det meste og det bedste af hvad vort Lands
Billedhuggerkunst har frembragt efter Thorvaldsens Impuls, og saaledes repræ-
senterer en Periode, hvor vort Land indtog en fremragende Plads i Europas Sculp-
turs Historie, særlig ved Bissens og Jerichaus Værker, og da det tillige indeholder
det, som vi ellers her i Landet savne, en Repræsentation baade af antik Kunst og
af Udlandets store Frembringelser i Nutiden, kunne vi kun ønske, at det maa faae
sin endelige Plads i Danmarks Hovedstad, og vi tilbyde det da herved som Gave
til vort Fædreland.

Det er vor Forudsætning, at Staden Kjøbenhavn afgiver den nødvendige Byggegrund, og at Byen og Staten hver for sig deeltage med Halvdeelen af den til Opførelse af en passende Bygning nødvendige Sum, ialt en Million Kroner.

Saafremt ovennævnte Tilbud maatte blive modtaget, ville vi oprette neden-
staaende Fundats, paa hvilken der til sin Tid vil være at søge allerhøieste Stad-
fæstelse.

Denne Fundats bør dog yderligere udarbeides, og vi henstille navnlig til Re-
gjeringens og Kommunalbestyrelsens Afgjørelse at fastsætte den Ordning af Valget
af Glyptoteksbestyrelsens Formand som maatte findes rettest, ligesom vi ikke
absolut fastholde den i Fundatsudkastets § 2 trufne Bestemmelse om en kvalifice-
ret Adgang for en af vore Sønner til at indtræde i Bestyrelsen.

OTTILIA JACOBSEN.   CARL JACOBSEN.

Ny Carlsberg, den 8. Marts 1888.

The printed deed of gift
of 8 March 1888.[16]

The construction of the Glyptotek in Copenhagen
was approved by law on 5 April 1888. Here the law
is reprinted in *Lovtidende*, the daily register of
laws and statues passed by parliament. The first
article confirms a state grant of 500,000 Danish
crowns to build the Glyptotek on condition that
Copenhagen City Council provides the same sum
and a building plot for the museum.[17]

Glyptothekets Overgang til Kjøbenhavn.

At the end of May Mayor Hansen sent points the council committee wanted to address to Carl Jacobsen. Progress was slow because no agreement could be reached on the location of the museum. Since 1885 four different locations had been suggested. Dahlerup had drawn up plans for them all. Dahlerup's first proposal from 1884/1885 was for a location between Dagmar Theatre and Vester Voldgade (1). In 1885 H.N. Hansen suggested locating the museum on the hill in Aborre Park (2) and later at present-day Israel Square facing Ørsted Park (3). The location eventually agreed upon was across the road from Tivoli Gardens (4). Panorama of Copenhagen from 1897 with proposed sites for the Glyptotek marked.[18]

Shortly after the construction of the Glyptotek in Copenhagen was approved by parliament in 1888 people started imagining statues marching from Valby to the city. Illustration from *Blæksprutten*, 1888.[19]

1889

On 23 September the city council approved the allocation of funding for the Glyptotek in Copenhagen and a plot next to Tivoli Gardens to build the museum.

The city council appointed a committee to supervise the board and building of the Glyptotek. The members of the committee, which was active from 1890 to 1897, were Carl Jacobsen, A.P. Weis, A. Asmussen, P. Koch and H.N. Hansen. Here they are shown with architect Vilhelm Dahlerup (second from right) in Julius Paulsen's painting *The Committee Appointed to Approve and Manage the Construction of the Glyptotek*, 1905.[20]

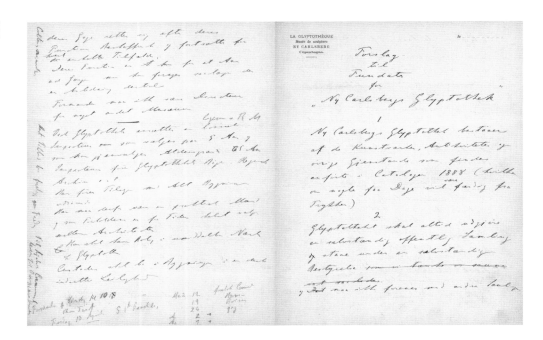

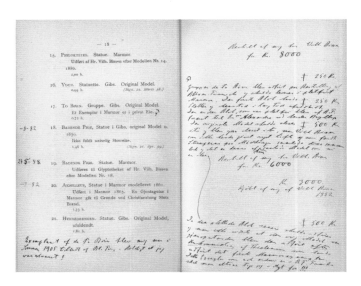

Over the years that followed the value of the Glyptotek's collection was frequently debated at city council meetings. The opposition questioned whether its value corresponded to a million Danish crowns and a valuable building plot in Copenhagen – the conditions of Carl and Ottilia Jacobsen's donation. The deed of gift included the items registered in the catalogue of the Glyptotek's collection from 1888 and 1889. Carl Jacobsen noted the price of many of the artworks in his personal copy of the catalogue from 1888.[21]

Carl Jacobsen's handwritten draft of the Glyptotek's trust deed. The deed was ratified at a meeting of the city council on 21 May 1891.[22]

1897

In April 1897 sculptures from the collection of 19th-century French and Danish art were moved from the old Glyptotek in Valby to the new Glyptotek in Copenhagen.[23]

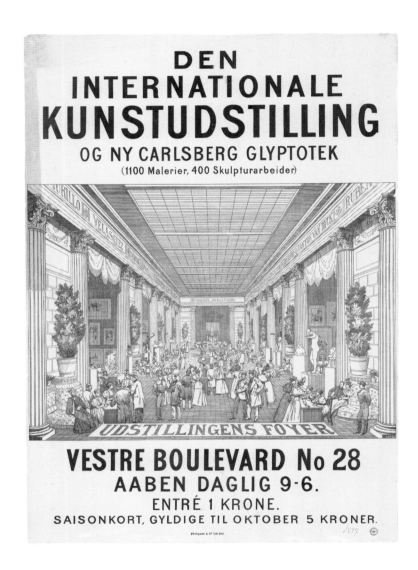

In the spring of 1896 Carl Jacobsen had the idea of opening a large international exhibition at the same time as the inauguration of Dahlerup's Glyptotek building. He presented the idea to the Ministry for Church and Educational Affairs in a letter dated 3 March.[24]

The *International Art Exhibition* was an ambitious, large-scale project. More than 1,200 works of art were brought to Copenhagen from all over Europe for an exhibition that was accompanied by a poster and richly illustrated catalogue. The exhibition was a huge hit. Between 16,000 and 18,000 visitors passed through the turnstiles on the opening day alone.

The temporary building for *The International Art Exhibition* was designed by architect Vilhelm Klein. The building was located between the side wings of Dahlerup's Glyptotek building where the Winter Garden is today. In 1888 Vilhelm Klein had designed the pavilion for *The French Art Exhibition* where Copenhagen City Hall Square is now located. He had also designed buildings for Carl Jacobsen at the brewery in Valby. Vilhelm Klein's ground plan clearly shows a peristyle courtyard for serving refreshments, a precursor to today's museum cafés. The photograph shows the refreshment area with Danish sculptor Hermann Ernst Freund's central fountain sculpture *Boy with Swan*.[25]

Peter Elfelt's photograph of Carl Jacobsen's speech at the inauguration of the Glyptotek and opening of *The International Art Exhibition* on 1 May 1897. The invited guests, including the royal family facing the podium, are seated in the main hall of the temporary exhibition building where the Winter Garden is today.[26]

152
Til Glyptotheket.

Udover Sekler hans Ry vil spænde,
I sene Slægter hvert Barn vil kjende
Ham og hans Værk som sin *A. B. C.* —
Men hvem erindrer da *N. V. D.?*

GAVEBREV AF 14. JANUAR 1899

Siden vi den 8. Marts 1888 tilbød vor daværende Kunstsamling til Oprettelse af Ny Carlsberg Glyptotek i Kjøbenhavn, er det lykkedes undertegnede Carl Jacobsen at samle et Museum for antik Sculptur, som i de forløbne 11 Aar er voxet til at blive en af de betydeligste Samlinger af denne Art, som existerer: »Det gamle Glyptotek paa Ny Carlsberg«.

De samme Motiver, som i sin Tid tilskyndede os til at overdrage den første Samling til Offentlighedens Eie og Opstilling i Kjøbenhavn, ere i endnu høiere Grad tilstede for »det gamle Glyptoteks« Vedkommende: Dels fordi denne Samling er langt større og værdifuldere end den første, dels og særlig, fordi antike Sculpturer jo aldrig kan erstattes, hvis de gaae til grunde, og det overhovedet ikke længere er muligt at bringe dem til Veje.

Vi tilbyde derfor herved at skjænke »Det gamle Glyptotek«, hvis Indhold er angivet i det medfølgende Catalog, samt i et separat Catalog over den ægyptiske Afdeling, som er under Udarbeidelse af Hr. Professor Valdemar Schmidt, til Offentligheden, under den Forudsætning, at det forenes med »Ny Carlsberg Glyptotek« i en ny Tilbygning, tilstrækkelig stor til at optage alle Kunstværkerne, og med eventuelle Forøgelser for Øie, samt at der til denne Bygnings Opførelse af Stat og Kommune ydes en Million Kroner, samt den fornødne Byggegrund.

Vi ville da tillige skjænke »Ny Carlsberg Glyptotek« de os tilhørende dér opstillede Kunstværker.

CARL JACOBSEN.   OTTILIA JACOBSEN.

Ny Carlsberg, den 14. Januar 1899.

Once Carl Jacobsen's wish for a Glyptotek in Copenhagen had been granted, he became a popular subject of caricatures. This 1897 drawing from the satirical paper *Puk* shows Carl Jacobsen, depicted in a similar vein to Michelangelo's *Moses* on the façade of the Glyptotek, sitting with the museum on his lap flanked by herm pillars featuring portraits of architects Vilhelm Dahlerup and Vilhelm Klein. The initials N.V.D in the short verse under the drawing is the painter and art reviewer Niels Vinding Dorph. Dorph had written a critical review of the Glyptotek's architecture in the newspaper *Politiken* the day after the museum opened.

Less than ten years after Carl and Ottilia Jacobsen's deed of gift of 8 March 1888 it was apparent that Dahlerup's building was too small to also house their antiquities collection. On 14 January 1899 they therefore submitted another deed of gift to parliament. The donation was again conditional on the city council and government providing a million Danish crowns between them and the council providing a building plot.

A seven-man committee was appointed. The members were Supreme Court Assessor P.F. Koch (chair) and Councillor of State R. Strøm, both appointed by the Ministry of Culture; Mayor Hansen, appointed by parliament; Member of Parliament Oscar Hansen; Mayor Dybdahl of the City Council Executive; Councillor Klausen from Copenhagen City Council; and Head Clerk A.P. Weis from the board of the Glyptotek. One of the city council's conditions was that three architects be invited to enter a competition to design the extension: Martin Borch, Andreas Clemmensen and Hack Kampmann. The committee chose Kampmann, partly because his proposal included the Central Hall, and partly because future extensions could be built without marring the building's exterior. The committee submitted its report and recommendations in August 1900.[27]

In his 1899 notebook Carl Jacobsen appraised the three architects' proposals for an extension to house his collection of antiquities. He made no secret about being most enthusiastic about Hack Kampmann's ideas, which he considered to be the most original of the three. He also emphasised Kampmann's proposal of skylights in all the galleries, which he considered to provide "by far the best light effects". On the Central Hall he wrote enthusiastically "add to this the magnificent Central Hall, which itself is a work of art of the highest calibre", and the mausoleum, the core of which he describes as a "pure pearl".[28]

Progress was slow. Carl Jacobsen wrote in his book: "We decided to make things run more smoothly by offering one million crowns, partly for the Central Hall, for which funds had yet to be found, and partly for new acquisitions and decorative elements. We were to make the payment, but the money was to be refunded to us or our estate by the New Carlsberg Foundation. That oiled the works and got the ship sailing."[29]

1903

On 12 December 1903 the New Carlsberg Foundation's board of directors approved the construction of a dome above the Winter Garden in accordance with Dahlerup's design.[30]

The Winter Garden and dome were expensive projects, and Carl Jacobsen had to mobilise all available means to build them. The brewer was so insistent that Michael Lunn, the family's lawyer and Carl Jacobsen's friend, warned chair of the Carlsberg Foundation Edvard Holm that Carl Jacobsen's plans could have direct financial consequences for the foundation.[31]

1904

In January 1904 Vilhelm Dahlerup recounted the story behind the Glyptotek's monumental dome to the weekly magazine *Illustreret Tidende* in an article illustrated with a drawing of the dome. Carl Jacobsen had always wanted the Glyptotek to have a dome and winter garden. As mentioned above, his first sketch in 1883 had been inspired by Dahlerup's proposal for a sepulchral monument to Victor Emmanuel II of Italy that also had a dome.[32]

1905

In 1905 the first works from the Jacobsens' collection of antiquities were moved from the old Glyptotek in Valby to the new Glyptotek in Copenhagen. To the left removal men (probably brewery workers) moving the statue of Pan out of Hack Kampmann's loggia on Ny Carlsberg Vej, and to the right a statue of Hermes from the Odescalchi Collection being made ready to be moved from the old Glyptotek.[33]

1906

Vilhelm Dahlerup's Winter Garden and Hack Kampmann's extension housing the Antiquities Collection were inaugurated with pomp and circumstance and the attendance of the royal family on 27 June. The photograph shows Carl Jacobsen holding his inauguration speech on the balcony of the Winter Garden. The speech included his thoughts on the meaning of art and his vision of making art accessible to everyone.[34]

A contemporary caricature shows Carl Jacobsen with a rose in his mouth and his second wife Lili von Kohl surrounded by well-known contemporary figures, including prominent art historian and painter Karl Madsen, architects Vilhelm Klein and Hack Kampmann, sculptor Stephan Sinding, and Carl Jacobsen's friend and advisor Andreas Peter Weis, chair of the board of the Glyptotek and a member of the board of the New Carlsberg Foundation for many years.[35]

Notes

1. The timeline is based on Carl Jacobsen's book *Ny Carlsberg Glyptoteks Tilblivelse* (1906) and a wide range of other sources including correspondence, meeting minutes, drawings, photographs and newspaper articles. A detailed presentation of the creation of the Glyptotek with links to the relevant sources can be found in Carl Jacobsen's Correspondence Archive: https://brevarkivet.ny-carlsbergfondet.dk/en

2. The museum has been renovated and extended several times since the inauguration of Kampmann's building in 1906. In the 1920s administration and library buildings were added, and in 1996 Henning Larsen's extension was built. In 2006 an extensive renovation of parts of the museum was completed, including the excavation and lowering of the floor in the basement below Dahlerup's building to create a large foyer. See also the timeline on pp. 332–333.

3. Jacobsen, Carl: *Ny Carlsberg Glyptoteks Tilblivelse*. Copenhagen: Ny Carlsberg, 1906, p. 15.

4. Carl Jacobsen in a letter to Wolfgang Helbig, 24 June 1890. Carl Jacobsen's Correspondence Archive.

5. The Glyptotek Archive.

6. *Fortegnelse over de ved det kongelige Akademie for de skjønne Kunster offentligt udstillede Kunstværker*. Copenhagen: Thieles Bogtrykkeri, 1883, p. 48 (No. 443). Vilhelm Dahlerup's drawing is held by the Danish National Art Library.

7. The Carlsberg Archive.

8. Letter from Carl Jacobsen to Vilhelm Dahlerup, 25 November 1884. Carl Jacobsen's Correspondence Archive.

9. Letter from Carl Jacobsen to P.V. Grove, 19 February 1885. Carl Jacobsen's Correspondence Archive.

10. Letter from H.N. Hansen to Carl Jacobsen, 24 February 1885. Carl Jacobsen's Correspondence Archive.

11. Danish National Art Library.

12. Letters from Carl Jacobsen to Vilhelm Dahlerup, 29 August and 29 September 1885. Carl Jacobsen's Correspondence Archive.

13. Letter from Carl Jacobsen to the Ministry for Church and Educational Affairs, 19 May 1885. Carl Jacobsen's Correspondence Archive.

14. The Glyptotek Archive.

15. Ibid.

16. Carl Jacobsen's Correspondence Archive.

17. The Royal Danish Library.

18. View of Copenhagen seen from Vesterbro, 1897. Copenhagen City Archives.

19. The Royal Danish Library.

20. Ny Carlsberg Glyptotek.

21. The Glyptotek Archive.

22. Carl Jacobsen's Correspondence Archive.

23. *Illustreret Tidende*, Year 38, No. 27, 4 April 1897, p. 431. The Royal Danish Library.

24. Letter from Carl Jacobsen to the Ministry for Church and Educational Affairs, 3 March 1896. The letter was written by a secretary and signed by Carl Jacobsen. Carl Jacobsen's Correspondence Archive.

25. Danish National Art Library.

26. The Carlsberg Archive.

27. Jacobsen, 1906, p. 58.

28. The Glyptotek Archive.

29. Jacobsen, 1906, p. 60.

30. The New Carlsberg Foundation Archive.

31. Letter from Michael Lunn to Edvard Holm, 17 December 1903. Carl Jacobsen's Correspondence Archive.

32. *Illustreret Tidende*, 1904, p. 266. Vilhelm Dahlerup's drawing is held by the Danish National Art Library.

33. The Carlsberg Archive.

34. The Glyptotek Archive.

35. Drawing by Alfred Schmidt, *Klods-Hans*, 8 July 1906.

Jesper Christiansen

Mondays at the Glyptotek

My mother had enrolled me in Askou-Jensen's drawing school at the Glyptotek. It was the mid 1970s. Frustrated that I had been declared unfit for high school, she had decided it would be a good idea if I had something to keep me occupied during the day, since I apparently had no idea what I wanted to be. One of the few successes I had at school was in 1973, when I won a bank magazine drawing competition because I was good at making flower-power drawings that looked like the cover of The Beatles LP *Yellow Submarine*. I went straight out and spent the 500 DKK cash prize on a Yamaha Western guitar. From that moment on my only dream was to be in a band.

Askou-Jensen taught his classes everywhere at the Glyptotek. In principle we could choose any room we liked and draw whatever we liked. Although our teacher did have some recommendations for new students, and his recommendation for me was to make a gigantic (130 by 80 cm!) charcoal drawing of the bust of Titus in one of the museum's round corner galleries.

Up until that point all I had really done were finicky fantasy drawings in a hippy style. I had never really tried to draw anything real – and certainly not with a coarse piece of charcoal that

crumbled as soon as it touched the paper. It soon became apparent to teacher and pupil alike that I possessed nothing like a sense of proportion or feeling for charcoal. But worst of all, I felt no urge whatsoever to draw cold greyish white marble sculptures. My drawings usually ended up as a big grey splotch in the middle of the paper because I kept rubbing what I had done out with a large cloth. I took a lot of breaks from drawing and spent most of my time walking around watching some of the older students knock out a man-size drawing of a Roman athlete before lunch.

I liked Mondays at the Glyptotek best, because that was when it was closed to the public. Which meant there were not as many people around to see how dreadful my drawings were. On days when the museum was open, I usually sat in the Winter Garden with a small drawing block sketching the plants or my classmates as they worked. Anything to avoid drawing those plaster and marble sculptures. When the course ended four or five months later I swore I would never set foot in the Glyptotek again.

Years passed, then out of the blue in 1981 I was asked if I would be the painter Jens Birkemose's assistant. He was making an exhibition in the loggia facing the Glyptotek's Winter Garden and needed some practical help.

I had, in the meantime, abandoned all hope of becoming a rock star. Now I dreamt about being a painter and jumped at the chance of helping a famous artist. Jens wanted to make works for the exhibition in materials he had never worked with before, including wax, neon light, paint on thin cotton canvas and chipboard. As Jens figured out how to use the different materials he taught me how an artist worked.

We worked in one of the small pavilions surrounding the King's Garden or at an atelier on Pilestræde. As he experimented on the thin fabric, Jens played opera full blast on a cassette player. I had no prior relationship to classical music but could soon tell the difference between Puccini, Verdi and Wagner – and knew why Alban Berg was the world's best composer. When we worked in the loggia, it was usually on Monday afternoons when the museum was closed. I soon acquired a taste for walking around the Glyptotek on my own when we had a break, looking at French masterpieces and the Danish Golden Age and having the art all to myself.

Working with Jens Birkemose I saw how much he trusted his intuition and how persuasive he was at arguing for his choices. I had been wondering why he had chosen the loggia next to the Winter Garden, because he only had three walls to hang his works. But Jens knew perfectly well what he was doing with the missing wall that was the Winter Garden, because it turned out that all his paintings and drawings were full of palms, turtles and jungle motifs. I think that was the first time I got a sense of how important the installation of paintings can be.

Since then, the loggia next to the Winter Garden has been one of my favourite places at the Glyptotek, because having a whole wall of living plants feels so generous.

In 2011 the New Carlsberg Foundation invited me to help celebrate the bicentenary of the birth of the brewer J.C. Jacobsen at the Glyptotek and to choose the gallery where I wanted to exhibit my work. I chose the smallest gallery I could find upstairs with the Golden Age painters to show what would turn out to be my first landscape paintings.

Naturally the hanging of the works had to be done on a Monday when the museum was closed, and once again I had the chance to wander around on my own looking at Monet, Corot and not least my newly discovered painting hero Bonnard.

Studying Bonnard's paintings and sculpture became a bit of an obsession. During the entire time I was a professor at the art academy from 2002 to 2008 I would drop by the Glyptotek on my way to or from work to say hello to Monsieur Bonnard at least once a week. I sketched and photographed his painting of the garden room (La salle á manger) endlessly, using the studies as inspiration for many of my own works.

Ironically, these days I find myself right back where I started, drawing stone sculptures down with the Etruscans and marble sculptures up with Rodin, and very occasionally going over to look Titus deep in his marble eyes, thinking how good it is that we experience life in small doses and do not have to comprehend and digest everything all at once.

One place, or function if you will, at the Glyptotek that has been crucial to my work as an artist over the years has been its bookshop. The bookshop has been in different places, had different owners and had just as many different profiles, but it has always been rooted in books on ancient works of art and French Impressionism. In 1994 there was an exhibition of the painter Richard Mortensen's last works. Mortensen had passed away the previous year, and in the catalogue for the exhibition his widow Charlotte Mortensen wrote a beautiful essay describing how he suddenly started painting again late in life. That essay became central for me, because Charlotte Mortensen described how she and their daughter Nanna helped the ageing artist by stretching his canvases and mixing paint in yoghurt pots, but most of all by listening to his artistic considerations. The text was both touchingly optimistic and highly instructive, because it was basically about the connection between pictures and language. Because how do you explain to someone else how to blend the exact colour you want? Through language. And how do you make sense of everything Mortensen had read about Matisse and talked about incessantly when painting? By seeing the brand-new form of Colourism and much freer brushwork he developed working via remote control.

The Mortensen exhibition played a major role in sparking a series of works I painted based on the letters of the alphabet that focused on this connection between pictures and language. And it is still the same. The first thing I do whenever I enter the Glyptotek (and most other museums, I now realise) is head for the bookshop. And if, like me, you appreciate books, but also more or less laudable museum shop items like copies of sculptures, drawing blocks with Bonnard covers or scarfs featuring details of works in the museum's special exhibitions, then the current bookshop is the perfect place.

I have moved to the countryside so am in Copenhagen less these days, but the Glyptotek is still my local museum. Whenever I am in the city I carve out the time to squeeze in a visit to make a small sketch, buy a book, see some works again or say hello to Bonnard – if he is home.

Kasper Lægring

COLLAGE OF A CENTURY

Architecture at the Glyptotek

The imposing edifice that meets the eye on Dante's Square in Copenhagen today is as manifold as the collections inside the museum. Three architects – Vilhelm Dahlerup, Hack Kampmann and Henning Larsen – spent a century shaping it. Whereas there are certain similarities in style and period between the first and largest museum buildings from 1897 and 1906 respectively, Henning Larsen's 1996 addition, which cannot be seen from the outside, deviates from the rest of the museum complex in being modernist and minimalist in style.

The result of the architects' work is a low block with two main façades, one facing Dante's Square and the other the museum garden. The garden and fenced area running parallel to Tietgensgade underline the solitary character of a building with stately gatehouse doors facing both side streets. These connect two very different buildings, which are, however, united by their brick façades and symmetry along a central axis extending all the way from the main façade to the north-east to the rear façade to the south-west. The walls of both buildings conceal a collage-like interior and the spatial porosity created by the Winter Garden, courtyards, gateways and atriums. What follows examines this collage of highly disparate styles and building types more closely.

The Dahlerup Building

The Dahlerup building consists of three wings built around a courtyard. The complex is comprised of five elements: three tall volumes aligned with the central axis of the building containing the main entrance and entrance hall marking the beginning of the axis, and wings with sculpture galleries parallel to the adjacent streets of Tietgensgade and Niels Brocks Gade. All three volumes are covered by low, slate hipped roofs,

the latter two with skylights. The main body of the entrance building is connected to the two side buildings by two lower wings, which together with the entrance comprise the main façade of the museum. Since these two sections are lower than the rest Dahlerup has furnished them with copper saddle roofs between the walls of the entrance and the end walls of the side buildings. The roofs here also have a long row of skylights, but also a slight drop creating a gentle S-shaped curve or ogee.

The Dahlerup building has a foundation of Allinge granite from the Danish island of Bornholm and walls of polished red brick with decorative elements in granite, limestone and terracotta. The building alternates between one and two floors.

Taking a closer look at the main façade, the triumphal arch creates a grand entrance and extends above the high-ceilinged ground floor and half way up the first floor. A cornice unifies the arched section with the length of the façade, and together with the lower side façades on each side creates a front façade in the Composite order. At the top there are reliefs of master artists and sculptors, the laurelled initials of Carl and Ottilia Jacobsen, and two kneeling centaurs facing each other holding an oak-leaf wreath framing a coat of arms with a sheaf of corn – a central ingredient in brewing beer. The central cartouche has the words "NY-CARLSBERG GLYPTOTEK" in gilded capitals. The sculpture was the creation of Frederik Hammeleff (1847–1916).[1]

The central triumphal arch also determines the compositional principles for the rest of the main façade. On each side of the central section there is a gallery comprised of three bays with semicircular arches resting on paired pillars of the Composite order. Both corners of the galleries end in imitation ashlars. This motif is repeated on the main body of the building behind, doubling the corner and underlining the protruding character of the gallery. The gallery interior is richly decorated. Here the limestone architrave is replaced by a terracotta Vitruvian scroll frieze.

The arches of the wide niches are decorated with large shells, and the remaining wall with a pattern comprised of diagonal terracotta tiles framed by a border of corresponding tiles. The narrow sections behind the paired pillars, on the other hand, have two recesses – an oblong with a square above – decorated with bronze trophies supporting a cartouche with the name of the artist portrayed in the bust below. The square has

The Glyptotek is comprised of three buildings designed by three architects: Vilhelm Dahlerup, Hack Kampmann and Henning Larsen. Here the glass dome of the Winter Garden is in the centre and the first building designed by Dahlerup to the right. Kampmann's building can be made out to the left. The latest extension by Henning Larsen is hidden inside an inner courtyard.

a terracotta plate with an oak-leaf wreath. Such details were not complete in time for the opening of the museum in 1897 but were added as and when the busts arrived. The same is true of the two niches flanking the entrance portal, which also have shell ornamentation at the top. Busts were installed over the years, although not in the large niches, which remain empty to this day.

In front of the main façade, steps lead up to a low paved platform with rounded corners and a geometrical pattern of red and slate-blue stone, which was restored in 1985–1986.[2]

Seen from the side streets, Dahlerup's wings are more understated. There are two buildings the same height as the entrance. The façades of the buildings, which are divided into five bays, are in red machine-made brick and also divided according to a classical order, although the dimensions are larger than the main façade and the volute capitals have been replaced by cornucopia. The buildings have three cornices, the main one surmounted by an attic rhythmically articulated by recesses. The upper part of each main bay has a large lunette window below which there is a large expanse of wall with panels of different custom-made bricks.

Elevation view of Vilhelm Dahlerup's façade, 1890. Dahlerup's building has three wings, one of which faces Dante's Square. The central section is comprised of the main entrance with a triumphal arch extending halfway up the first floor. There are three identical bays on either side of the entrance with semicircular arches resting on paired pillars. The entire façade is ornately decorated.

Paired pillars divide the façades of both
side wings into five bays. There is a large
lunette window at the top of each bay
above decorative panels of hand-moulded
bricks. Each putto relief in the centre of
the panels is different.

In sharp contrast to the material richness of the main façade, the sides are decorated with cement plaster. In the middle the panels are interrupted by a central, rectangular relief with a putto, a motif repeated with variations from bay to bay.

The Entrance Hall

The interior of the Glyptotek is comprised of different rooms meeting different needs of a practical or symbolic nature, all of which are unified by a highly original floor plan. From the entrance hall, suites of rooms extend like arms to the Danish sculpture collection on one side and the French sculpture collection on the other.

The entrance hall is precisely that, a hall or basilica, and the most monumental room of Dahlerup's original museum building. Its inward orientation underlines the central axis running through the middle of the building, and at the same time makes it possible to look and pass through the main body of the building from the street to the courtyard. The high-ceilinged, barrel-vaulted space spanning the entire height of this central section has two levels, with a platform or stylobate with four Corinthian columns along the long sides. This Corinthian order continues in the end sections of the entrance hall, but with pilasters instead. The barrel-vaulted ceiling has opulent gilded coffering.

At each end of the entrance hall there is a semicircle. Above the entrance this takes the form of a lunette window, whereas the opposite end has a recess. In gilded letters on the frieze under this is Carl Jacobsen's motto, "LABOREMUS PRO PATRIA" ('Let us work for the Fatherland'). The wall of the entrance hall and pilasters are painted in contrasting colours, with a predominance of olive green.[3]

The floor is chequered black and white marble in a diagonal pattern. The podiums on the sides have inbuilt staircases in blue-grey granite, whereas the podiums and staircase panelling are covered in red-speckled granite. The steps to the podiums are located symmetrically and axially in the second and fourth bay of each row of columns. The first of these closest to the street is in line with the entrances to the adjoining galleries, whereas those further along are in line with the long flight of stairs to the upper floors of the building. Since the latest renovation there are now also stairs in the third bay leading down to the converted basement. Regardless of whether it leads to an

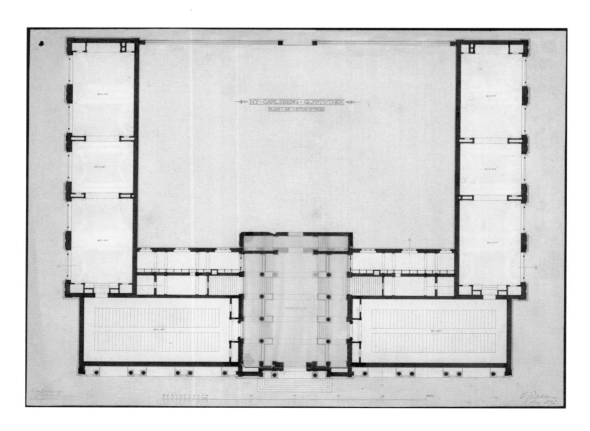

Vilhelm Dahlerup: Ground floor plan, 1890. The ground floor has an entrance hall on the central axis of the building with staircases on either side leading to the galleries above. The building originally had three wings and an open courtyard where the Winter Garden is today.

The entrance hall is one of the most impressive rooms of Dahlerup's building, here seen from the landing leading to one of the sculpture galleries. Reminiscent of a basilica, the entrance hall has a barrel-vaulted ceiling with gilded coffering and a podium on both sides leading to the sculpture galleries.

opening or not the wall of each bay is slightly recessed and framed by a simple surround of red granite. The recesses are profiled and covered with stucco arabesques, also painted green. The floors of the colonnades are terrazzo.

The Floor Plan of the Side Wings

The ground floor of the Glyptotek was devoted to sculpture, whereas the floors above were more mixed with space for busts and paintings alike. The entrance hall still provides access to all the floors and galleries of the museum, but more often than not visitors have to go back to the beginning to choose another destination. The floor plan on both sides is basically identical, with the same height and dimensions. Only the side-lit galleries facing the side streets vary in the division of the rooms.

Gallery 41 and Gallery 33 are at a right angle to and accessed from the entrance hall. Both are long and double height, with vaulted ceilings and skylights. From floor to ceiling they are divided into three zones: plain painted walls, then plaster friezes, and finally barrel-vaulted ceilings with gently curving elliptical arches featuring two rows of skylights, the concave glass of which is embedded in the coffering that covers both ceilings. This is a steel construction in which the visible skylights channel light from the outer windows on the sloping copper roof of the building.

The ceiling is grey stucco with symmetrically repeated decorations in the form of

Vilhelm Dahlerup: Ceiling design, undated.

arabesques, medallions, acanthus vines and cartouches. The white ornamentation is primarily classical in style against a contrasting background of painted sections, borders and edging. The overall impression is eclectic, with a ceiling that is inspired by the French Beaux-Arts and its free use of elements of historical architecture rather than being purely classical.

Each of these large skylit galleries provides a view into the quadratic corner galleries of the building – Gallery 42 and Gallery 34 – which are slightly raised in relationship to the galleries with skylights and side windows. The corner galleries also have skylights, but just as two of the corners of the room are rounded, the transition to the ceiling has been softened by the use of a cavetto moulding. Visually the corner galleries open up onto the skylit galleries via large portals with corner corbels.

Gallery 45 and Gallery 36 are museum highlights, with richer and more varied ornamentation than that of their neighbours. Both galleries were created for specific sculptures. Whereas Gallery 45 represents the culmination of the floor plan of the Danish section and has an apse as its *point de vue*, Gallery 36 is halfway through the French section and changes orientation along the axis leading to the Winter Garden.

Ornamentation, Colours and Furniture

Dahlerup's interior design focuses on surface rather than solidity, entirely in keeping with contemporary historicism. As a result, his Glyptotek is a *tour de force* by the plasterers and painters who worked on the interior. Even the lavish use of different kinds of marble looks more like apparel than creating the impression of something solid. There are, however, some departures where three-dimensionality comes to the fore. Examples include the entrances to the two large skylit galleries with their monumental portals of the Corinthian order crowned by a segmental gable influenced by the style of the Early Renaissance.

The galleries on the ground floor of the Dahlerup building have friezes as central motifs, primarily by Danish sculptors Herman Wilhelm Bissen and Jens Adolf Jerichau.

All the floors are terrazzo with a central rectangular mosaic. This often has stylised flowers flanked by narrower bands. Attic-style braided bands and interlocking meanders form a frame incorporating a swastika. This ancient Sanskrit symbol of prosperity and well-being was the logo of the Carlsberg brewery prior to the inauspicious connotations it developed with Nazism. This floor design is used throughout the ground floor, often with a central mosaic in lighter hues surrounded by a darker, contrasting border.

The walls are painted in the classical colours of historicism: burgundy, dark umber, marine blue, olive green, ochre and red iron oxide. The mouldings are usually a stony grey colour. The galleries are full of contrasts between dark walls, lighter mouldings on the ceiling and sides, and chalk-white friezes.

The interior design of Dahlerup's building is a mix of serious and humorous mottoes, symbols of the past and present, and public and private references. Ancient mythology, Christianity, personal memories, artist myths, corporate trademarks and memory culture are interwoven to form a remarkable synthesis.

The Staircases

Paradoxically, the most opulent parts of Dahlerup's building are the two narrow staircases leading to the suite of galleries grouped around the Winter Garden and the long skylit galleries at the top of each side wing.

The two granite flights of steps mirror each other. Spatially and structurally they are the same, but there are a number of differences in the decorative scheme. The area is crowned by an arched ceiling with inset skylights. In the one to the south-east, bright colours have been used to paint realistic plant and bird motifs against an azure background. A rose, blackberry flower and passionflower can be identified on the panes, whereas the north-west version is in colder, more muted colours and abstract and geometrical in design like a pattern of tiles.

The walls of the staircases are divided into polychrome marble with granite panels below and an upper zone with a lower edge defined by the top landing in white stucco. The details of both kinds of ornamentation vary, and Dahlerup himself only had sketched plans for them. The south-west staircase has sections with medallions of famous artists on the walls, whereas the north-west staircase has allegories of different art forms: sculpture, painting, dance, music, poetry, architecture and landscape gardening. Both staircases are also richly decorated with cartouches, arabesques, centrepieces, medallions, festoons and trophies.

The size and order of the galleries on both sides of the main wing are almost identical but the interiors are all different. The walls in Galleries 41 and 33 are divided into three zones: first a plain painted wall, then plaster friezes, and finally the beginning of the low-arched, barrel-vaulted ceiling with rows of skylights.

The Dahlerup Building in Summary

Dahlerup's contribution to the Glyptotek is a visual lesson in the historicist view of architecture, where the articulation of tectonic and construction principles is secondary to lining the building with panels, frescoes, stucco, glass and marble. Dahlerup designed a building that is simultaneously a whole and its parts. That it is comprised of individual volumes is apparent in the different kinds of roof (a principle taken from the Baroque), but they are united by a consistency of materials, a shared adherence to classical rules of proportion, and a stylistic monopoly by the Italian Renaissance.

The meticulousness and *horror vacui* of the Glyptotek's main façade is typical of Dahlerup and the Early Renaissance, his favourite period in terms of style. Combining features of classical architecture with a focus on surface and an extensive use of reliefs is highly characteristic of the period's style, which Dahlerup was partial to combining with Mannerist ornamental features. The façade of the museum represents his constant efforts to facilitate the transition between the bays and fill every available surface.

The roof construction is entirely hidden, and heating and ventilation vents have been made

The long galleries of the main wing lead to quadratic corner galleries at the top of marble steps. The corner galleries also have skylights and the same vertical wall zones as the other galleries.

Rather than designing all the ornamentation himself, Vilhelm Dahlerup chose to work closely with artists and artisans. This was not always a smooth collaboration. There were numerous clashes and occasions when he complained to Carl Jacobsen about their failure to understand his architecture.

MATHÆVS

JEG · ER · A · OG · Ω
BEGYNDELSEN · OG
ENDEN JEG JEG VIL
GIVE · DEN · SOM · TØR·
STER · AF · LIVETS · VANDS
KILDE · UFORSKYLDT.
AAB · 21 · 6

into ornamental features. The individuality of the different parts of the building is toned down in favour of harmony and flow. The widespread and differentiated use of marble and granite at the Glyptotek is a major contributor to the museum's opulent atmosphere. International historicism and French-influenced Beaux-Arts in particular were also based on traditionally built architecture hewn in stone.

The degree of enthusiasm and care the builder, architect and many craftsmen involved invested in the museum is palpable, making the Glyptotek a veritable treasure trove of painstakingly chosen details and exquisite materials, and creating spaces like the entrance hall that are second to none in Denmark.

The Winter Garden

The Winter Garden at the heart of the Glyptotek is a creative transformation of one of the leftover open courtyards of Dahlerup's building into an Italian-inspired inner courtyard flanked by two arcades with a central staircase leading to the Kampmann building.

The first Glyptotek building from 1897 was an unfinished torso, and the courtyard resembled a paltry backyard.[4] At the time of the opening visitors had to constantly return to the entrance hall when they reached the end of either wing on the ground floor, the narrow corridors on the first floor, or the upper painting galleries. There was no passage between the two sides, and even though an exit to the Winter Garden was established in 1914,[5] the general experience of the Dahlerup building was one of suites of galleries leading to a dead end. This was primarily due to the fourth wing planned to complete the complex to the south-west never being built.

The Winter Garden replaced the original plan of a stone domed building in Dahlerup's very first proposal in 1884.[6] It was revived as an idea in 1902, and construction began in 1904. It was completed in 1906 at the same time as the Kampmann building. The solution on the ground floor was to construct two deep arcades along the side wings, whereas the main wing only had a modest shell structure added. A central section with a double staircase led to the new Kampmann building. The side sections were merely shell structures with windows facing the goods yard separating the two buildings.

The two arcades running along Dahlerup's original side wings, as well as the mock façade

Two granite staircases with arched ceilings and painted skylights lead from the entrance hall to the floors above.

81

Vilhelm Dahlerup: Elevation view of staircase, undated. The walls of the staircases
are divided into a lower zone covered with
marble and an upper zone of white stucco.
The latter includes wall panels with
medallions portraying famous artists.

with an inbuilt staircase to Kampmann's building, form a single façade covering the ground and first floors. The arcades occupy the entire ground floor, apart from two full-height windows facing the inaccessible yard behind them. Today the window to the south-west opens onto the glass corridor leading to the Henning Larsen building.

The façades adhere to the Corinthian order, and the mouldings and architrave above the capitals follow the same line as the row of columns in the entrance hall of the older building. The pilasters that divide the façade vertically are, however, somewhat taller than the columns in the entrance hall due to sunken floor of the Winter Garden.

The cornice running across the façade – interrupted by pilasters – compensates for the height difference. The first floor is lower, almost like a mezzanine, and has simple pilasters, whereas the windows here are vertical apertures in groups of three or four.[7] Whereas the long façade along the central axis of the building is symmetrical with a triumphal arch around the staircase, the short sides with arcades are asymmetrical. This is due to the composition of the façade – three bays leading to the main building in staggered formation and a single broader bay – following the axes determined by the dome construction. Along the arcades the floor juts out below the façade, creating a podium for sculptures and the back wall of the flowerbeds below.

The steps that connect to the Kampmann building are the most monumental element of the Winter Garden. The base of the central bay forms a semicircular niche with a circular pool that has a decoratively scalloped outer edge. At the back of the pool, which also contains a fountain, is a circular plinth with Marius-Jean-Antonin Mercié's (1845–1916) sculpture *Gloria Victis* from 1874.

The floors of the arcades and steps are multicoloured terrazzo in a simple pattern with a narrow red-and-white chequered border framed by dark-green terrazzo. The interior of the arcades ends in a cross vault, but whereas the arches of the façade are semicircular, the ceiling of the arcade is elliptical. The barrel vaults are decorated with stucco flowers, and the entire ceiling is whitewashed.

The façades are walls of hand-hewn stone with limestone cornices and ornamentation.[8] In gilded iron lettering on the architrave running along the façades are mottoes in Latin and Danish chosen by the brewer Carl Jacobsen. The capitals

There are many kinds of marble on the walls of Vilhelm Dahlerup's building as well as on its columns, door surrounds and other decorative features.

are also decorated with a monogram: the intertwined initials C and O of Carl and his wife, Ottilia. To the left of the portal facing the Kampmann building are the words "NY CARLSBERG FONDET BYGHERRE" ('Built by the New Carlsberg Foundation') and to the right "VILHELM DAHLERUP BYGMESTER" ('Architect Vilhelm Dahlerup').

The Dome Construction

The twelve slender cast-iron pillars supporting the dome form a square juxtaposed with the new, affixed screen façade along the main wing. Each side of the square is divided into three bays by pillars, the largest slightly wider than the others. These middle bays are located on the central axis from the street to the courtyard and the side axes from the middle to the side wings respectively. The location of the dome construction is thus entirely determined by the existing axes. The square framework of the dome has been placed precisely where the symmetry axes of the main wing and entrance hall and the windows and room divisions of the side wings meet. This is a solution that has the added advantage of shifting the dome towards the boulevard so it can be seen from the outside.[9]

All the cast-iron pillars of the dome are made of three pieces joined to reach its full height. They were treated with red lead and painted a grey-green colour.[10] Despite its industrial materials, the dome is a classical construction divided into a tambour, a pendentive vault, and a lantern crowned by a small dome and weathervane. The foot of the dome has a row of identical palmettes, the contours of which, like the ribs of the dome, were originally gilded. The tambour is surrounded by a quadratic platform enclosed by a balustrade. The steel trusses of the glass roof rest on the cornice between the ground and first floors, and the divisions follow those of the façade. The incorporation of iron constructions in traditional architecture was high on the agenda during the 19th century, and as a result the Winter Garden is both a modern construction of industrial extraction and a classical Italian inner courtyard, or *cortile*.

The Kampmann Building

As mentioned above, a fourth wing was intended to complete the Glyptotek in Carl Jacobsen's 1884 sketch[11] but was never built. Dahlerup's complex was U-shaped, and the fate of the fourth wing remained undecided. In the end it was abandoned

In the early 1900s the building Vilhelm Dahlerup had envisioned was finally completed with the construction of the Winter Garden. At the opening he said: "I am so glad the dome is now complete. Before people asked: Where is the Glyptotek? And people showed them the way, and all roads lead there, but tourists still could not find it. Now we can just point at the dome: The Glyptotek is there! And when the sun shines on its green glass it looks like a ripe fruit, a wonderful round ripe fruit in the sun!"

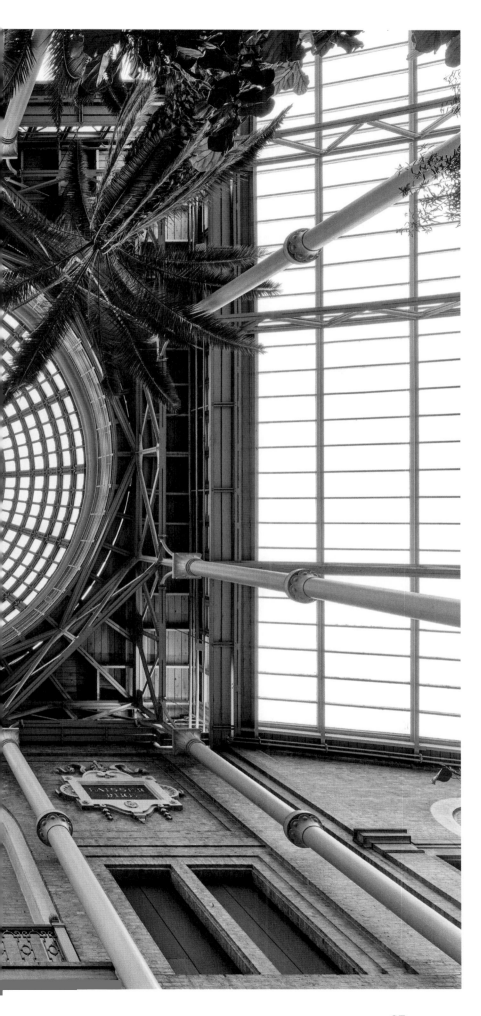

The dome of the Winter Garden is supported by twelve slender cast-iron columns. Its quadratic frame is on the central axis of the building, but not in the middle of the garden. Instead, it is juxtaposed with the yellow-brick façade of the former courtyard, making it more visible from the road in front of the museum.

in favour of the Winter Garden with a new architect – Hack Kampmann – at the helm.

Unlike Dahlerup's highly composite complex, Kampmann's building has the appearance of a single, large block. Kampmann also designed the two gatehouses bridging the two buildings. Kampmann's building follows the same central axis as that of Dahlerup's, and the height is around the same as the tallest wing of Dahlerup's building. Instead of a central inner courtyard Kampmann's building has two separate ones. With the exception of the Winter Garden Dahlerup chose to use machine-made bricks, whereas Kampmann's façades are made of handmade bricks, with a darker hue and more variation in tone and texture. The bricks were custom made to specific dimensions to reduce the size of the mortar joints. The façade was then polished with carborundum (silicon carbide).[12]

Whereas Dahlerup used every thinkable kind of stone from Denmark and abroad to create an interplay of colour and contrasts, granite dominates Kampmann's exterior. Finally, while Dahlerup divided his complex into legible sections, Kampmann's façade is a consistent, continuous expanse.

Vilhelm Dahlerup's and Hack Kampmann's buildings are connected by two gatehouse buildings facing the side streets. The double doors have granite surrounds reminiscent of Egyptian architecture.

The ground plan of Kampmann's building is rectangular, with the long sides adjoining Dahlerup's pre-existing building and the museum garden, and the short sides running parallel to the side streets. All three visible – and symmetrical – façades have a long avant-corps resulting in slightly recessed corners that create turret-like structures. The façades only have two floors. The upper floor has no windows and therefore appears as a separate brick surface.

The difference between Kampmann's and Dahlerup's views of architecture begins with the plinth. Here there are three highly unusual granite steps inspired by the platform or crepis at the base of Greek temples.[13] After the profiles of ovolo and cavetto mouldings, comes the plinth zone itself marked by large blocks of granite surmounted by a dentil cornice. This zone houses the ground floor, which is more like a closed cellar. The surface of the granite has light, evenly distributed marks of hewing that add life to the large expanse.

Above the cornice the façade changes to bare brick, and the entire upper floor of the façade is divided by paired pilasters. The pilasters are made of the same brick as the façade, but their capitals are made of the same light-coloured, Norwegian granite as the base, beams and cornices.[14] The avant-corps on the side façades have five bays, increasing to nine on the main façade including the central section.

Along the plinth zone the bay divisions are marked by regularly spaced upright rectangular windows divided into two almost quadratic halves by a broad granite mullion. The windows in the four corner sections, however, appear as individual apertures. All the windows have bars of black wrought iron. The ornamentation is geometrical and harmonises with the granite blocks of the lower façade, where slight protrusions, shifts in colour and differences in hewing techniques create a clear sense of rhythm.

Unlike the windows in the avant-corps, the single windows of the corner sections are flanked by swastikas – the original logo of the New Carlsberg brewery – at the top of the stone frames. These have only been preserved on the sides facing the museum garden. Those on the side façades were re-carved as crosses during the Nazi occupation of Denmark.

The overall aesthetic impression left by the ground floor is one of abstract forms. This is, however, disrupted by a series of animal

Each corner of Hack Kampmann's building has a relief of a winged female figure. Created by the Danish sculptor Ludvig Brandstrup, they symbolise dawn, noon, evening and night.

The base of Hack Kampmann's building has high granite steps followed by the actual plinth zone: large blocks of granite surmounted by a dentil cornice below a façade of hand-moulded red bricks.

heads protruding from the upper mullions of the double windows. They are the works of Karl Hansen Reistrup (1863–1929),[15] whose contribution to the façade of this part of the Glyptotek assembles a veritable zoo.[16]

The drainpipes located in the inverted corners created by the ressaults are encapsulated by the granite heads of cows, buffaloes, goats and baboons, creating a subtle yet cheerful contrast to the spartan façade.

The exterior of the main floor is, as mentioned, simply a brick wall divided by paired pillars. Yet even here we find some strange hybrids. The bases of the columns, for example, are of the Ionic order whereas the capitals are more akin to the Doric or Tuscan order. This combination of classical codes continues moving up to the beam of the pilasters, which is of the Ionic order. The three layers of the beam consist of an architrave – also trisected – a plain frieze shaped by coarser hewing and a cornice with a dentil frieze.

The pilasters here, which continue around the corner, are wider and made of granite, and each of them has a full-length relief of a winged female figure by Danish sculptor Ludvig Brandstrup

90

The otherwise closed and controlled façades have a row of animal heads carved by the Danish sculptor and ceramicist Karl Hansen Reistrup.

(1861–1935) resting on a small consol. Each of the four reliefs symbolises a time of day: dawn, noon, evening and night.

In the centre of the large façade facing the museum garden there is a small, bronze door set in a deep casing that tapers slightly towards the top, giving it an Egyptian twist. Each leaf of the door has a window above three carved wreaths of laurel, ivy and oak leaves surmounted by the year 1906 in Roman numerals. Above the doorway is Carl Jacobsen's motto, "Semper Ardens" ('Forever Burning').

On the main floor level there is a central loggia behind two polished granite Ionic columns embedded in the façade. The loggia is flanked by two limestone reliefs by Danish sculptor Carl Aarsleff (1852–1918). To the left are figures of Ottilia and Carl Jacobsen. The full-length figures are statuesque, formally posed, and dressed in ancient robes. The relief on the right includes figures symbolising city and state.

The Ionic columns create a portico that is similar in structure to a Greek ante-temple. Above the columns the frieze on the beam is decorated with no less than five bronze laurels. But the element that really gives this central section its character and endows the entire Kampmann building with monumentality is the large granite step pyramid. It is set slightly back from the façade line, creating space for an attic with six plinths, two of which are larger than the others. The attic is flush with the façade. The two broad plinths on either side house two free-standing bronze sculptures of horses modelled on the central pair of four gilded horses in the Basilica di San Marco in Venice, which are in turn copies of Roman sculptures from the 3rd century CE. At the top of the pyramid there is a full-size bronze copy of the statue of Athena Velletri, which itself is a Roman marble copy from the 1st century BCE of a bronze original from circa 420 BCE.[17]

Each wing except the one facing Niels Brocks Gade has a pitched roof with large sections of skylights made of pounded glass with copper beading creating an extended ridge light. The recessed cubic corner sections, on the other hand, have distinctive pavilion roofs with lanterns. These lanterns have steep mansard roofs of glass with decorative triangular gables on either side and rise with slightly sloping sides crowned by a low copper dome.

The only windows in Hack Kampmann's building are on the ground floor. Above them the brick façades are divided by paired pilasters of the Corinthian order. A loggia is built into the façade facing the museum garden. It has two Ionic granite columns and is crowned by a large step pyramid.

There is a limestone relief on either side of the columns. The one to the left portrays Carl and Ottilia Jacobsen, and the one to the right has two figures personifying the city and state. The step pyramid is made of granite and set slightly back from the façade line. The pyramid is flanked by freestanding bronze sculptures of horses inspired by those at the Basilica di San Marco in Venice.

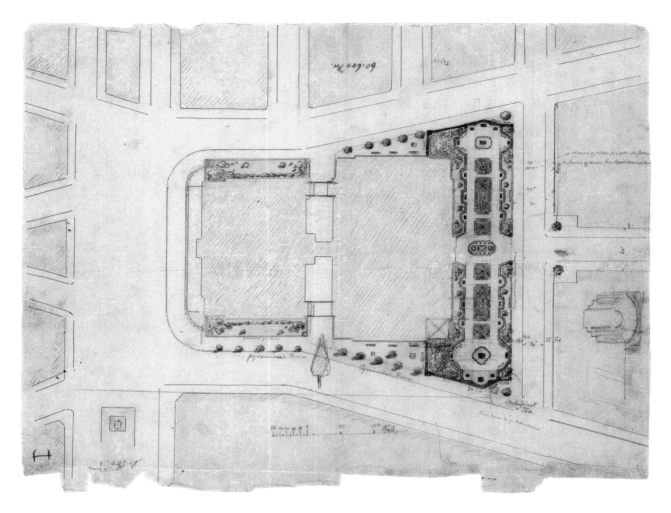

Galleries of Different Shapes and Sizes

The interior of Kampmann's building differs from Dahlerup's building in style, floor plan, and materials.

Kampmann's ground plan is no less symmetrical than Dahlerup's, but unlike the existing U-shaped structure Kampmann's building for the Antiquities Collection is designed with connecting rooms enabling free passage from one end of the building to the other on the same level. The ground plan is a block with open courtyards. There is a broad wing in the middle surrounded by narrower wings.

The uniformity, stringency and unity of the building are also reflected in the interior, where the Central Hall occupies the middle of the broad wing with all other rooms repeated according to a set scheme. The result is a monumental, high-ceilinged first floor with a series of elongated barrel-shaped galleries (Galleries 1, 6, 8, 10 and 12) connected at the corners by quadratic or circular galleries (Galleries 4, 7, 9 and 13). Whereas Dahlerup used windows facing different directions, Kampmann mainly uses skylights. Furthermore, the architecture is based on simple geometrical effects seen, for example, in the highly similar

Hack Kampmann: The museum garden, undated. The overall plan for the museum garden was designed by Hack Kampmann in 1907 after the inauguration of his building. The City of Copenhagen's head gardener Valdemar Fabricius Hansen was responsible for the flowerbeds and planting.

94

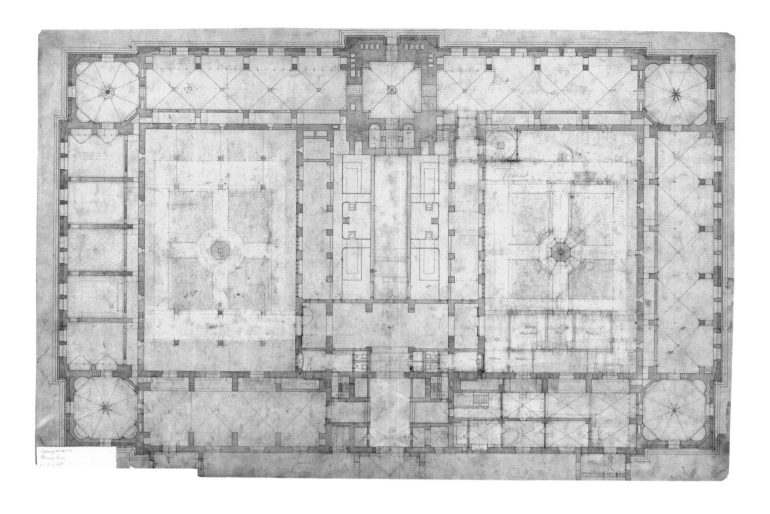

Hack Kampmann: Ground floor plan, undated. Unlike Vilhelm Dahlerup's building, it is possible to walk around the entire building. The plan is like a block with two courtyards and a wing in the middle housing the Central Hall. One of the courtyards has since been reduced by the addition of a building housing the museum's administration and library, whereas the other now contains Henning Larsen's extension.

terrazzo floors. The mouldings and cornices are also both simple and sparingly used.

Even though the artefacts in the Antiquities Collection were very different in origin and character – Egyptian, Greek and Roman – the presence of different periods in the interior was to be discrete and stylised. The intention was not to recreate the interiors of the ancient past, the sole exception being the Central Hall. Instead, we are presented with paraphrases, albeit ones that are more consistent and historically accurate in shape than Dahlerup's highly composite interior. Another difference is that Kampmann designed almost all the ornamentation himself.

The five long, barrel-vaulted galleries are designed in the same way, with polished terrazzo floors, plain walls, a simple cornice and a ceiling with large skylights of pounded glass mounted in narrow strips of copper. The entrances to the galleries are simple portals made of various kinds of granite.

The two lantern galleries on the corners facing Tietgensgade are simple, quadratic rooms where the mansard shape of the lanterns continues down to the cornice via slightly sloping walls. On the opposite side of the building, the

The four long galleries in Hack Kamp-mann's building look alike and all have barrel-vaulted ceilings and skylights. The architecture is simpler in style than Dahlerup's. The walls have narrow skirting boards and plain painted walls topped by a cornice. Above this is a vaulted ceiling with stucco ornamentation that differs from gallery to gallery. The floors are mosaic and terrazzo.

corner galleries are rotundas with conical roofs and a round opening or oculus as a transition to the square lantern.

Between these two round galleries adjacent to Niels Brocks Gade the interior design is somewhat different. Instead of a long gallery with skylights, there are five small galleries *en enfilade* – arranged in a row with each opening onto the next. The small galleries are barrel-vaulted and three of them also have an apse. The ceilings are richly decorated with a stucco design of plant motifs on an espalier-like lattice pattern, and the meandering plant motifs on the floors are less controlled than those in the long galleries. The small galleries were to alternate between yellow, red and green. They still do, although the colours today are not identical to the original colours as a sectional view by Kampmann shows. Here the contrasts are accentuated by the use of clear, luminous colours.

Kampmann's interior design for the Antiquities Collection alternates between elements referencing ancient civilisations like the papyrus and lotus, Danish or Nordic elements like summer flowers, and symbols of the founder Carl Jacobsen's profession like barley and hops – or his private life like the thistle, the national flower of Scotland where Ottilia Jacobsen was born. Stylisation remains a principle throughout these themes.

The Lion Hall

From the arcade of Dahlerup's staircase from the Winter Garden a flight of dark granite steps leads to the entrance to Kampmann's building, the Lion Hall. Before reaching this there is a small barrel-vaulted transitional space with the last steps of the Winter Garden, which was designed by Kampmann.

Turning around to face the Winter Garden, a lunette window can be seen above an inscription under a medallion with white symbols on an oxblood background. The medallion depicts a trowel, a compass and a bricklayer's hammer joined by an unfurling measuring tape. Below it are the words:

LITTLE GOOD DOES IT DO FOR THE
MASTER TO BUILD
IF THE LORD DOES NOT BUILD WITH HIM
TO MAKE THE FOUNDATIONS SECURE
⇓ THE HOPES OF MAN ⇓
IF THE LORD DOES NOT HEED HIS CALL
ARE BUT FLEETING SHADOWS

The long galleries on the first floor are connected to the short sides of the building by circular or quadratic corner galleries. A row of smaller galleries faces Tietgensgade. They have different floor designs, ceiling ornamentation and colours on the walls that often mirror the collections on display.

An imposing double door made of teak with riveted brass plates leads to the Lion Hall, named after the four sculptures guarding its corners. This quadratic room ends in a cross vault with a skylight at the top drawing light from the ridge light on the roof above.

Whereas the entrance to the Central Hall is on one level, there are steps to the right and left of the Lion Hall leading to the identical Gallery 1 and Gallery 6.

The doorway to the Central Hall lies on the central axis. Above it is a tympanum or pediment with three black dots ornamentally placed in the centre surrounded by winding words telling that the building was built by State, the City of Copenhagen and the New Carlsberg Foundation.

The Central Hall and Mausoleum

Whereas the Lion Hall with its ceremonial atmosphere borders on being early Christian in style, the Central Hall is more classical and celebratory. The hall forms a natural pivotal point for the Antiquities Collection and contains Roman statues, reliefs and sarcophaguses. This is the only room Kampmann designed to emulate a classical setting and provide a context for the treasures on display. Rather than reconstructing a specific historical environment, however, he has chosen to paraphrase. This sets it apart from contemporary museum architecture elsewhere, where accurate reconstructions were the ideal. Instead, the hall evokes an atmosphere, something Carl Jacobsen often expressed as his goal in building the Glyptotek.[18]

The Central Hall is designed as a classical peristyle: a courtyard surrounded on three sides by twenty columns connected by square pillars in the corners. The columns and pillars are of the Ionic order, with fluting and columns of polished, white, black-veined Pavonazzetto marble. The bases and capitals are in white-veined Statuario marble. The capitals of the corner pillars have an egg-and-dart frieze above a frieze with roundels.

The back wall inside the colonnades has a horizontally trisected marble dado. Statuario marble and white-flame Italian Hemelino marble are also used on the floor of the colonnade, which is raised slightly above the floor of the hall and covered with square tiles. The wall has been painted *al fresco*. Today it is Pompeian red, but it was originally ochre, something we know from Kampmann's drawings and newspaper reviews at the time.[19] This has also been reconfirmed by the latest architectural paint research.[20]

Kampmann's winning project originally had a monumental descending staircase in the middle of the Central Hall. This was soon abandoned and replaced by a shallow square pool or impluvium, the bottom of which is decorated with an authentic Roman mosaic: *Europe and the Bull*.[21] The pool was filled with water for the opening.

The marble floor of the Central Hall is richly decorated with squares framed by narrower bands with rhombuses. A combination of Pavonazzetto marble, red antique Spanish Rouge marble, green Greek Verde marble, and honey-coloured, grey-flame Italian Giallo di Torri marble has been used.

The ceiling of the Central Hall is constructed as a saddle roof with rafters made of white steel beams. The spaces between them are almost entirely occupied by skylights. Unlike the classical peristyle, the industrial-style ceiling is a patently modern construction.

At the opposite end of the Central Hall, adjacent to and opening directly onto the mausoleum, another row of columns can be seen with an avant-corps and temple façade of the Ionic order approached by seven steps in white Norwegian Furuli marble. It has been made using the same kind of columns in the same materials and proportions as the colonnade and is crowned by a triangular pediment with a niche in the middle in the shape of a small, stylised portico. In gold capitals on the architrave are the names Carl and Ottilia Jacobsen. At the back the two middle Ionic columns are mirrored, but in the style of the mausoleum, where the bases have differently rolled edges and the columns are red-and-black variegated granite from the Trondheim area. The capital does not belong to the classical orders and has a heavy cornice with a frieze below that has two rosettes on either side. The shift in colour and style in the mausoleum creates a more sombre atmosphere. Whereas the light and porous Central Hall expands the sense of space, the mausoleum creates an impression of condensed, compact solidity. Whilst axially connected to the Central Hall, the dark colour scheme and smooth, reflecting surfaces represent its antithesis. The walls are entirely covered with green-black porphyritic diorite to create the illusion of solid walls and heavy ashlars. The depth of the door openings to the neighbouring galleries is heavily accentuated

by door frames made of polished black Scanian diabase. The floor is richly decorated like that of the Central Hall. Facing the Central Hall, but also the museum garden bringing light in from the side, are solid, free-standing square pillars around a loggia. From the very beginning this was sealed with large panes of glass mounted in thin bronze frames.

The room is topped by a coffered, white-plastered dome under the step pyramid on the roof. It has a square base that tapers to a smaller square at the top.

The Ground Floor and Etruscan Collection

The lower floor of Kampmann's building clearly plays a secondary role, and today almost half of it is used for museum administration and closed to the public. The three main wings of the ground floor facing the exterior resemble a crypt or cellar. They have heavy barrel vaults and granite pillars that follow the same pattern. Today this long, unbroken sequence is divided by display cases and podiums. The four corner rooms are isolated spaces akin to turrets, octagonal with niches in both the inner and outer walls. The barrel vaulting

Steps from the Winter Garden lead to the foyer of Kampmann's building – the Lion Hall – providing access to the Central Hall and two long galleries. The Lion Hall is on the central axis of the building, making it possible to see both the main entrance to Dahlerup's building and the museum garden. The quadratic hall has skylights.

mirrors this in being parasol-shaped. Only in the wing facing Niels Brocks Gade are there smaller rooms of the same format as those on the first floor. The original mosaic floor of oxblood terrazzo with a simple pattern of white studs has also been preserved here.

Signs of the Times in Dahlerup and Kampmann's Buildings

Kampmann's extension to the Glyptotek is no different to Dahlerup's original building in terms of complexity, but whereas the individual wings and sections of Dahlerup's architecture can be clearly seen – both separately and connected – from the street, Kampmann has built a single, coherent block behind a continuous façade of the same height, dictated and structured by a system of stepped platforms, plinths, walls and cornices. That the building contains galleries and exhibitions is not apparent from the outside. Rounding the façade there is a sense of the same basic forms being repeated. This is not to say that Kampmann's building is less functionally communicative, but the interior is less spatially differentiated than Dahlerup's building, and the integrated style of architecture Kampmann was aiming for does not

Kampmann's building was made to house Carl and Ottilia Jacobsen's collections of ancient Greek, Roman and Egyptian art and artefacts, collections the Central Hall echoes in a classical peristyle with colonnades on three sides. The fourth side has a protruding temple façade providing access to the mausoleum behind it. There is a sunken Roman mosaic in the marble floor. The hall is dominated by marble of many kinds and colours. The ceiling is a glazed pitched roof.

The step pyramid is located above the mausoleum. The ceiling inside its square dome form is coffered and plastered white.

103

allow for any osmosis between the building and the outside world.

Kampmann was as well-schooled in historicism as Dahlerup, and both architects were capable of combining the styles of different periods when required to do so. The new departure with Kampmann's façade, however, is that it is unequivocally classicist in style and archaic in atmosphere. Only small deviations – the trapezoid Egyptian portal in the middle of the main façade and again at the entrances in the side façades – reveal other sources of inspiration than Greek–Roman. Overall there are no eclectic disruptions to the overall impression of a building with a design from classical antiquity. Only the building's red bricks point to the influence of National Romanticism.

As the latest architectural paint research shows, the old and new Glyptotek buildings both had a distinctive palette of colours. The interior of Dahlerup's building was dominated by dark, muted, earthen tones, whereas Kampmann used lighter, clearer, stronger colours, alternating from room to room to maximise the contrasts. White walls actually dominated,[22] something also confirmed by architectural paint research.[23] In

Whereas the Central Hall is light and festive, the mausoleum has a much more sombre atmosphere, despite large windows looking out onto the museum garden. The walls are covered with green-black porphyritic Diorite, creating a dark, intense atmosphere offset by the light ceiling.

104

Kampmann's approach to the Glyptotek, it is the formation of the rooms that held full sway over the architectural experience. Ornamentation is kept to an absolute minimum and stylised rather than naturalistic.

Only a few years passed between the construction of Dahlerup's and Kampmann's buildings, yet the differences between them are more conspicuous than the similarities, which can primarily be seen in the central axis, symmetry, and extensive use of marble, granite and stone. There are, however, a number of parallels. The façades of both buildings provide no clues as to the disposition of the rooms inside, especially where traditional windows have been forsaken in favour of skylights, but in Kampmann's building this contrast between the inner and outer structure is also pronounced. Seen from the outside, at ground level there is a step formation that alludes to Greek temples, whereas inside the floor plan is more Roman and probably actually more influenced by the Renaissance.

It would be easy to exaggerate the differences between Dahlerup and Kampmann's views and schools of architecture – the older historicist European versus the younger National Romantic – but with the Glyptotek they both appear to occupy a kind of hiatus. The intrusive urban modernity of city life leaves no direct mark on the architecture itself, yet is still addressed indirectly. With Dahlerup this can be seen in the stucco façades of Copenhagen rubbing off on the interior and having a synthesising effect. At the same time, he aims for a flexible passage between the galleries and rooms, softening every sharp corner with curves or ornamentation despite the pathways through the museum leading to dead ends and visitors having to retrace their steps.

The overall impression created by Kampmann's building is more wilful, more unapproachable and less urban, although also more timeless, concentrated and monumental than Dahlerup's. In terms of functionality, it also forms the back of the complex. This influences how the architecture is perceived – a show façade for the museum garden – as well as the ornamentation, which enhances the impression of a protective bastion for the treasures the building holds.

Kampmann's design is imbued with a high degree of clarity. The different areas are like modules rhythmically succeeding each other. There is no wasted space or dead ends like those in Dahlerup's building, and the continuous path parallel to the outer walls that forms a closed circuit on both sides is truly unique. At the floor-plan level Kampmann's building has better circulation than Dahlerup's, although its closed nature cannot be denied. Visitors are more secluded from the life and sounds of the city in the Antiquities Collection than the Danish Collection and French Collection where the side wings offer a view of the Tivoli Gardens and Copenhagen's roofscape. This powerful sense of timelessness seems to have been an objective in its own right. Even the Central Hall is cut off from the surrounding city and modern life.

Kampmann has abandoned marble from southern climes in favour of Norwegian marble, German porphyry, Swedish and Danish granite, and Finnish soapstone. Only in the Central Hall and mausoleum, both more accurate imitations of historical structures, is French, Italian and Greek marble used. Kampmann's National Romantic and Nordic focus is thus present in his careful choice of materials, which have a very different effect than those of Dahlerup, who was aiming for imitation, decoration and to create an atmosphere rather than organic or processual symbols of the creative powers of nature. The materials used in Kampmann's building draw more attention in their own right than in processed form, and they also form part of a tectonic context, making structural elements visible.

Another difference can be seen in the use of spatial effects. Whereas Dahlerup was aiming for a synthesis where the qualities of individual materials were subservient to the unified effect with a focus on surface rather than three-dimensionality, Kampmann developed a radical division into floor, wall and ceiling zones that do not merge or overlap in design or theme.

A final difference is that Kampmann retained full aesthetic and artistic control of every aspect of the building process, entirely in keeping with the Romantic spirit of the 'creative genius', whereas Dahlerup was far more pragmatic and willing to delegate the specifics of the interior to skilled craftsmen. Kampmann thereby stands as the ultimate creator, whereas Dahlerup was less particular about which stucco relief accorded to which iconographic programme.

The Henning Larsen Building
In 1996 an architecture competition led to the completion of another important chapter in the architectural history of the Glyptotek: the creation of a contemporary building for the museum's

French painting collection by Danish architect Henning Larsen. The extension was built in one of the unused courtyards of the Kampmann building, an idea Carl Jacobsen himself had anticipated and encouraged.[24]

From the left side of the Winter Garden a tunnel-shaped corridor entirely encapsulated in opaque, milk-white glass leads to the Kampmann building. The corridor has a simple steel structure painted anthracite grey and a floor of dark-grey granite. After the passage through the outer wall to the Kampmann building comes one of the ground floor's barrel-vaulted rooms, painted white with a floor of plain grey granite tiles.

The basic structure of the Henning Larsen building is remarkably simple. The ground plan follows that of the courtyard on a smaller scale, leaving a broad shaft between Kampmann's original building and Larsen's addition. The main body of the building, which has two long and two short sides, has slightly slanting façades without windows divided by high vertical recesses placed at regular intervals. The building's discretely slanting profile provides optical compensation to prevent the building feeling overwhelming or out of balance.[25] The recesses continue almost to the top of the building, where they are replaced by a series of box-shaped apertures. The walls are clad in stucco marble, creating a smooth, gleaming surface. The existing outer walls of Kampmann's building have been covered with a thin layer of sand-coloured plaster that allows the texture of the brick wall beneath to be traced. The two walls thus differ in both colour and texture.

The independent block in the courtyard has a crown slightly higher than that of the Kampmann building, creating a sloping roof between the old building and the new. The glass roof is divided by simple white steel battens, bathing the perimeter shaft in light and casting silhouettes of the battens onto the walls.

After the initial flight of marble steps in the corner entrance, visitors can turn left into a corridor with a staircase in anthracite-grey steel. This is the first of several entrances to the four floors of the building. On either side of the corner greeting visitors upon arrival the recesses are both significantly deeper and open on each main floor, providing a view of a loggia on either side. The loggia has a glass shield framed in grey steel to match the staircase.

The other corridor on the long side of the building takes visitors to the broad main entrance

In 1992 Henning Larsen won the competition to draw an extension to the Glyptotek in one of the courtyards of Hack Kampmann's building. What stood out in Larsen's proposal was that it did not fill the courtyard from wall to wall but was surrounded by a staircase with skylights.

This corridor with a chequered floor has a row of sculptures by Danish sculptor Herman Wilhelm Bissen and runs between the Central Hall and the staircase in Henning Larsen's building. The gallery in the Kampmann building facing the museum garden can be accessed from the corridor.

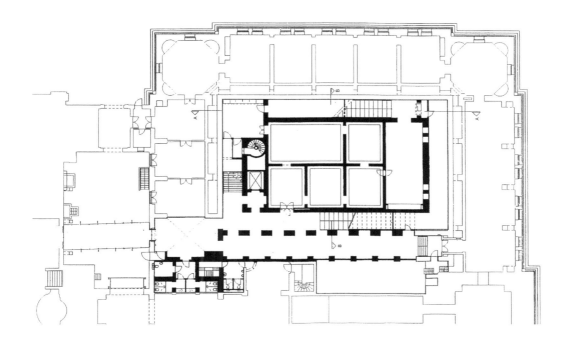

of the building. The portal marking the entrance deviates from the rest of the building in being placed in the middle of the lesene (a pilaster without a capital) separating the second and third recess. The entrance has a glass door.

The staircase starts further along the façade, halfway along the fourth recess. It has deep Carrara marble steps on a low incline. Following the ascent of the staircase the recesses become gradually shorter. It is a quarter-turn staircase with L-shaped landings in the corners that spirals around the interior, although not all the way to the top, where a roof terrace crowns the museum building. This serves a dual practical and aesthetic purpose. The low gradient of the staircase is due to several factors. After the second flight passing the short side of the building, the stairs reach the second landing with a door leading to the galleries on the first floor. The staircase then continues along the long side of the building, where the low gradient means that instead of being blocked the lunette windows in Kampmann's façade receive light from the new atrium. The last corner landing repeats the single-bay arcade of the ground floor and provides access to the second-floor galleries.

The galleries differ in size. Larsen has used classical proportions, with smaller galleries half the size of the larger ones, although rather than following any time-honoured system their dimensions are determined by the ground plan of the building. This in turn is determined by the dimensions of the original courtyard. The galleries have artificial lighting and a strictly controlled inner climate.

Spatial Duality

Henning Larsen's continuation of the Glyptotek's long architectural history is exceptional in its simplicity and stringency. The building is an expression of a turn in late modernism in which a self-referential approach to specific architectural elements verges on the postmodern. It also exemplifies Henning Larsen's trademark aesthetics. At first glance his building has characteristics of modernist architecture: it is an entirely white clear cubic volume devoid of ornamentation divided into modules – perhaps most clearly in the elements of the staircase – and using modern materials such as steel and glass as an integral part of the architecture.

At the same time, other elements point to a more traditional, classical and premodern

A quarter-turn staircase with L-shaped landings winds around the body of the building to the second floor. The building has slightly sloping walls rendered with polished marble plaster. The steps of the staircase are made of Italian marble from Carrara, and the adjoining wall of Kampmann's building is rendered with a thin layer of sand-coloured plaster. Above the staircase a skylight spans the gap between Kampmann's and Larsen's buildings.

The architectural style of Dahlerup's, Kampmann's and Larsen's buildings is very different, but they share the use of skylights to allow daylight inside. In Henning Larsen's building the skylights are made of white steel battens and clear glass.

understanding of architecture. These include the symmetry axes that influence the articulation of the building with recesses, the steel staircase structure, the mirroring of the two arcade bays in the corners, and not least the construction of the roof terrace.

There are also a number of archaic elements: the slanting walls paraphrase a distinctive feature of primarily Egyptian architecture, with portals, obelisks and of course pyramids slanting at various angles, whereas the arcades and connecting arches are based on the architecture of ancient Rome. The slanting façades can also be seen as the kind of optical finesse seen in ancient Greek temples, where entasis (the convex curve of the column) and the slight rounding of the outer perimeter walls served to optically counteract any experience of distortion from a distance. This antiquated effect is not created through ornamentation but via the revival of certain features of ancient architecture in abstract form on phenomenological terms. The evocation of the past is a primarily bodily experience. There are no identifiable historical models for Larsen's approach, just some generalised features of the architecture of the past. The use of stucco marble, an ancient technique with an aura of exclusivity, also distances the building from the present, something accentuated by its secluded location inside another building at the museum.

Finally, the major role played by light when walking around the atrium can be seen as characteristic of Nordic, Scandinavian or regional architecture. The modulation of natural light has been emphasised as a central architectural element in Scandinavia time and time again. Here the effect exceeds its practical role. Rather than being channelled into the monolithic building, it is used to create a dramatic contrast between the artificially lit chambers, the dark mummy vault below ground, and the corridors full of natural light surrounding them.

Unlike early modernism, where for the most part the avant-garde cultivated an architecture liberated from any reference to the past, Henning Larsen's building presents a far more self-referential and perhaps more complex form of modernism.

The Collage of a Century

The Glyptotek is characterised by the gradual, unpredictable and adaptable process of creation that marked all of Carl Jacobsen's building projects. His enterprises had a public didactic goal, but they were also part of his own personal learning process. His willingness to revise plans, change his mind and find new ways has resulted in a richly multifaceted building complex, which like a collage has continued to develop and grow since it was built.

Another general characteristic of the Glyptotek is its synthesis of many different symbolic universes to form an integrated whole in which patriotism, business, religion, education and the personal are placed on an equal footing. Instead of being kept separate, these different symbolic realms cross-pollinate each other.

Almost every major style from over a century is thus gathered at one address. Of these the presence of modernism can be disputed, given that Henning Larsen's building actually lands somewhere between modernism and postmodernism.

Paradoxically, Dahlerup fell victim to Jacobsen's acceptance of the historicist idea of a building's purpose corresponding to a fixed style. For whilst in material and detail Kampmann's building is influenced by National Romanticism, it pays even greater homage to the legacy of the

The galleries differ in size, but their dimensions relate to each other with smaller galleries half the size of the larger galleries. All the galleries in the building have artificial lighting.

The dark subterranean mummy gallery
can be accessed from Hack Kampmann's
building but was first built in connection
with Henning Larsen's extension.

ancient past. This is perhaps why the elements of Kampmann's building are less differentiated and more schematic. Whilst his building as a whole is more unified and block-like, it reveals less about the functional organisation of the interior than Dahlerup's building, influenced as it is by the social circulation of the city. Kampmann's building is still an exercise in style, just a more stringent style than Dahlerup's focusing on the primacy of spatiality and the power of abstraction. Finally, there is the Winter Garden, which appropriately adds architectural engineering to the repertoire of styles gathered at the Glyptotek at the same time as marking the culmination of urban sociality's penetration of the museum walls. Larsen's contribution to the process succeeds in gathering all the former motifs and spaces in a sophisticated paraphrase that manages to be a striking reproduction of the archetypal urbanity represented by marketplaces and squares, as well as a bold statement of architectural autonomy. As such, the architecture of the Glyptotek provides not only examples and illustrations but also a visual index of major changes in the art of building over the past century and more.

From the perspective of style history, the unadulterated classicism of the Central Hall and mausoleum were unique at this point in Danish architectural history. Functionally it emerged that the brewer Carl Jacobsen's insistence on a Central Hall was a wise one. Then, as now, it provided a setting for the events and gatherings that are part of every museum's life.

Notes

1 Willerup, 1896.
2 Minutes of the Glyptotek board meeting held on 20 November 1984 (Vol. 9, pp. 1114–1127), The Glyptotek Archive.
3 Simonsen, 2021, p. 27.
4 O.R.L., 1906.
5 Minutes of the Glyptotek board meeting held on 25 March 1914 (Vol. 2, pp. 9–13), The Glyptotek Archive.
6 Dahlerup, 1904.
7 Minutes of the Glyptotek board meeting held on 19 December 1914 (Vol. 2, pp. 159–160), The Glyptotek Archive.
8 O.R.L., 1906, p. 409.
9 Ibid., p. 407.
10 Simonsen, 2021, p. 30.
11 Jacobsen, 1906, p. 58.
12 Anonymous, 1906, p. 413.
13 Ibid.
14 Ibid.
15 Ibid., p. 414.
16 Zoologist Mikkel Stelvig has assisted in identifying the animals represented. Facing Niels Brocks Gade they are water buffalo, bear, tiger, hippopotamus and male lion. Facing the museum garden they are moose, gorilla, female lion, Cerberus (the Hound of Hades), lynx, female lion, male lion and Asian elephant. Facing Tietgensgade they are female lion, male lion, black rhinoceros, baboon and Bactrian camel. Some of the heads are supplemented by small reliefs of symmetrically composed animal pairs, but these are less evenly spaced and only on the façades facing the museum garden and Tietgensgade. Represented here are polecat/weasel, cobra, young crocodile, lungfish and lizard. Østergaard, 2011, pp. 9–10.
17 Ibid., p. 17.
18 Christensen and Frederiksen, 2021, p. 185.
19 Anonymous, 1906, p. 415.
20 Simonsen, 2021, p. 35.
21 Jacobsen, 1906, p. 62; Anonymous, 1906, p. 414.
22 Arvid, 1906.
23 Simonsen, 2021, pp. 35–37.
24 Jacobsen, 1906, p. 64.
25 "That the vertical wall slants is an important detail. If it hadn't, I think it would have felt as it the building was toppling down on them." Gram, 1996, p. 26.

Bibliography

Anonymous: "Musæumsbygningen for antik Kunst", *Architekten – Meddelelser fra Akademisk Architektforening*, Year 9, No. 38 (1906), pp. 412–415.

Arvid: "Glyptoteket. Et Kunstværk til 3 Millioner – Før Indvielsen", *Ekstra Bladet*, 28 May 1906.

Asmussen, Marianne Wirenfeldt: "Hack Kampmann und die 'Ny Carlsberg Glyptotek'", *Hafnia – Copenhagen Papers in the History of Art*, Vol. 9 (1983), pp. 89–112.

Bruun, Andreas: *Jens Vilhelm Dahlerups Liv og Virksomhed*. Copenhagen: H. Hagerups Boghandel, 1907.

Christensen, Julie Lejsgaard, and Rune Frederiksen: "Collecting with Passion – Towards Carl Jacobsen's Museum in the Late 19th Century", in: Christine Horwitz Tommerup and Anna Manly (eds.): *Auguste Rodin – Displacements*. Copenhagen: Ny Carlsberg Glyptotek, 2021, pp. 178–196.

Dahlerup, Vilhelm: "Ny Carlsberg Glyptotek", *Illustreret Tidende*, Year 45, No. 15 (1904), p. 266.

Glamann, Kristof: *Øl og Marmor – Carl Jacobsen på Ny Carlsberg*. Copenhagen: Gyldendal, 1995.

Gram, Dorte: "Arkitekturen beskytter kunsten", *Byggeforum*, Year 59, No. 6 (1996), pp. 24–26.

Jacobsen, Carl: *Ny Carlsberg Glyptoteks Tilblivelse*. Copenhagen: Ny Carlsberg, 1906.

"Ny Carlsberg Glyptothek – Bygningen", *Jyllands-Posten*, 5 August 1906.

O.R.L. [Osvald Rosendahl Langballe]: "Ny Carlsberg Glyptotek", *Architekten – Meddelelser fra Akademisk Architektforening*, Year 8, No. 38 (1906), pp. 401–412.

Pryd, Per: "Glyptotekets Bygmestre – To Interviews", *Politiken*, 27 June 1906, p. 4.

Simonsen, Anne Jonstrup: *Ny Carlsberg Glyptotek – Farvearkæologisk undersøgelse*. Copenhagen: Københavns Konservator, 2021.

Willerup, O.: "La nouvelle Glyptothèque de Copenhague", *La Construction moderne*, Year 12, No. 6 (7 November 1896), p. 67, https://portaildocumentaire. citedelarchitecture.fr/pdfjs/ web/viewer.html?file=/Info-doc/ged/viewPortalPublished. ashx?eid%3DIFD_FICJOINT_ FRAPN02_COM_1896_45_PDF_1

Zanker von Meyer, *Dorothee: Die Bauten von J.C. und Carl Jacobsen – Zur Bautätigkeit einer Industriellenfamilie in Dänemark*. Berlin: Deutscher Kunstverlag, 1982.

Østergaard, Jan Stubbe: "*Semper Ardens* – Facaden af Hack Kampmanns bygning til Glyptotekets antikke samling", *AIGIS, supplementum*, No. 1, May 2011.

Eva Tind

In the Winter Garden

I go down the steps and enter an almost thirty-metre-high subtropical garden. Seen from above the Winter Garden is a glass globe in the middle of cold Nordic Copenhagen. To plant yourself in an enormous hothouse – the green heart of the museum – and let your head fall back as your eyes seek the sunlight streaming through the honey-coloured glass of its vast domed roof creates the perfect illusion of eternal sunshine. The Winter Garden is the element that unifies the Glyptotek architecturally. The dome itself is borne by twelve iron columns. Glass roofs connect the heavens it frames to architect Vilhelm Dahlerup's building from 1897 and Hack Kampmann's 1906 extensions. As Carl Jacobsen once said: "We Danes know far more about plants than about works of art, but it is my hope that in the winter the garden will draw people inside, and as they look at the palms maybe they will also give some thought to the statues." The Winter Garden was to attract visitors to take a stroll indoors in winter, wandering between vast date palms, orange hibiscus, and bougainvillea plants as a respite after seeing solid white sculptures standing mutely grouped in the high-ceilinged galleries. The triumph of white marble, the art of immortalising the moment. Not with a simple click but with the enduring labour of the human body, through strength of hand, by hewing stone into the shape of a vision as the bones of the sculptor are ground down and the sharpness of the tool is dulled as that of the sculpture emerges.

I move towards the open loggia with its view of the garden. A reclining white marble body catches my eye. It is *The Water Mother* from 1921 raising her left arm with her elbow bent so a bright white, polished baby can sit on her upper arm like the branch of a tree. *The Water Mother*'s little finger supports the baby's head, this light touch enough to support the small being's entire body. Two babies identical to the first suckle at each nipple, drawing life from the mother as still more white marble babies crawl around her naked body. Like a litter of identical baby animals they climb from the water between umbrella papyrus and swimming goldfish to clamber up the maternal body. Close to *The Water Mother* hangs Cupid, and a sarcophagus with winged cherubs also stands silently in the Winter Garden, between heaven and earth, between perishable plants and solid marble. Amidst all this carved testimony to the past I have the fleeting feeling of hovering between then and now, between life and death, between pride and the sublime fall. Everything crumbles over time.

Even the hardest stone perishes. But the plants, even the most tender of them, cast seeds and multiply. Fear of death sits like the heads of flowers lightly on their stems. The dome is an eye turned towards the unconquered universe above, and the clouds blow past and away, for winter never comes to the Winter Garden.

Martin Søberg

CONCEPTION AND TYPOLOGY

Principles of Architectural Composition at the Glyptotek

During the second half of the 19th century the number of art museums in Europe exploded in the face of an increasing interest in history, the new power position of the bourgeoisie, and the rapid growth of the continent's metropoles. With their concentration of art and relics of the past in the centre of Europe's cities, art museums represented an opportunity for aesthetic contemplation, as well as providing a didactic tool for education and edification. Like many other public institutions of the period, museums were often permeated by both positivist ideals of progress and concepts of national identity.[1] Architectural ideas of the past were recycled, first and foremost the design and organisation of buildings made for princely collections. As art historian Steen Hammershøy Andersen points out in his analysis of the grand boulevard Ringstrasse in Vienna, the second half of the 19th century was witness to the rise of a bourgeoisie who instead of wanting to overthrow the Court culture of the past transformed its aesthetics. This led to what he calls an imitative relationship, at least in the adoption of princely aesthetic effects such as stucco façades.[2] Beneath the surface, however, the situation was more complex, and new ideas were brought to bear on those of the past.

At the opening of the extension of the Glyptotek and its Winter Garden in 1906, the brewer Carl Jacobsen published a short book on the conception of the Glyptotek.[3] The text was a personal account of events leading up to the opening of the museum, including the origins of the collection, the deeds of gift involved, and the construction of its first and second buildings. Jacobsen's account of the architectural aspects of creating the museum is relatively brief, so in this article I dig a little deeper, exploring the architectural foundations of the Glyptotek in the context of other 19th-century museum buildings. My primary focus is on architectural forms and spatial composition, as well as the ways Danish architects Vilhelm Dahlerup and Hack Kampmann drew on existing architectural typologies, adapting and updating them in dialogue with basic principles of architectural composition during the creative process.[4]

Types of Museum Architecture

In 1882 Carl and Ottilia Jacobsen opened their private art collection at the New Carlsberg brewery complex in Valby to the public. Two years later, a fire at Christiansborg Palace destroyed almost the entire royal art collection, including the Danish sculpture collection. The loss resulted in the Jacobsens donating their collection to the state and what was to become the Glyptotek. In 1906 Carl Jacobsen wrote:

> "I called the collection the 'Glyptotek' to make known that it was not an ordinary museum, with all the requirements of scientific order and comprehensiveness that would imply, and where works of art often stand frozen, estranged from one another [...]."[5]

The term *glyptotek* is Greek for a place for storing sculptures. It also referred to the Bavarian king Ludwig I's (1786–1868) Glyptothek in Munich, a collection of ancient sculpture open to the public and housed in a building built 1815–1830 designed by German architect Leo von Klenze (1784–1864). The building had a quadratic floor plan with four wings surrounding an open courtyard, and temple façades at the front and back, all underlining the central symmetrical axis. Carl Jacobsen made the first sketch of the Glyptotek in Copenhagen himself. It was heavily inspired by the Glyptothek in Munich: a quadratic floor plan comprised of four wings, but with a domed rotunda in the centre instead of an open courtyard (see p. 43).[6]

One way to approach the relationship between Klenze's building and Jacobsen's sketch is their shared architectural typology. As Austrian architect Andreas Lechner writes, the term typology refers to repeated and 'typical' architectural forms and spaces that go beyond the individual building and also relate to its function. Architects can draw on such typologies or position themselves in relationship to them in other ways when developing new architecture.[7] Typology reflects not only a certain stability in architecture but also the passing down of meaning: a form of collective memory in which types are identified and analysed in existing architecture, as well as in imagining new buildings.

Types of museum buildings can thus be analysed to find connections and differences from a typological perspective.[8] There are, however, blind spots to this approach. As British museologist Suzanne MacLeod writes, typology can be connected to mistaken ideas about the history of architecture as a continuous process of development, progressing from one stage to the

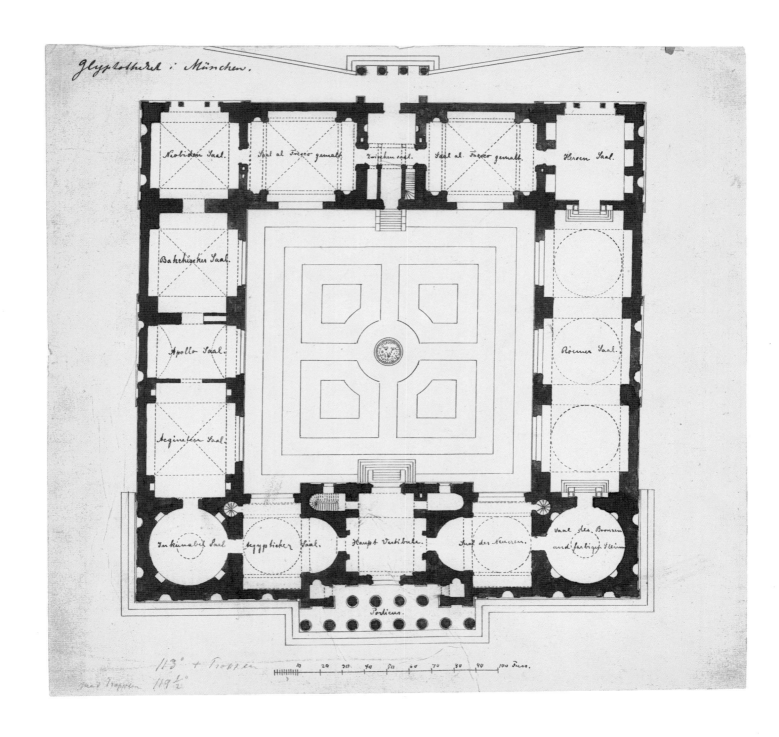

Leo von Klenze: Glyptothek, 1815–1830,
Munich. Traced drawing by Vilhelm
Dahlerup, undated. Carl Jacobsen drew
a proposal for the Glyptotek in Copenhagen himself based on the Glyptothek
in Munich. As the drawing shows
the museum was also a key source of
inspiration for Dahlerup in developing
the architecture of the Glyptotek in
Copenhagen.

Leo von Klenze: Glyptothek, 1815–1830, Munich. This lithograph of the museum by an unidentified artist (1880) shows the main entrance facing Königsplatz with a temple front and Ionic columns of the Classical order. The niches in the façade contain sculptures representing the collection of ancient sculptures inside the museum.

next towards a pinnacle of achievement. Furthermore, MacLeod argues that a typological approach to museum architecture can be tied to an understanding of architecture as free of content, seeing architecture as a pure work of art that fails to take the contents and social practices of the museum into account, just as changes in physical conditions over time are rarely included in typological analysis.[9] Instead MacLeod sees museum architecture as an aspect of social and cultural production, a technology that involves human bodies, usage and identity.[10] A typological approach can, nonetheless, be useful in understanding aspects of form and spatiality, including how the architecture was created and the other types it relates to. This does, however, demand awareness of aspects of the architecture this excludes, such as how the building functions, how it is experienced and how it has changed. These are valid considerations, but beyond the scope of what follows.

Princely collections were an important phenomenon during the Renaissance, leading to the creation of designated rooms – usually a central room or long gallery – to exhibit them.[11] Not until the mid 18th century were such collections actually open to the public. These included the Fridericianum museum in Kassel (1769–1777), commissioned by Frederik II, Landgrave of Hesse-Kassel (1720–1785) and designed by German architect Simon Louis du Ry (1726–1799). The building had a temple front and housed collections of art and natural history specimens. Around the same time the Pio Clementino Museum at the Vatican was extended (circa 1773–1780) by architects Michelangelo Simonetti (1724–1787) and Giuseppe Camporesi (1761–1822). The Neoclassical complex included a rotunda with a coffered dome, semicircular windows and niches for ancient sculptures – the type of space that was particularly popular in subsequent museum buildings, combining monumental architecture rooted in antiquity and the display of sculptures.

Growing interest in the public museum as an institution and type of architecture was already apparent in the Prix de Rome competitions arranged by the influential French Académie d'Architecture. Museum design was the subject of the competition numerous times between 1778 and the beginning of the 19th century. In 1778–1779 two first prizes were awarded, one to Guy de Gisors (1762–1835) and the other to François-Jacques Delannoy (1755–1835). Both architects had proposed a building plan based on a square divided by a Greek cross creating four courtyards, which in Delannoy's proposal had a rotunda in the middle – an early example corresponding to Jacobsen's later sketch. A similar configuration was presented by French architect Étienne-Louis Boullée (1728–1799) in a museum proposal from 1783, although his building had a much larger rotunda and semicircular colonnades on each side of the square.

Whereas the French examples above only existed on paper, at the beginning of the 19th century several museums were actually built in Germany, museums that were to have a major influence on later European museum architecture. The quadratic museum was finally realised with Klenze's Glyptothek in Munich. The building was the result of a competition to which Klenze submitted three entries in different styles – Greek, Roman and Renaissance – in an early demonstration of the plurality of styles that was later to flourish in the 19th century as historicism and eclecticism. At the Altes Museum in Berlin (1823–1830), German architect Karl Friedrich Schinkel (1781–1841) combined a rectangular plan with a classical colonnade, monumental staircases, two inner courtyards and a central rotunda with pendentive vaulting to display ancient sculptures, just like the rotunda at the Pio Clementino Museum.[12]

At the Pinakothek in Munich (1824–1836), Leo von Klenze continued to develop the gallery as a basilica structure comprised of a central hall with skylights, side-lit alcoves along the sides and a long gallery with arched arcade windows. The ground floor housed storage, a library and a print room. The architecture inspired other European museum buildings, including the Gemäldegalerie in Dresden (1847–1855) designed by German architect Gottfried Semper (1803–1879), and the Kunsthistorisches Hofmuseum in Vienna (1871–1891) designed by Semper in collaboration with Austrian architect Carl von Hasenauer (1833–1894).[13]

According to Andreas Lechner, the development of existing types like the gallery, basilica, rotunda and atrium were influenced by the illustrated publications of French architect Jean-Nicolas-Louis Durand (1760–1834). Durand saw architecture as a formal system in which what might be called 'samples' today could be assembled in various combinations according to classical principles of composition.[14] As an architectural discipline, composition also played a central role in the architecture classes taught at the influential French École des Beaux-Arts, especially in equipping architects to design an entire ensemble of buildings and building parts to create a homogenous whole.[15] Combinations of this kind were seen in 19th-century historicism, and not least in the eclecticism also practised by Vilhelm Dahlerup and Hack Kampmann. The goal was not archaeological accuracy in recreating specific styles or building types but using architectural types and motifs in new contexts. Art historian Mette Bligaard explains eclecticism as a form of "free imitation" in which styles were not to be simply copied but improved upon.[16] She takes the interest of Danish architects in Lombardian brick architecture as an example easily converted using Danish building methods and materials. As Ferdinand Meldahl (1827–1908) wrote to fellow architect Gustav Friedrich Hetsch (1788–1864) in 1854: "I consider central and northern Italy to be the perfect larder for Scandinavian architects."[17] Style and materials emerged in the interaction of the building's form, function and spatial composition. The type formations of the early 19th century played a crucial role, transferring theoretical, imaginary architecture to real buildings, like the museums of Klenze and Schinkel. As I explore below, this also applies to the architecture of the Glyptotek.

Variations on a Type:
The Dahlerup Building

The sketch Carl Jacobsen based on Klenze's Glyptothek was the starting point for Vilhelm Dahlerup's development of the project.[18] Dahlerup also said that his 1882 monument to Victor Emmanuel II (1820–1878) in Rome, which Jacobsen had seen at the 1884 Charlottenborg Exhibition, was a further source of inspiration.[19] The monument was a cylindrical building on a quadratic platform. The cylinder was decorated with frescoes and reliefs, and inside there was a corridor spiralling along the perimeter and a Pantheon-like central area with a coffered dome and niches for sculptures. The quadratic floor plan recurred in Klenze's Glyptothek, as well as in Dahlerup's monument to Victor Emmanuel, and formed the basis for Dahlerup's proposal for the Glyptotek.[20] A central rotunda is another key feature of the architecture of ancient Rome and the Renaissance. References to ancient Rome in museums and the other monumental architecture of the period had multiple threads, the goal being to display classical or classically inspired sculptures in a classical setting, not only to create a harmonious whole but to connote classical architecture's ideals of civic education and edification. Some of Dahlerup's sketches for buildings whose function is unknown also explored the construction and decoration of a Pantheon-like rotunda, as well as locating the rotunda in a larger building with a monumental façade and steps. These drawings are from Dahlerup's sketchbook, and he probably made them from 1854 to 1858 while still a student. On the same theme, in 1833 the Copenhagen art society Kunstforeningen had held a competition for the design of a museum inside the uncompleted rotunda of Frederik's Church. The winning project was G.F. Hetsch's proposal for a sculpture museum, which he reworked as a proposal for a national art museum. The 1837 project was based on a quadratic floor plan surrounding a central rotunda, the same configuration Hetsch used for his proposal for Thorvaldsen's Museum in 1838. As Hetsch's student, Dahlerup must have been familiar with these projects.[21]

We do not know the exact order of Dahlerup's many proposals for the Glyptotek, but they

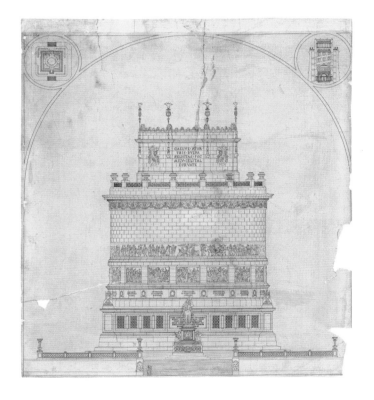

Vilhelm Dahlerup: Monument to Victor Emmanuel II, 1882, Rome. In 1882 Dahlerup entered an international competition to design a monument to the Italian king Victor Emmanuel II in Rome. In 1884 the project was shown at an exhibition at the Royal Danish Academy of Fine Arts, which is where Carl Jacobsen saw it. The round building with a rotunda was the model for the domed structures in various proposals Dahlerup drew for the Glyptotek. The glass dome of the Winter Garden stemmed from such ideas.

Vilhelm Dahlerup: Proposal for the Glyptotek, 1888/1889. Dahlerup drew many different plans for the Glyptotek in different Copenhagen locations. The one here is undated and the location unidentified. The floor plan looks like Carl Jacobsen's preliminary design for the museum and the façade like the museum that was finally built.

must all have been made between 1888 and 1890 when construction began. One drawing shows a ground plan close to the one in Jacobsen's sketch, with a series of larger and smaller galleries in a square around the rotunda. It could be Dahlerup's first proposal, but since in many ways it resembles the final building it could also be from a later stage of the design process. This is true, for example, of the façade with three bays on either side of the entrance and the long staircases next to the front galleries. Before turning to the museum that was finally built, it is worth taking a closer look at some of the alternatives.

The location of the Glyptotek was a decisive factor. Carl Jacobsen wanted it to be built opposite the site for the new City Hall, where Copenhagen City Hall Square is today. This was where the temporary building for the exhibition of French art Jacobsen organised in 1888 was located. Dahlerup's proposal for this location is an almost rectangular, symmetrically structured building with five bays facing the square and an entrance hall that leads directly into the rotunda. The front part of the building consists of two floors connected by a semicircular staircase. The main disposition is the same as Jacobsen's sketch, with four wings surrounding a courtyard with a domed rotunda as the main feature. Here, however, the square has become a rectangle, making the front of the building significantly shorter. From a typological perspective it is reminiscent of Klenze's Glyptothek, but even closer to Thorvaldsen's Museum (1839–1848), Denmark's first art museum designed by Danish architect Michael Gottlieb Bindesbøll (1800–1856). Thorvaldsen's Museum also has a rectangular ground plan, five bays facing an open square, side-lit galleries on the long sides and a central open courtyard.

Copenhagen's mayor suggested an alternative site on a square facing Ørsted Park, where Israel Square is today, and Dahlerup drew up a proposal for a building that spans almost the entire width of the square. At first glance the plan looks almost identical to Jacobsen's: quasi-quadratic and the same on both sides of the central axis. Four wings surround a central building comprised partly of a lower corridor with skylights and four chapel-like rooms marking the diagonals of the complex, and partly of a rotunda with nine niches containing sculptures. Above these are semicircular windows, and at the top a coffered dome like that on the rotunda at the Pio Clementino Museum.

Spatially, however, the building is far more differentiated than Jacobsen's sketch. The front and back wings are tall, one-storey buildings with skylights and an entrance hall modelled on the ancient Arch of Constantine in Rome. This is crowned by a quadriga – a sculpture of a chariot with four horses abreast like that at Thorvaldsen's Museum. Visitors to the museum pass beneath this archway to reach a rectangular hallway with access to galleries on both sides and the rotunda directly ahead. Stairs from the front galleries lead to central wings with two floors. Each side wing of the lower floor, which is slightly below ground level, has two large galleries and six smaller alcoves in which one large and two smaller sculptures appear to have been installed, just as at Thorvaldsen's Museum. The galleries on the first floor have skylights and are presumably for paintings. This kind of building, with sidelights on the lower floor and skylights on the floor above, was widespread in contemporary museum and gallery architecture, as seen at the Pinakothek in Munich and Charlottenborg in Copenhagen. There are free-standing sculptures along the façade facing the park, turning the narrow space in front of the building into an outdoor exhibition space just like the Glyptotek today. The building's close interaction with its surroundings is further underlined by an entrance free of monumental steps. Unlike many museums and other monumental buildings of the period it is level with the terrain.

A park location at Helmer's Bastion, where Jarmer's Square is today, was also considered. Here the setting was more open, with two new, main boulevards in Copenhagen – Vestre Boulevard (now H.C. Andersen's Boulevard) and Nørre Voldgade – meeting at an obtuse angle. It would thus be seen more at an angle than the orthogonal façade of the building facing Ørsted Park. This would make it more like the National Gallery of Denmark, which was at the planning stage and also designed by Dahlerup and fellow architect Georg E.W. Møller (1840–1897). Both are oblique buildings on high ground facing Copenhagen centre, creating a monumental wall surrounding the city and, not least, life on the boulevards.

On 23 September 1889 the city council opted for a site next to Tivoli Gardens. A drawing by Dahlerup shows the dome with a sculpture group at the top instead of a lantern. The windows of the façade, which is divided into nine bays of almost equal width, look into the exhibition halls behind them, and the central section is much more understated than the final design of the Glyptotek. A cross-section of another version shows the double construction of the dome: a solid base continuing in the brickwork of an inner dome divided into octagonal coffers with an outer dome of cast-iron grating. The dome appears to float above an open tambour comprised of narrow walls pointing to the centre and inside this ring of walls caryatids on the railing of the gallery. An elevation drawing of the east façade shows the arcade theme of the front continuing all the way round the building, although on the sides the columns have been replaced by pilasters and the shells by flat, blind arcades framing circular relief portraits in profile called *tondi*. In another drawing, which in places closely resembles the museum that was eventually built, the dome's gallery has disappeared and the dome itself is so low that it cannot be seen from the outside. The same proposal included a fourth wing comprised of a large hall with skylights and access to a large, glass-covered hall, possibly an atrium of sorts with a direct connection to the inner courtyard. The domed glass ceiling and colonnades resemble the conservatory at J.C. (1811–1887) and Laura

Vilhelm Dahlerup: Proposal for the Glyptotek on the square next to Ørsted Park,
1888/1889. This virtually quadratic plan
with galleries arranged around a central
rotunda features in several proposals for
the Glyptotek. Here the building is located
on the Copenhagen square facing Ørsted
Park.

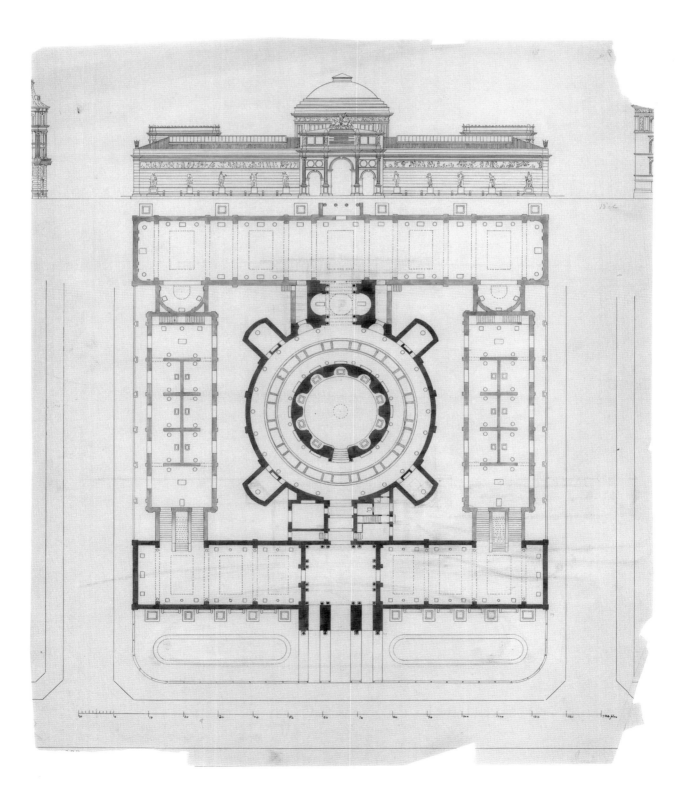

Jacobsen's (1819–1911) villa at the old Carlsberg brewery complex.

The construction of the Glyptotek began in the spring of 1890. The project had been reduced in a number of ways before the official opening on 1 May 1897. The rotunda and dome had to be done without, and the range of materials was also more limited. As a result, the side wings were built of bricks and cement instead of limestone and granite as originally planned. The larger exhibition galleries were located in three wings: a single-storey main wing with skylights facing the street, and two taller side wings facing the streets of Tietgensgade and Niels Brocks Gade respectively. These have side-lit sculpture galleries on the ground floor, and painting galleries with standard skylights on the floor above. The triumphal arch had been reduced to a large *serliana* (a tripartite opening) the central part of which is arched whereas the two sides end in beams. Dahlerup used the same feature at the National Gallery of Denmark, but at the Glyptotek the two side openings are reduced to niches containing sculptures. Sculptures in shell-headed niches are a common feature of Renaissance architecture, and Dahlerup also included them in the side

Vilhelm Dahlerup: Proposal for the Glyptotek on Vestre Boulevard, 1889. Elevation of the east façade. The arcade of the front façade continues around the building. The façades of the side wings eventually built were simpler with semicircular windows.

ressaults for his competition entry to build a joint national and art museum.[22] The remainder of the façade is comprised of three niches on either side of the central section, which extends to approximately the same height as the side wings. Seen in perspective, the building is comprised of three tall parallel wings connected by a lower wing at the front. This is similar to the proposal for Israel Square with its lower entrance and two-storey side wings. Whereas the triumphal arch of the older project emphasises the entrance, this central focus is more underplayed in the actual façade of the Glyptotek where the central arch is repeated by the six arches of the arcade, creating a façade of rhythmical repetitions.

Completion and Change: The Kampmann Building and the Winter Garden

When the Glyptotek opened in 1897, Dahlerup's building was like a torso. The fourth connecting wing, creating a continuous path between the wings like that at Klenze's Glyptothek and Schinkel's Altes Museum, had never been built. Neither had the domed rotunda. Not until several years later, when the open courtyard of

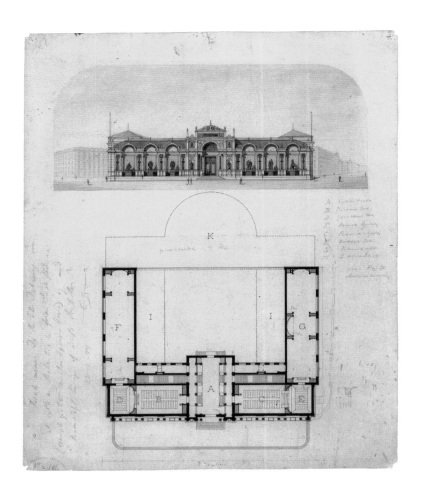

Vilhelm Dahlerup: Proposal for the Glyptotek on Vestre Boulevard, 1889/1890. The drawing shows the actual façade and ground plan of the building constructed from 1890 to 1897. The rotunda, dome and rear gallery wing of earlier designs are no longer included.

Dahlerup's building was closed in by a wing for the Antiquities Collection, was a dome built — and by a different architect. Hack Kampmann's winning 1901 competition entry for an extension to the Glyptotek, which was largely carried out as planned, was rectangular in floor plan and followed the pre-existing main axis. Whereas Dahlerup, as seen above, drew many different plans for his building, Kampmann's building was largely given from the outset by the pre-existing wings of the museum and the terms of the competition. The wing with the Antiquities Collection is connected to Dahlerup's building via two lower gatehouses but is slightly wider. The Central Hall lies on the central axis between the side wings, and takes the form of a covered colonnade with a temple front at the rear marking the culmination of the axis. Beyond the temple front there is a square room with a steep, vertical coffered ceiling inside an equally steep step pyramid on the roof above. The pyramid was modelled on the ancient Greek Mausoleum of Halicarnassus in present-day Turkey, described by both the Roman author Pliny the Elder (23–79 CE) and the Roman architect Vitruvius (c. 70–25 BCE). In 1852 the British archaeologist Charles Thomas Newton's (1816–1894) excavations and surveys resulted in a drawn reconstruction. It is also worthy of note that Kampmann's competition entry had quadratic exhibition halls in three of the four corners of the building, whereas the final plan has two quadratic and two round halls in the corners marking a change of direction between the wings, like Klenze's Glyptothek but turned ninety degrees. The indentation of the corners in relationship to the side wings were not part of Klenze's museum but are seen in Dahlerup's early proposals for the Glyptotek.

Kampmann's building does not create a continuous path between Dahlerup's three wings but is built so visitors can walk through all the large exhibition halls before returning to the starting point, circling the two inner courtyards and central hall. Typologically, the rectangular plan with two inner courtyards is connected to Schinkel's Altes Museum, although without the Berlin museum's central rotunda, which has been replaced by an atrium-like central hall. Kampmann's building thus relates, perhaps slightly surprisingly, to another of Dahlerup's projects, namely his competition entry for a combined national and art museum mentioned above, which also has a rectangular complex with two courtyards and a central albeit uncovered atrium.

The wing for the Antiquities Collection has two floors: the lower ground-floor exhibition hall, which from the outside is hidden behind the high plinth wall, and the Egyptian, Greek and Roman collections in galleries mainly lit by skylights. On this kind of light Carl Jacobsen wrote:

> "At Chatsworth House in England I saw the splendid hall the Duke of Devonshire had built for his wonderful sculpture collection. Light comes from "lanterns" in the ceiling, which has a very pleasing effect and adds grandeur to the room. I built my central hall in the same way, modelled closely on Chatsworth, and we used similar lanterns in the four corner galleries of Kampmann's new building at the Glyptotek."[23]

As seen above, two-storey buildings were popular for museums, although galleries with skylights were usually intended for the display of paintings, as in Dahlerup's building at the Glyptotek or Klenze's Pinakothek. Kampmann's disposition, with lower-ceilinged galleries below and higher ceilings in the galleries above as a kind of *bel étage*, followed the disposition at the Pinakothek rather than Dahlerup's building. Kampmann proposed that the basement level should be accessed via a monumental staircase in the middle of the Glyptotek's Central Hall. Carl Jacobsen was against the idea, so a significantly smaller staircase was moved to the corner of the hall, and a water basin or impluvium with an original Roman mosaic at the bottom was installed in the middle of the floor instead.

Different ideas for the façades of the building were tried out. Kampmann initially thought they should be covered in either red or white marble plaster, the only ornamentation being

Vilhelm Dahlerup: Proposal for the Glyptotek on Vestre Boulevard, 1889/1890. Perspective drawing showing the two-storey side wings and lower front wing with a raised entrance hall. The composition creates a rhythmical sequence of differently sized buildings framed by arcades.

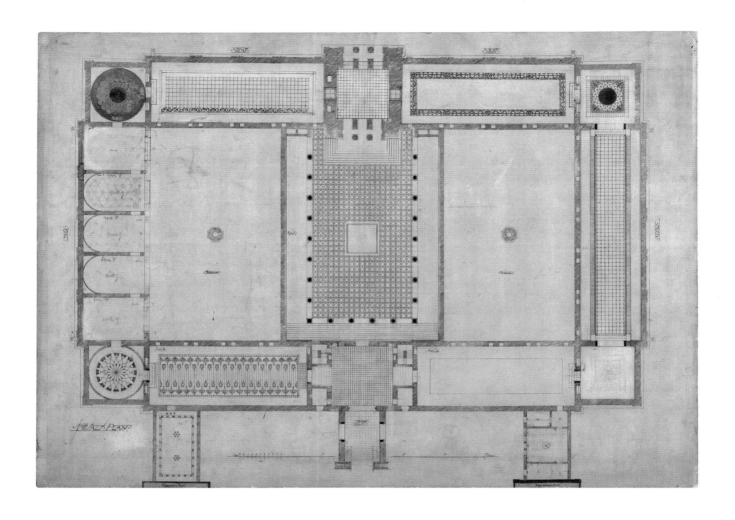

Hack Kampmann: The Glyptotek, 1900. The rectangular ground plan for the extension to house the museum's Antiquities Collection has four gallery wings surrounding a hall on the central axis, creating two inner courtyards.

around the windows of the ground floor and the mausoleum-like central section. He did, however, experiment with ornamentation in several drawings. In one, the high plinth wall is covered by a relief, not unlike the fresco by Danish painter Jørgen Sonne (1801–1890) covering the lower part of the walls at Thorvaldsen's Museum. In other sketches angels hold cartouches with inscriptions or reliefs. Kampmann also considered light from the side in the north and south wings. He tried a number of solutions: a repetition of the semicircular windows of Dahlerup's side wing, a row of Ionic columns making the wings look like the sides of a temple, trapezoid windows indebted to Thorvaldsen's Museum and linking back to Egyptian and Etruscan architecture, and rectangular windows divided in the middle and the same size as the windows on the ground floor. The emphasis on vertical lines also varies. The angels of the corner pavilions are added, emphasising the four corners of the building reinforced by skylights with domes instead of flat pyramids. Large brick surfaces are broken by coupled pilasters, a simplified continuation of the use of pilasters in Dahlerup's side wings throughout the complex as a whole.

The use of the pyramid in museum architecture had not been seen before. This made it a new typological invention, although the pyramidal tower marking the central axis of Oxford University Museum of Natural History (1855–1860), designed by Irish architects Thomas Newenham Deane (1828–1899) and Benjamin Woodward (1816–1861), has a similar spatial effect. It has been considered whether Kampmann imagined Carl and Ottilia Jacobsen being buried in the mausoleum section, or indeed whether it should be seen as a mausoleum at all.[24] Danish archaeologist Jan Stubbe Østergaard has suggested that it could be a *heroon*: a shrine to a hero for commemoration or worship.[25] Another explanation could be that the Mausoleum of Halicarnassus was a hybrid of different styles: the Egyptian pyramid (albeit via Greek architecture) and the peripteral Greek temple. Kampmann's version is not a replica of the mausoleum in Halicarnassus but his own interpretation in which the pyramid is placed above a Greek ante-temple, as well as being connected to an atrium, a familiar feature of Greek and especially Roman architecture. Furthermore, we find pyramids in Etruscan and Roman sepulchral architecture. This combination of types

Hack Kampmann: Proposal for the extension to the Glyptotek, 1900. In his first proposals Kampmann envisioned the façades of the museum being rendered with white or red stucco marble. In this drawing the central section of the west wing has a row of Ionic columns.

Hack Kampmann: Proposal for the extension to the Glyptotek, 1900. Perspective drawing of the building from the west. Dahlerup's building can just be made out behind. The skylights of the corner pavilions now have the domed tops that were later built.

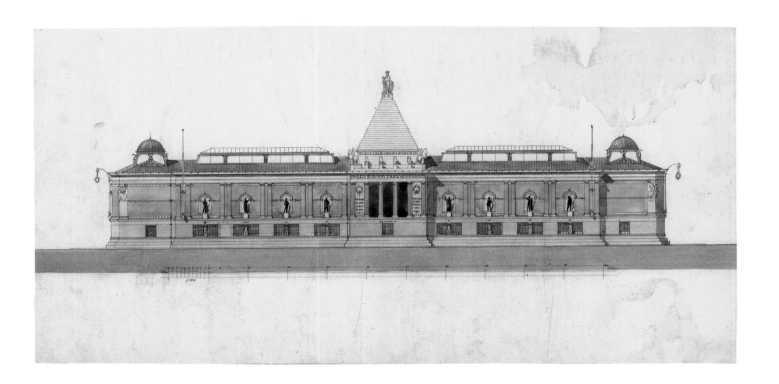

Hack Kampmann: Proposal for the extension to the Glyptotek, 1900. Here Kampmann has drawn sculptures in the bays of the façade that correspond to the ones in the arcade bays on Dahlerup's entrance façade.

reflects the contents of the museum, its collection of Egyptian, Greek and Roman artefacts. The result is synthesis rather than eclecticism, bringing key architectural features together to form a new whole.

This synthesis should also be seen in light of the didactic intentions of the Glyptotek. As art historian Carol Duncan argues, there is a long tradition of museum architecture being modelled on historical, ceremonial structures, meaning buildings emphasising spiritual transformation. According to Duncan, 19th-century art museums were to cause wonder but also have a civilising and edifying effect.[26] Like much museum architecture of the period, the wing for the Antiquities Collection was not a neutral setting for artefacts but intended to evoke the ancient world. This is underlined by the unrealised murals Kampmann had intended to decorate the walls of the galleries. The murals depicted major buildings of the ancient world, making the context the artefacts came from visible. The Mausoleum of Halicarnassus features twice in the mural designs: once in a sketch of a painting for the semicircular end wall, and in more simplified form in a sketch for the stucco decoration in the exhibition of

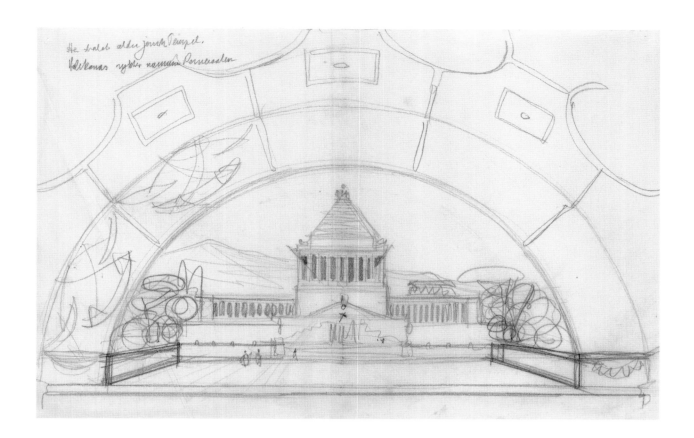

Greek–Roman art located directly south of the central mausoleum. This represented a way for Kampmann to establish a coherent world, a *Gesamtkunstwerk*, in which the connection between the artefacts, images of ancient architecture, reliefs midway between painting and sculpture, and the actual entry into an architectural space form a panorama-like continuum.[27]

With the extension, the Glyptotek was finally given its dome. Dahlerup had drawn the Winter Garden covered by a dome and a direct connection to the wing with the Antiquities Collection. As Carl Jacobsen wrote in 1906: "[...] there had to be a dome, it was a debt of honour we owed to Dahlerup".[28] Some of the drawings, which may predate the architectural competition for the antiquities wing, show how Dahlerup had imagined the dome being directly connected to the entrance hall. The dome itself is not much higher, but the outer cast-iron dome structure rises significantly above it. The Winter Garden was intended as a place of respite, where visitors could rest their eyes, but also as a museum attraction in its own right.[29] One model for the glass roof above the courtyard was the Industrial Exhibition Hall in Copenhagen (1870–1872), designed by Danish

Hack Kampmann: Proposal for a mural in one of the smaller galleries, the Glyptotek, 1900. Drawing of a mural of the Mausoleum of Halicarnassus, which was the model for the central section of the rear façade. It represents Kampmann's efforts to establish a connection between the interior and exterior of the museum and between its exhibits and architecture.

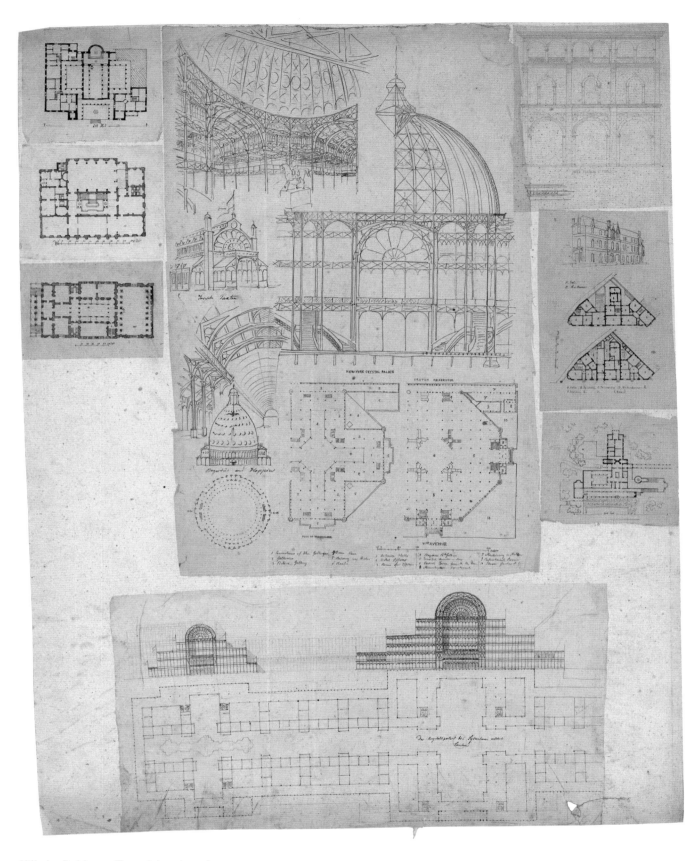

Vilhelm Dahlerup: Traced drawing of
international glass and cast-iron structures, undated. The drawings demonstrate
Dahlerup's interest in exhibition architecture and the industrial materials he used in
the Glyptotek's Winter Garden. The large
drawing in the middle is New York Crystal
Palace (1853) and below it Crystal Palace,
London (1851).

Vilhelm Dahlerup: Proposal for the rotunda, the Glyptotek, 1901. Here Dahlerup has drawn the cast-iron and glass dome supported by stone columns and arches.

architect Vilhelm Klein (1835–1913), although there were many other contemporary examples. Dahlerup sought international inspiration for its typology and construction. His sketchbook contains traced drawings of, for example, Crystal Palace in London (1851) and New York Crystal Palace (1853), the latter with a glass dome in the centre. The glass-covered sculpture courtyard at École des Beaux-Arts in Paris, designed in 1863 by French architects Félix Duban (1797–1870) and Ernest-Georges Coquart (1831–1902) and built in 1871–1874, could also have been a source of inspiration. That Dahlerup hoped to build at least part of the dome in stone can be seen in a perspectival cross-section where the tambour is lower down, creating a circular structure borne by pillars and arches. Each section of the tambour is divided into two bays marked by arches, creating a clearly articulated hierarchy. The style here is much more heavily influenced by the Early Renaissance than the dome that was eventually built with a light, filigreed cast-iron construction.

In his review of the Glyptotek, Danish art historian Vilhelm Wanscher (1875–1961) wrote that the building had been "adorned by a dome, which like the light domes on the St.

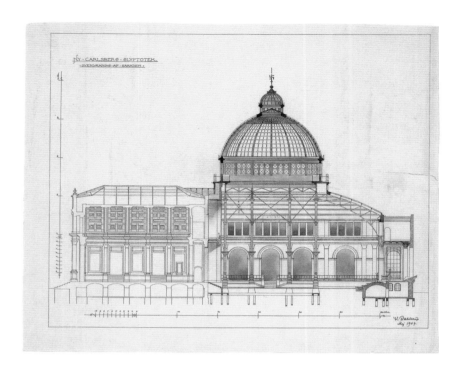

Vilhelm Dahlerup: Dome and Winter Garden, the Glyptotek, 1901. In its final form the dome and rest of the Winter Garden's roof was made of glass and cast iron. A light, elegant construction resting on the existing building in continuation of the vestibule seen in cross-section to the left.

Mark's Basilica in Venice and other buildings of north Italian architecture rounds softly above the arches of the façade, granting them an indirect supportive role [...]".[30] At the same time, the dome made the Glyptotek more akin in typology to another major museum building of the period, the previously mentioned and far more imposing Kunsthistorisches Hofmuseum in Vienna. Here, however, the dome is built of brick and flanked by four smaller towers also with domed roofs.

The Glyptotek's Architectural Family

The subsequent landscaping of the Glyptotek's garden and the renovation of Vestre Boulevard made the museum a *grand ensemble*: an imposing complex in an urban setting with scenic elements. The major American and European world fairs of the late 19th century were developed precisely as such ensembles.[31] As this article shows, however, the creation of the Glyptotek's architecture was in dialogue with the city surrounding it from the very beginning, and the wing for the Antiquities Collection was also in dialogue with Dahlerup's building. The architecture of both wings is furthermore connected to existing types of museum and gallery architecture and also incorporated entirely different types of architecture, such as the pyramid. Dahlerup and Kampmann's work with the principles of composition was highly typological rather than stylistic in nature, prioritising architectural forms and spatial composition.

For Dahlerup, the range of potential sites for the Glyptotek provided an opportunity to experiment with its design, including different levels, different volumes, and different dome locations and sizes. The resulting spatial effects relate to but also rethink existing typologies. Kampmann's project was more restricted, not least because it was an extension to Dahlerup's building. Nonetheless, he managed to create spatial,

ornamental and material connections to what already existed at the same time as bringing the architecture into play as a didactic tool. In their work at the Glyptotek Dahlerup and Kampmann alike turned to key types of 19th-century museum architecture for inspiration, not least Leo von Klenze's Glyptothek and Pinakothek and Karl Friedrich Schinkel's Altes Museum. Dahlerup and Kampmann's buildings became part of an architectural family but with unique traits of their own, including original forms of synthesis and new typological variations.

Vilhelm Dahlerup: Façade of the Glyptotek, 1901. Dahlerup had always hoped the Glyptotek would be crowned by a dome. With the roof of the Winter Garden his vision was realised with a monumental dome surmounting the entire museum complex.

Notes

1. Giebelhausen, 2003, p. 5; Poulsen, 1992.
2. Andersen, 1994, p. 38.
3. Jacobsen, 1906.
4. The architecture of the Glyptotek has also been a subject of study in the past, although never with a focus on the connection between its conception and typology. See "Ny Carlsberg Glyptothek", 1901; Zanker von Meyer, 1982, pp. 161–204; Asmussen, 1983; and Kasper Lægring's articles in this publication. Danish museum architecture in general, however, is a relatively well-covered field. See Jørgensen, Lund and Nørregård-Nielsen, 1980, pp. 171–173; Villadsen, 1983; Villadsen, 1998; and Pedersen, Troelsen and Nielsen, 2009.
5. Jacobsen, 1906, p. 19.
6. Ibid., p. 24.
7. Lechner, 2021, p. 156. For more on types and typology see, for example, Moneo, 1978, and Jacoby, 2015.
8. Pevsner, 1976. See also Marotta, 2013.
9. MacLeod, 2013, pp. 18–19.
10. This perspective is inspired by, among others, Tony Bennett's groundbreaking book *The Birth of the Museum* (1995). Using the French philosopher Michel Foucault's analysis of power, Bennett examines the museum as an apparatus to create a particular kind of citizen, a specific culture and certain patterns of social behaviour. Another dimension, which Pevsner also shows little interest in and that a typological approach has difficulty grasping, is the experiential, i.e. the museum as a stage set or generator of atmosphere, most recently dealt with in a special issue of the architectural journal *Oase*. Liefooghe, Çiçek and Engels, 2022. A phenomenological approach to architecture can, for example, be found in Pedersen, 2006.
11. Pevsner, 1976, p. 112.
12. Jørgensen, 2009, p. 115.
13. Pevsner, 1976, p. 130.
14. Lechner, 2021, p. 196.
15. Lucan, 2012, pp. 65–81.
16. Bligaard, 2008, Vol. 1, p. 184.
17. Quoted from ibid., p. 222.
18. Bruun, 1907, pp. 82–88.
19. Pryd, 1906.
20. Typologically, Dahlerup's monument to Victor Emmanuel II is also related to Klenze's Befreiungshalle ('Hall of Liberation') in Kelheim, Bavaria (1842–1863), a rotunda structure with an inner pendentive vault.
21. As Danish art historian Kjeld von Folsach has pointed out, the disposition in the 1838 project bears a striking resemblance to German architect Karl von Fischer's 1815 competition entry for the Munich Glyptothek. Folsach, 1988, pp. 116–129. See also Plagemann, 1967, pp. 48–49, illus. 18–19.
22. The façade's similarities to Scuola Grande di San Marco and St. Mark's Basilica in Venice have been identified elsewhere, but I would like to suggest another possible source of Venetian inspiration, i.e. the Loggetta on St. Mark's Square (1538–1546), by the Italian sculptor and architect Jacopo Sansovino. The Loggetta's arcade structure, sculptures in shell-headed niches paired pillars and winged figures in relief around the opening could well have inspired Dahlerup.
23. Jacobsen, 1906, p. 29.
24. See also Vilhelm Wanscher's description of the mausoleum. Wanscher, 1906, p. 28.
25. Østergaard, 2011, p. 20.
26. Duncan, 1995, pp. 9 and 16.
27. For more on *Gesamtkunstwerk*, see Munch, 2012.
28. Jacobsen, 1906, p. 61.
29. Ibid.
30. Wanscher, 1906, p. 28.
31. Lucan, 2012, pp. 192–196.

Bibliography

Andersen, Steen Hammershøy: "Fortrængningens kulisser – Om Ringstraße i Wien og betydningsdannelser i den historicistiske bys rum", *Passepartout*, Year 2, No. 4 (1994), pp. 23–45.

Asmussen, Marianne Wirenfeldt: "Hack Kampmann und die 'Ny Carlsberg Glyptotek'", *Hafnia – Copenhagen Papers in the History of Art*, No. 9 (1983), pp. 89–112.

Bennett, Tony: *The Birth of the Museum – History, Theory, Politics*. London and New York: Routledge, 1995.

Bligaard, Mette: *Frederiksborgs genrejsning – Historicisme i teori og praksis*, Vols. 1–2. Copenhagen: Forlaget Vandkunsten, 2008.

Bruun, Andreas: *Jens Vilhelm Dahlerups Liv og Virksomhed*. Copenhagen: H. Hagerups Boghandel, 1907.

Dahlerup, Vilhelm: "Ny Carlsberg Glyptotek", *Illustreret Tidende*, Year 45, No. 15 (1904), p. 266.

Duncan, Carol: *Civilizing Rituals – Inside Public Art Museums*. London and New York: Routledge, 1995.

Folsach, Kjeld von: *Fra nyklassicisme til historicisme – Arkitekten G.F. Hetsch*. Copenhagen: Christian Ejlers' Forlag, 1988.

Giebelhausen, Michaela: "Introduction. The Architecture of the Museum – Symbolic Structures, Urban Contexts", in: Michaela Giebelhausen (ed.): *The Architecture of the Museum – Symbolic Structures, Urban Contexts*. Manchester and New York: Manchester University Press, 2003, pp. 1–14.

Jacobsen, Carl: *Ny Carlsberg Glyptoteks Tilblivelse*. Copenhagen: Ny Carlsberg, 1906.

Jacoby, Sam: "Typal and Typological Reasoning – A Diagrammatic Practice of Architecture", *The Journal of Architecture*, Year 20, No. 6 (2015), pp. 938–961.

Jørgensen, Hans Henrik Lohfert: "Fra panoptikon til synoptikon – Museet som scenografi for spektakulær selvudstilling", *Passepartout*, Year 14, No. 28 (2009), pp. 109–126.

Jørgensen, Lisbet Balslev, Hakon Lund and Hans Edvard Nørregård-Nielsen: *Danmarks arkitektur*, Vol. 5: *Magtens bolig*. Copenhagen: Gyldendal, 1980.

Lechner, Andreas: *Thinking Design – Blueprint for an Architecture of Typology*. Zurich: Park Books, 2021.

Liefooghe, Maarten, Asli Çiçek and Jantje Engels: "Staging the Museum", *Oase – Journal for Architecture*, No. 111 (2022), pp. 1–6.

Lucan, Jacques: *Composition, Non-Composition – Architecture and Theory in the Nineteenth and Twentieth Centuries*. Lausanne: EPFL Press, 2012.

MacLeod, Suzanne: *Museum Architecture – A New Biography*. Oxford and New York: Routledge, 2013.

Marotta, Antonello: "Typology Quarterly – Museums", *The Architectural Review*, Vol. 232, No. 1391 (2013), pp. 76–85.

Moneo, Rafael: "On Typology", *Oppositions*, No. 13 (1978), pp. 22–45.

Munch, Anders V.: *Fra Bayreuth til Bauhaus – Gesamtkunstwerk'et og de moderne kunstformer*. Aarhus: Aarhus University Press, 2012.

"Ny Carlsberg Glyptothek", *Architekten: Meddelelser fra Akademisk Architektforening*, Year 3, No. 7 (1901), pp. 77–80 and 98–100.

Pedersen, Simon Ostenfeld: "Museumsarkitektur", *Agora – Journal for metafysisk spekulasjon*, No. 3 (2006), pp. 123–136.

Pedersen, Simon Ostenfeld, Anders Troelsen and Tina Lerke Nielsen (eds.): "Museumsarkitektur", *Passepartout*, Year 14, No. 28 (2009).

Pevsner, Nikolaus: *A History of Building Types*. London: Thames & Hudson, 1976.

Plagemann, Volker: *Das deutsche Kunstmuseum 1790–1870 – Lage, Baukörper, Raumorganisation, Bildprogramm*. Munich: Prestel-Verlag, 1967.

Poulsen, Hanne Kolind: "Videnskabens bastion – Om Julius Lange og opførelsen af Statens Museum for Kunst", *Kunstmuseets Årsskrift*, Vol. 70 (1992), pp. 116–145.

Pryd, Per: "Glyptotekets Bygmestre – To Interviews", *Politiken*, 27 June, 1906, p. 4.

Steenstrup, Johannes: *Carl Jacobsens Liv og Gerning*. Copenhagen: New Carlsberg Foundation and M.P. Madsens Boghandel, 1922.

Villadsen, Villads: "Om kunstmuseumsbyggeri i Danmark", *Kunst og Museum*, Year 18 (1983), pp. 14–27.

Villadsen, Villads: *Statens Museum for Kunst 1827–1952*. Copenhagen: SMK – National Gallery of Denmark and Gyldendal, 1998.

Wanscher, Vilhelm: "Glyptotheket", *Architekten – Meddelelser fra Akademisk Architektforening*, Year 9, No. 3 (1906), pp. 28–30.

Zanker von Meyer, Dorothee: *Die Bauten von J.C. und Carl Jacobsen – Zur Bautätigkeit einer Industriellenfamilie in Dänemark*. Berlin: Deutscher Kunstverlag, 1982.

Østergaard, Jan Stubbe: "*Semper Ardens* – Facaden af Hack Kampmanns bygning til Glyptotekets antikke samling", *AIGIS, supplementum*, No. 1, May 2011.

Jakob Ingemann Parby

A METROPOLIS COMPLETED?

The Glyptotek and the Making of Modern Copenhagen

In the latter half of the 19th century, Copenhagen broke out of the city's gated ramparts and started to expand. Over the following decades the city grew dramatically. From 1850 to 1920 the area and population of the city more than quadrupled. At the same time, the modernisation that was underway radically changed the housing, self-perception and everyday lives of Copenhageners. The change took place in three phases, culminating in the new neighbourhoods of Vesterbro, Nørrebro, Østerbro and Amagerbro merging with the old city centre as the ramparts were transformed into parks, boulevards, institutions and residential districts. City Hall Square and the Rysensteen quarter where the Glyptotek opened in 1897 were a key part of this transformation, which fuelled ideas about the Danish capital as a world city – a metropolis. This article frames the building of the Glyptotek in the broader context of Copenhagen's urban history and examines why the museum, like many of the new buildings and monuments of the period was met by such contradictory reactions.

When the brewer Carl Jacobsen opened his art collection to the public at the first Glyptotek in Valby in 1882, it had been thirty years since the demarcation terrain between the Copenhagen lakes, Jagtvej and Valby Hill was freed for development and the city gates demolished. This was in part the result of heavy pressure from business owners and citizens in Copenhagen, spearheaded by Carl Jacobsen's father, J.C. Jacobsen.[1] As early as 1846 he moved his brewery from the city centre to Valby in order to expand and modernise production. Part of the reason for choosing the new location was indications of rich subterranean water deposits in the area, although these failed to materialise.

The Valby location was, however, advantageous for other reasons. The low price of land, for example, as well as the new railway between Copenhagen and Roskilde, which opened in 1847 and ran right past the brewery – an ideal way to transport raw materials and the finished product.[2] Among the drawbacks to being outside the city centre was the distance workers had to cover to reach the workplace. Until the passport control and the payment of customs duties and tolls at the city gates was abolished in 1856, their opening and closing times were an issue for the businesses that had been granted dispensation to move beyond the ramparts, especially in winter when the gates did not open until 7 a.m. and the working day usually began at 6 a.m. People could pay to get out of the city via Nørreport (North Gate) after hours, but that cost around five per cent of an unskilled labourer's daily wages. This made recruiting workers difficult.[3]

The opening hours of the city gates was one of the most critical stumbling blocks the new industrial class faced in the hierarchical, militarised society of the absolute monarchy, which was a poor match for industrialism's ideals of growth, productivity and the utilisation of manpower. As well as the issue of labour-force mobility, the city gates were bottlenecks hindering movement and the circulation of goods and raw materials. Prior to the railway between Copenhagen and Roskilde being built, the commission behind it made a survey of the traffic passing through Vesterport (West Gate). On an annual basis 40,000 tons of goods, 50,000 farmers in carts, and 30,000 others travelling either by mail coach or in their own horse-drawn vehicles passed through the gate,[4] on top of which came people on foot. Five hundred thousand people a year went beyond the ramparts to Frederiksberg Gardens on Sundays and public holidays, most of them on foot, although some took an omnibus or hired a carriage outside the city gates. During the year 1843, for example, 140,000 people took an omnibus from Vesterport to the gardens.[5]

The city gates were seen as a symbol of the absolute monarchy's lack of ambition for Danish industry, and an unnecessary restriction on the life of Copenhagen's citizens. In the 1840s the brewer J.C. Jacobsen joined protests against gate-closing times and tolls to the city council by industrialists such as foundry owner Anker Heegaard (1815–1893) and factory owner Johan Christian Drewsen (1777–1851). Their complaints initially went unheeded, but they did ensure the matter continued to be discussed.[6]

In 1852 the Danish military lifted building restrictions on the other side of Copenhagen's lakes. More and more properties were built beyond the ramparts, creating even more congestion at the city gates. As a result in 1856 the gates were slated for demolition. In 1858 Østerport (East Gate) was the last to go. All that remained were gaping holes in the city ramparts.[7] A cast-iron bridge was installed where Nørreport had been so people could still walk along Nørrevold (the northern rampart) without descending to street level. Later the bridge was incorporated into the pathways in Ørsted Park where it remains to this day.

A City Unbound

The removal of building restrictions on the former demarcation terrain sparked a new and increasingly hectic race between landowners, urban planners and property speculators to build new housing and industrial districts. These new neighbourhoods on the other side of the bridges were named after the cobbled main roads passing through them from the surrounding countryside to the city gates: Vesterbro, Nørrebro, Østerbro and Amagerbro. The suffix *bro* stems from *brosten*, the Danish word for cobblestone. Initially they only referred to the roads but now became the names of whole neighbourhoods.

Suburbs were already emerging before the former demarcation terrain was freed for development, mainly along the roads Vesterbrogade and Nørrebrogade leading into the city. These early suburbs contributed to the way the neighbourhoods subsequently developed. Vesterbro, for example, had a cattle market and slaughterhouses, as well as inns and places of entertainment. Such activities gave the district a distinct identity that took a new turn when the amusement park Tivoli Gardens opened in 1843, followed by the modernised Meatpacking District in 1879, alongside breweries, theatres, hotels and dance halls. In 1847 the construction of railways to Roskilde and Korsør and expansion of the harbour to supply the newly built gasworks and meatpacking district made it a colourful neighbourhood, reinforcing its reputation as the first port of call for everyone from circus artists and musicians to farmers and travelling salesmen. Nørrebro, on the other hand, was dominated by the rapidly growing iron industry, which together with densely built areas of small working-class flats made it a stronghold for the labour movement later in the 19th century.[8]

The neighbourhoods of Østerbro and Frederiksberg were where Copenhagen's wealthy merchants and the city elite built their villas and summer residences. Later in the 19th century Østerbro in particular but also parts of Frederiksberg experienced an influx of industries and working-class housing that changed the demographics of the area, which led to some wealthier residents moving further north.[9] The inner part of Amagerbro was constrained by military building regulations right up until 1909, when it was developed systematically and efficiently by multiple building contractors. Further away from the city, an industrial district with poor-quality housing for workers evolved from the 1860s onwards. In 1901–1903 the area of Sundbyerne in the northern part of Amager became part of Copenhagen and the general urbanisation of the city. The explosive development of the modern city from 1852 onwards was mirrored demographically, with a population that grew from around 135,000 in 1850 to more than 560,000 in 1921.[10]

City Formation

Parallel to the development of the new neighbourhoods, the old city within the ramparts also changed dramatically. The cholera epidemic of 1853, which killed almost 5,000 Copenhageners and infected thousands more, revealed how vulnerable the city was to infectious diseases that thrived in overcrowded conditions with open gutters and damp basement flats.[11] This led to the development of new kinds of housing, like the terraced houses built by the Danish Medical Association in Østerbro. Construction here began as early as the autumn of 1853. They were designed by Danish architect Michael Gottlieb Bindesbøll, which was unusual at a time when architects rarely made working-class housing. The medical association envisioned such terraces becoming a standard model for housing as the city expanded, and they did inspire individual developments by, for example, the Danish Workers' Building Society. They were never, however, implemented on any major scale.

In the meantime, increased awareness of the city's poor state of health was somewhat cynically exploited by both the city council and private developers. A report by medical officer F.F. Ulrik (1818–1917) on the area around Peder Madsen's Passage, for example, provided the basis for slum clearance by a private construction company headed by C.F. Tietgen and I.C. Jacobsen. This was tied to building the new Hotel d'Angleterre and the street Ny Østergade, all part of Copenhagen's growing trade and consumer culture. Both the hotel and the new street were applauded in the press as an important boost to Copenhagen's status as a metropolis and destination for Europe's travelling elite,[12] but neither the city government nor the construction company considered helping the impoverished inhabitants of the area. They were evicted from their homes as part of the slum clearance and left to find new places to live on their own, either in the new neighbourhoods across the lakes or the remaining slums of the old city.[13] The same thing

Peder Madsen's Passage, c. 1870. The passage ran from Grønnegade and ended in a gateway next to a chemist's shop at Østergade 18. At its narrowest point it was only three metres wide. The passage disappeared with the construction of Ny Østergade in 1872–1876.

This photograph gives an idea of the scale of slum clearance in Copenhagen during the decades around the turn of the century. Here buildings in Grønnegade and Regnegade being demolished to make way for the extension of Ny Øster-gade in 1908.

Hotel d'Angleterre after a total renovation in 1880. The main guardhouse disappeared when the hotel was modernised. A new street was established next to the new headquarters of the Great Northern Telegraph Company seen here to the right of the photograph with Stephan Sinding's sculpture *Elektra* on the roof.

Pavement café at the Etablissement National across from the main entrance to Tivoli Gardens, c. 1910. The author and journalist Herman Bang captured all that was new in his articles and novels. He was the incarnation of the modern flâneur, who in conscious opposition to harried passers-by sauntered about town or sat observing the crowds from one of the many new pavement cafés that opened during the period. Being a flâneur in the modern city was often associated with authors and artists.

happened following subsequent slum clearances in the medieval part of the city centre. As a result, the population of the area dropped from 68,000 in 1855 to 33,000 in 1916.[14]

Along what is now Strøget – Copenhagen's main pedestrianised shopping street – shops with window displays were first seen in the 1820s, tempting customers with dreams of luxury. After the demolition of the city gates and emergence of the new neighbourhoods, the transition of the city centre was faster and more systematic. Many properties were turned into veritable palaces of consumption, often extending over several floors. They supplanted traditional businesses where shopkeepers and master craftsmen had their accommodation, stock and workshops on the same premises as their business and often lodgings for apprentices and assistants. Now both business owners and staff lived in new, private homes outside the city centre, commuting to their place of work.[15]

Busy people hurrying to and from work and pouring in and out of the city's theatres and entertainment venues became a symbol of the city and a theme of literature and art. The teeming masses and hectic life of the city were viewed with both

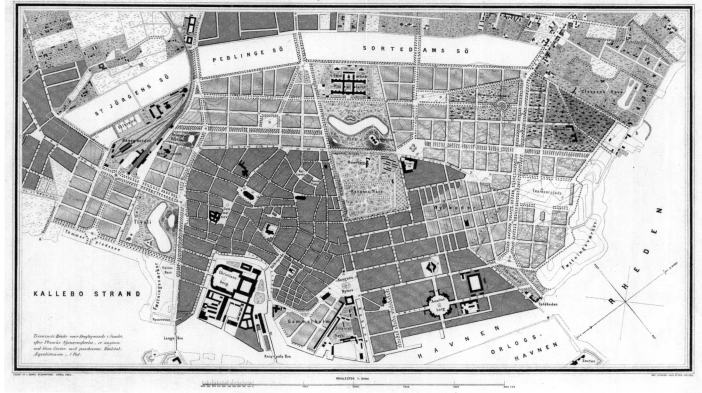

PLAN

til Bebyggelse af Terrainet mellem Kjöbenhavns Demarcationslinie og den indre By, efter Fæstningsvoldenes Slöifning.

(Udarbeidet ved den af Krigsministeriet d. 8 September 1858 nedsatte Commission).

enthusiasm and irony, for example by Herman Bang (1857–1912) in his novel *Stuk* ('Stucco', 1887):

> "Like a military formation, workers flocked along the pavements across the bridge – a regimented march beating against the paving stones; and on the tracks running down the middle of the street illuminated theatre carriages went clanging past, three in a row, crammed with cheering women in hats hanging onto the edge of the platforms."[16]

Connecting the City

At the same time as the new neighbourhoods and city were developing in the 1860s and 1870s, pressure to transform Copenhagen's ramparts was increasing. Any work on this vast defensive earthwork and moat separating the old city centre from new districts was a vast undertaking in terms of administration and construction. Despite the fact that the first plans based on similar projects in Vienna, Berlin and Paris had been drawn up as early as the 1850s, it took until 1871 for a plan to finally be approved and the ramparts sold to the city council with the proviso that at least 600,000 square feet (the equivalent of eighteen football

The building plan of the commission for the demolition of Copenhagen's ramparts, 1865. The commission wanted to make densely built areas on the former rampart terrain, a plan that met resistance from several fronts.

163

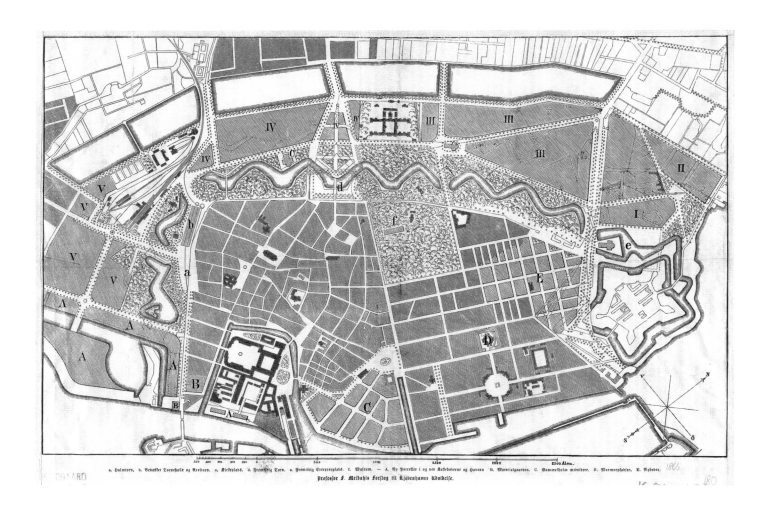

a. Halmtorv. b. Bebastet Torvehalle og Krettorv. c. Kirkeplads. d. Fremtidig Torv. e. Fremtidig Erercerplads. f. Museum. — A. Ny Parceller i og ved Kassedoberne og Havnen. B. Materialgaarden. C. Gammelholm medvidere. D. Marmorpladsen. E. Nyboder.

Professor F. Meldahls Forslag til Kjøbenhavns Udvidelse.

Ferdinand Meldahl's alternative plan for the rampart terrain, 1866. Meldahl's plan introduced the idea of a much larger recreational area.

The approved plan, 1871–1872. There was
as yet no plan for the Rysensteen quarter,
where the Glyptotek was to be located.
Aborre Park, which no longer exists, is
seen between Ørsted Park and Copenhagen's second railway station, which was
in use from 1867 to 1910.

pitches) be designated park areas. This proviso was the result of a debate following in the wake of the demolition commission's plan of 1865. The plan had proposed maximal use of the area with densely built housing, but was criticised for not making space for the trades and industries that were to provide the inhabitants with a livelihood or any green spaces. In 1866 Danish architect Ferdinand Meldahl presented an alternative plan that included a long, connected belt of parks and a serpentine waterway to replace the moat that had surrounded the ramparts. The final plan was a compromise between the two. The need for parks and green spaces was, however, acknowledged, and the designated area for parks eventually doubled, to 1,200,000 square feet.[17]

Running parallel to the park belt were two new boulevards. Borrowed from French, the term originally referred to the flat surface of a rampart. Over the years, however, its meaning had changed to denote a broad street lined by trees and houses with a promenade or bridle path in the middle. Luxury apartments for the upper middle class were built facing the parks and main streets, whilst small flats like those in the new neighbourhoods were to be found in the side streets and backstreets. In 1878 there were as many as 1,200 flats measuring between twenty-five and thirty-one and a half square metres.[18]

The process of converting the embankments into parks, boulevards and residential areas, as well as building institutions and museums, lasted into the 20th century. Copenhagen City Council had built a new, ultramodern hospital on the glacis beyond the northern ramparts in 1863. In the 1870s the Botanical Garden (1871–1874), Ørsted Park (1876–1879) and Linné Square, which was Copenhagen's fruit and vegetable market from 1889 to 1958 and renamed Israel Square in 1968, were established and apartment buildings and flats built in the surrounding streets and side streets.

Further east a new development was built by the Workers' Building Society, comprised of eleven streets of terraced houses between the old eastern ramparts and Sortedam Lake. The development of the eastern ramparts was slow and cautious. In 1876–1877 a footpath was made cutting through them (now the street Sølvgade), and the same year it was decided that the three bastions east of this should be made into a park. In 1885–1886 Quintus Bastion was chosen as the building site for the new National Gallery of Denmark, which was inaugurated in June 1896. Like the Glyptotek, the National Gallery was designed by Vilhelm Dahlerup. From the very beginning, the area covered by the museum was restricted by a planned underground railway to connect the train stations of Copenhagen. The plans were realised in 1917 and led to the demolition of the remains of the eastern ramparts.

The conversion of the ramparts to the west and south continued in the 1880s with the removal of the western rampart and building of Vestre Boulevard, and from 1892 with the addition of the new city hall and City Hall Square as well as the Rysensteen quarter where the Glyptotek was later built.

From Meldahl to Ambt

Whereas the neighbourhood around Nørrevold was built according to architect Ferdinand Meldahl's rectangular street plan, the areas around Vestervold (the western ramparts) and the Rysensteen quarter were the creation of Copenhagen's first city engineer, Charles Ambt (1847–1919). The switch from Meldahl to Ambt reflected a general shift in the balance of power between architecture and engineering in the 1880s, with the latter gaining a stronger hold on urban planning. This was connected to the increasing importance of infrastructure in urban development – tramlines, water, electricity, gas supplies and underground sewers – as well as the growing development of the city into functional zones: industrial districts, residential neighbourhoods, commercial areas and larger institutional complexes, all of which required the skill and expertise of engineers.

This shift in power was based not only on different professions, but also what became known as 'the polytechnic breakthrough' in Denmark. After 1850 students at Denmark's Polytechnic Institute were increasingly trained to work in the country's growing trades and industries, whereas in the past the focus had been more academic. The networks that developed between industry and the public sector, which also employed engineers, tipped the balance of urban planning in engineers' favour.[19]

Charles Ambt, Copenhagen's city engineer from 1886 to 1902, is a clear example of this shift. Whereas Meldahl's influence was based on his position as a professor at the architecture school of the Royal Danish Academy of Fine Arts and the resulting influence he had on the entire field of Danish architecture, Ambt was able to assume an almost equally powerful position despite being

The digging of Vestervold, 1885, when
Jarmer's Tower, part of Copenhagen's
16th-century fortifications, was uncovered. Later the ruin formed part of the
bastions and ramparts built in the 1670s.
The end of Vester Voldgade and the
chimney of the waterworks can be seen
in the background.

a mere council official and neither politically
elected nor a formal representative of any specific style or school. Ambt managed to secure an
exceptional position compared to other officers
in the city department established in 1858 to cover
Copenhagen's urban planning, infrastructure,
health and fire service. He was actively involved
in all council meetings on the development of the
city's railways, its Free Port and the question of
turning the commons into parks and residential
areas. This coordinating role made it possible to
imagine urban planning on a much larger scale
rather than district by district as had been the
case under Meldahl.[20]

City Hall, City Hall Square, Vestervold and Rysensteen

The growing power of the city engineer over
urban planning was very apparent in the districts
recently brought under the governance of Copenhagen City Council,[21] as well as in Ryvangen and
in the area around the gasworks port, which from
the 1880s onwards demonstrated the increasing
drive to develop on a larger scale with street plans
that ensured the circulation of traffic, sewage,
water, fresh air and light. Expansion and major

Vesterbro Passage with *The French Art Exhibition* to the right. Carl Jacobsen built a temporary exhibition hall as an addition to the Nordic Exhibition of Industry, Agriculture and Art out of his own pocket. Located where City Hall Square was later built, the exhibition included works by some of the best contemporary French painters and sculptors.

new roads such as Tagensvej, Strandboulevarden and Åboulevarden testified to the growing power of engineers and their focus on infrastructure and the flow of traffic in urban development. The Vestervold neighbourhood was home not only to Tivoli Gardens from 1843, but also to the city's first modern waterworks built in 1856–1859 on the glacis of Helmer's Bastion and from 1863 opposite Copenhagen's second train station. This is also where the Industrial Association's exhibition hall was located from 1872.

In the 1880s more places of entertainment opened in the area around Vesterbro Passage, including Etablissement National, the Circus Building and the Dagmar Theatre. The passage was the innermost part of Vesterbrogade, which in 1867 had been made into a broader arrival zone to the city from the west by filling in the moat and building Axel Square and Jernbanegade. Both Vesterbrogade and Jernbanegade ended at Halmtorvet – Straw Square in Danish – where hay and straw were sold. In 1888 this market and its name moved to its current location near the new Meatpacking District in Vesterbro, whereas the old square became the new City Hall Square.

As early as the summer of 1888 the capacity and uses of the new urban hub were put to the test with the Nordic Exhibition of Industry, Agriculture and Art, the largest exhibition ever to be held in Denmark.[22] During the 138 days it ran the exhibition had almost 1.4 million visitors.[23] Martin Nyrop (1849–1921) was the exhibition's head architect and designer of the main exhibition hall, a domed structure with a daring timber construction, corner turrets, dormer windows, façade carvings and painted decorations.

The experience Nyrop had from the exhibition gave him an advantage over other architects when the city council announced a competition to design a new city hall. He had already had hands-on experience of the area where it was to be built, and his work on the 1888 exhibition had met with wide acclaim. Many Danish and a few international architects submitted a total of fifteen entries to the competition, ranging from Valdemar Koch's (1852–1902) gothic castle complex, inspired by the 13th-century Cloth Hall of Ypres in Flanders, to Theophilus Hansen's (1813–1891) Byzantine complex.[24] Following a number of complications and adjustments Nyrop's project was chosen. The cornerstone was laid, and work on the foundations began in 1892. In 1898 the roof of the 105.6-metre tower was raised, in 1900 the bells of Copenhagen City Hall rang in the New Year for the first time, and by 1903 the interior had reached a point where the council could start working from City Hall. The official inauguration, however, was not until 1905.[25]

While Copenhagen City Hall was being built plans were underway for the rest of the Vestervold area from Vesterbro Passage to the Rysensteen quarter closest to Langebro Bridge. Here, as mentioned above, the city engineer Charles Ambt played a central role.

Plans for the Vicinity of the Glyptotek
In planning the new area Ambt drew inspiration from German architect Josef Stübben (1845–1936) and Austrian urban planner and architect Camillo Sitte (1843–1903). He presented some more general observations on urban street planning in a lecture at the Technological Society in 1888, where he warned against rectangular chessboard plans like those used in the early bridge districts and the Nørrevold area. Uniform, straight streets resulted in uniform perspectives and a lack of distinctive character:

The main hall of the Nordic Exhibition of Industry, Agriculture and Art in 1888. Among the trees to the right of the hall is an over-dimensioned brown Tuborg bottle housing Denmark's first elevator, and to the right of that a lighthouse installed at the Carlsberg exhibition symbolising the one built at the brewery in 1883 to mark the introduction of electric lights. The main hall was designed by Martin Nyrop who just years later won the competition to build a new city hall in almost the same spot. Painting by Rasmus Carl Rasmussen: *The Exhibition Hall*, 1888. Museum of Copenhagen.

Ambt's plan for the Rysensteen quarter of Copenhagen, 1899. The plan that was finally approved incorporated a number of Ambt's ideas about diagonal streets and bends, which together with squares provided more varied perspectives and experiences than the rectangular plan of the bridge districts. Plans for a church and locating the Royal Library on Vestre Boulevard were, however, dropped.

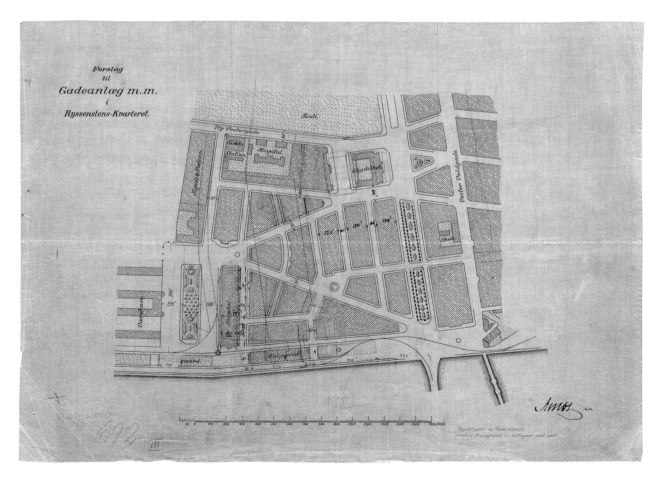

A temporary Langebro Bridge was
built in 1930. To the right Christian IX's
revolving bridge from 1903 and in the
background Rysensteen public baths.

"All the streets are equally long, equally dull and, in part, equally ugly. Indeed, if greenery had not been added here and there, or public buildings or shopping streets did not provide some life, there would be no distinguishing the individual streets [...]".[26]

Diagonals and staggered streets, on the other hand, made them distinctive and provided more interesting perspectives. Diagonal streets were to run between the points of intersection of radial and ring roads and the squares that were created naturally at such points.

Over the next ten years Ambt drew endless plans for the Rysensteen quarter with diagonal streets inspired by the ideas of Sitte and Stübben, although not without opposition. The mayor Christian K. Øllgaard (1841–1915), for example, was reluctant to abandon the chessboard principle, so in 1880 he asked Professor Julius Thomsen (1826–1909) to draw up a plan for the area between Vestre Boulevard and Vester Voldgade with this kind of grid. It is in revised versions of Thomsen's plans from 1888 and 1889 that the Glyptotek figures for the first time in its current location on Dante's Square. In 1890 Thomsen's plans for the area between Vestre Boulevard and Vester Voldgade were finally approved by the city council. Ambt went along with them despite his opposition to the chessboard principle. This represented a temporary defeat, but Ambt continued to develop his own plans for the neighbourhood on the other side of Vestre Boulevard, and in 1899 a new plan largely true to his original vision was approved.[27]

Vestre Boulevard itself (renamed H.C. Andersen's Boulevard in 1955) was constructed in 1891–1892, initially as an area for promenading far removed from the heavy traffic seen today. When the boulevard was asphalted in 1896 it was world news. According to the Copenhagen newspaper *Dannebrog*, in April 1896 the American newspaper *The World* published a large photograph of "the new boulevard in Copenhagen" with City Hall and part of the long, wide, asphalted boulevard in an attack on the lack of asphalt on Fifth Avenue in New York. The photograph demonstrated just "how far ahead of New York (!) the capital of little Denmark is. The new part of town was completed just recently (!) while Fifth Avenue is left with utterly scandalous paving".[28] Comments of this kind fuelled Copenhageners' dreams of their city becoming a world capital.

The first steps towards the transformation of the boulevard into the main traffic artery it is today were taken when Christian IX's Langebro Bridge was built in 1903, a cast-iron swing bridge capable of bearing the weight of goods trains and trams. The level of traffic increased further when a wider temporary bridge was built in 1930, followed by the current bridge designed by Danish architect Kaj Gottlob (1887–1976), which opened in 1954 to accommodate the steep increase in motoring of the post-war years. The boulevard became an eight-lane road, which radically reconfigured the original plan for arriving at the Glyptotek via Dante's Square.

The Glyptotek and the Museum's Neighbours

The area the Glyptotek moved into was still in the making when the museum opened in 1897. In many ways the area represented the last stage of the transformation of the rampart terrain into a new fashionable recreative area with a mix of institutions, parks, entertainment venues and residential areas. It was across the road from Tivoli Gardens with City Hall and the main fire station to the east and to the west present-day Christians Brygge, an area that had been diked and reclaimed, increasing the area of the city and the depth of its harbour. Until 1870 Tivoli Gardens was next to a row of timber yards and shallow waters. Over the following decades these were gradually filled with building materials and earth, partly from demolished sections of the northern and western ramparts.

Photographs of the Glyptotek taken shortly after the construction of City Hall's tower clearly show that the land surrounding the city's new museum was still marshy, and the timber yards can still be made out in the background.

Carl Jacobsen had envisaged a grander setting in 1888, when he and his wife Ottilia Jacobsen decided to donate their art collection to the people of Denmark on the condition that the city council and government provided a suitable building plot. Carl Jacobsen was made chairman of the museum board, which also included state and council representatives. Before the museum could be built there was a long process of negotiation during which other locations were proposed, first between the Dagmar Theatre and Vester Voldgade (directly opposite the new city hall) and then a plot between Ørsted Park and Aborre Park.[29] Both proposals were dismissed

Arial photograph taken from the tower of City Hall, 1898. The photograph shows the newly opened Glyptotek, Vestre Boulevard and the Arena Theatre in Tivoli Gardens, and behind them the waters of Kalvebod and the timber yards.

by Jacobsen, who reacted particularly negatively when a third option between Vendersgade and Ørsted Park was presented. He was appalled that the mayor would consider turning one of the city's few green oases into a building site.[30] Aborre Park disappeared a few years later when the city council gave part of it to the Danish State Railways as a prelude to the construction of a new underground railroad between Copenhagen Central and Østerport Station.

Instead the city council proposed the Glyptotek's current location, which Carl Jacobsen initially also rejected. He considered the plot too remote and not conducive to the sense of calm and cultivation that the new museum building was to instil in its visitors to open their minds to experiencing art. He found the neighbourhood and the "plebeian" Tivoli Gardens in particular problematic.[31] The construction of Dante's Square, which was approved in 1888, was the council's attempt to placate the brewer and ensure that the building would "play a prominent role" in the city as Mayor Øllgaard put it.[32] This also included the section of Vestre Boulevard in front of the museum being kept free of trees to provide a clear view of the museum from the new square.

172

Brewer Jacobsen was presumably also not enthusiastic about the proximity of the Rudolph Bergh Hospital, built in 1886 for patients with venereal diseases. These included sex workers, who from 1874 to 1906 were easy to spot since the legalisation of sex work during this period was conditional upon the women wearing specific clothing and being checked regularly for sexually transmitted diseases by the police surgeon.[33] On the other hand, he probably found it fitting that the city's western power plant was inaugurated in 1898 on the corner of Tietgensgade and Bernstorffsgade. It had a small 'lighthouse' that could be seen as mirroring the lighthouse at the Carlsberg brewery and certainly reflected the contemporary fascination with the possibilities of electricity.

Living Art Belongs to the Living

When Carl and Ottilia Jacobsen opened their art collection to the public in 1882 everything was in one room of the couple's villa near the brewery in Valby. In the years that followed their collection grew exponentially. The first Glyptotek saw the light of day at Carlsberg in 1885 and was gradually extended with new galleries. The idea of a new

Arial photograph taken from the tower of Copenhagen City Hall, 1909. The view is the same as in the previous photograph, but the area has changed dramatically. The Glyptotek has been extended with Hack Kampmann's new building from 1906, and the Rysensteen quarter has shot up around the museum and is now home to the Royal Danish Academy of Music and the Royal Danish Academy of Science and Letters. A newly built area along the quay of Islands Brygge can be seen in the background.

173

museum in the heart of the Danish capital was entirely in keeping with Carl Jacobsen's belief that "living art belongs to the living". He also believed that art belonged as much to "the common man" as the wealthy and educated.[34]

In reality, both the old and the new Glyptotek had a more select audience, as shown by the texts and catalogues published during the first decades of their existence, the understanding of which demanded a certain level of prior knowledge and education. The location of the new Glyptotek in the Rysensteen quarter, however, alongside government and city council funding and board members contributed to a gradual change in profile and visitor numbers. Opening hours were extended, and the council insisted that free admission on Wednesdays and Sundays be written into the museum's trust deed. In 1900 the Glyptotek had almost 37,000 visitors, 29,000 of them on days with free admission.[35]

Over the decades that followed further development of the Rysensteen quarter in keeping with contemporary urban planning ideals changed the Glyptotek's surroundings. At the beginning of the new century rows of apartment blocks and institutional buildings spread throughout the area. But the identity of the neighbourhood did not fully crystallise until Copenhagen's third and current Central Station opened in 1911. In 1916 plans for a new police headquarters were also approved. The architect was Hack Kampmann, who had also designed the extension for the Glyptotek's Antiquities Collection, inaugurated in 1906. Before long the Glyptotek was no longer remote but part of a bustling new neighbourhood with housing, offices, schools and central infrastructure connecting the capital to the rest of Denmark – and via the new main post office, Copenhagen Central Station and Langebro Bridge, the rest of the world.

This new connectivity helped the Glyptotek become the national and international tourist attraction it continues to be today. Located close to City Hall Square – the new city centre – the museum also contributed to Copenhagen's transition from a smaller urban centre to a modern metropolis comparable to city centres in the United States and elsewhere in Europe. In his collection of prose fragments *Asfaltens Sange* ('Songs of the Asphalt', 1918) Danish author Emil Bønnelycke (1893–1953) wrote about City Hall Square with a futuristic faith in progress:

"In the heart of the Metropolis, at City Hall Square in the centre of the world city of Copenhagen, I spend hour upon hour, heedless of my fate, joyfully immersed in a flood of teeming impressions. The crowds, the maelstrom, are the streaming river in which I bathe in speechless, humble ecstasy."[36]

For Bønnelycke Copenhagen was a young capital, a new capital mirroring the metropoles of the world with its "immense arena of shining asphalt where trams revolve, automobiles steer through the current, harnesses on carriages ring, and the national convoy of bicycles sing [...]".[37]

In the eyes of some Copenhageners and tourists the Glyptotek fulfilled Copenhagen's metropolitan ambitions by giving people access to ancient sculptures and modern art in the heart of the new city centre.[38] But not everyone approved. The formerly fêted architect Vilhelm Dahlerup's building in particular came under fire. His reputation had already suffered with his building for the National Gallery of Denmark in June 1896, which was criticised for its position at an angle to the surrounding streets and compared to children's building blocks. As one reviewer wrote, the main building of the gallery was considered unnecessarily "pretentious" and its outer wings lacking in "solidity". The walls were described as a "ghastly dark brown" and the ornamentation inside and out as lacking "grandeur". All in all it was "not difficult to find things that are wrong with the building. It is more difficult to find anything good to say about it".[39]

After such tirades Dahlerup was probably dreading reviews of the building he designed for the Glyptotek. After the opening on 1 May 1897 a journalist from *Social-Demokraten* wrote that it lacked "nobility and grandeur in style. There are too many frills and tasteless flourishes inside and out. Free of these is the high-ceilinged, vaulted vestibule with two rows of polished granite pillars and eight reclining sphinxes". The reviewer also found the colours of the walls pleasing and the light in the galleries good. It was, however, tasteless to make a gallery into a chapel with quotes from the Bible on the walls, just as the decorations on the painted skylights above the staircase to the painting collection seemed "gaudy and vulgar". The collection, on the other hand, was described as outstanding, something for which the people of Denmark owed thanks to its creator:

"It is among the best in Europe, with numerous first-rate works of art. It will permeate people's minds with beauty. [...] City dwellers need such sacrosanct places where they can rest while contemplating fine art and leave uplifted and pure of mind, fortified to return to the daily grind and grime. Beauty is perhaps the best educator of the people, the most edifying of teachers. Let us rejoice in this new temple to art that has arisen in our city. It is of more use than eight churches!"[40]

Even before it opened the author Henrik Pontoppidan (1857–1943) was equally scathing in his criticism of the building in one of his monologues in the newspaper *Politiken*. In March 1897 he called it a "monstrosity of tastelessness" and "a changeling begot by rape and born in stealth". It looked, he wrote, like a "barn" from one side and "the entrance to a huge waxworks" from the other. Pontoppidan claimed that the building should immediately be screened by five-storey buildings instead of "artists of the world being invited to witness our shame", a reference to the pavilion exhibition of international art Jacobsen had arranged in connection with the opening of the Glyptotek and accessed via the main entrance to the museum.[41] The exhibition drew huge crowds and functioned as intended to promote the Glyptotek and attract visitors during its opening months. During the final week of the exhibition admission was free and people flocked to see it. In just seven days there were more than 34,000 visitors, 18,363 of whom came on the last day, a Sunday:

> "People queued along the boulevard under police supervision waiting for their turn to get in. The crowds inside were overwhelming, and it is doubtful that many saw much of the art [...]. In the afternoon, as the number of people peaked, the cloakrooms had to give up – they could not cope with the vast numbers of canes, umbrellas and parasols. A reserve exit to Ny Vestergade was also opened so the crowds could pass through the building unimpeded."[42]

A Source of Pride or Shame?

In light of the number of visitors to the Glyptotek today, and the positive responses to the museum's programme of special exhibitions by visitors and reviewers alike, it can be difficult to understand the critical reactions it provoked when it opened in 1897, many of them focusing on the museum building. What made people like Pontoppidan feel what amounted to shame about the architecture, and how could a new museum in the Danish capital generate such conflicting opinions? The debate testifies to a period and a city on the threshold between tradition and radicality, between nostalgia and metropolitan dreams, between popular appeal and the avant-garde.

Caught in the crossfire between such positions, contemporary urban development, monuments and museums were often the subject of vehement and sometimes brutal altercations, reflecting how passionate many felt about the image and international reputation of the Danish capital. Public debates on the Glyptotek and National Gallery of Denmark were similar to those on Peder Madsen's Passage and Hotel d'Angleterre, Copenhagen City Hall and City Hall Square, as well as the Stork Fountain on Amager Square close to the city centre, where the members of the Society for the Embellishment of Copenhagen who funded and installed it were criticised for spoiling "one of the few places in Copenhagen that has the air of a metropolis!".[43] Such strong opinions reveal how much people considered to be at stake. At the end of the day it was about the kind of city people wanted to create and the kind of national identity they wanted to present to the world through their endeavours. The Glyptotek was one of many key initiatives with a dual focus in Copenhagen. Its goal was to enhance and encourage the education of ordinary people and increase their access to art and culture, but it was also an important way to enhance the image of the Danish capital in an increasingly competitive battle over prestige among expanding cities worldwide.

Notes

1 The demarcation terrain was opened for development in 1852 and the city gates demolished between 1856 and 1858. The general account of Copenhagen's urban development is primarily based on Parby, 2022; Thelle, 2015; Knudsen, 1988; and Holm and Johansen, 1940. The author would like to thank the editors of the book and the anonymous peer reviewer for their insightful comments and suggestions.

2 Lauring, 2009, p. 14.

3 Copenhagen City Archives: *Magistratens 2. Sekretariat*, incoming cases, 1844, no. 2903 and 3298; Parby, 2022, p. 12; Christensen, 1912, p. 7.

4 Christensen, 1912, pp. 362–363.

5 Ibid., pp. 106–107.

6 Copenhagen City Archives: *Magistratens 2. Sekretariat*, incoming cases, 1840, no. 347, and 1841, no. 138. See also Christensen, 1912, p. 6.

7 Preserving the city gates was considered at the time, but the art academy, which operated in an advisory capacity to the state, did not consider them worthy of preservation "on artistic terms". See Meldahl and Johansen, 1904, p. 505.

8 Parby, 2022, pp. 17–56. For a more general account of industrialisation in Copenhagen see Hyldtoft, 1984. For the consequences of industrialisation for the soundscapes of Copenhagen see Parby, 2021.

9 Ibid., p. 58 ff.

10 The figure for 1921 includes the municipalities of Frederiksberg and Gentofte, which were included in statistics for Copenhagen from that year.

11 Bonderup, 2008; Hübertz, 1855.

12 For more on this subject, see Parby, 2022, p. 71 ff.; Ulrik, 1871; and, for example, *Illustreret Tidende*, 13 June 1875, p. 367.

13 See Parby, 2022, p. 71 ff.; Mortensen, 2004, pp. 52–76.

14 Jørgensen, 1987, pp. 3–17.

15 Toftgaard, 2012, pp. 6–32; Jørgensen, 1986. On the impact of city formation on conservation legislation see Jensen, 1919, and Morgen and Bendsen, 2018.

16 Bang, 1987 (1887), p. 9. Translated into English for this publication. See also Zerlang, 2007.

17 Holm and Johansen, 1940, p. 17 ff.

18 Willerslev, 1979, p. 82.

19 Wagner, 1999.

20 Jørgensen, Knudsen and Møller, 1989, pp. 85–107.

21 From 1901 to 1902 Valby, Sundby and Brønshøj councils were incorporated in Copenhagen City Council.

22 See Skyggebjerg, 2017, and Jensen, 2015.

23 Skyggebjerg, 2017.

24 Haugsted, 1996, pp. 6–15. Drawings from the competition are held by Copenhagen City Archives and can also be seen at www.kbhbilleder.dk

25 Haugsted, 1996. See also Thelle, 2015.

26 Ambt, 1888–1889, p. 83.

27 Jørgensen, Knudsen and Møller, 1989, pp. 91–94 and 100–102.

28 The article was reported with pride in the Copenhagen newspaper *Dannebrog*, 12 April 1896.

29 Letter from H.N. Hansen to Carl Jacobsen, 24 February 1885. Carl Jacobsen's Correspondence Archive, Nos. 298–299.

30 Jacobsen, 1906, p. 36.

31 Jacobsen, 1906, pp. 36–37 and Claus Grønne's contribution to this publication.

32 Bramsen, 1998, p. 466.

33 On the regulation of sex work, see Pedersen, 2000, and Pedersen, 2007.

34 Østergaard, 2006, pp. 126–127. The quotes are taken from Jacobsen's opening speech at the inauguration of the Glyptotek's extension and Winter Garden in 1906.

35 Ibid., p. 128.

36 Bønnelycke, 1918, pp. 58–59. Translated into English for this publication.

37 Ibid., pp. 62–63.

38 *Stubbekjøbing Avis*, 4 May 1897. Copy held in Carl Jacobsen's Correspondence Archive.

39 Review in the newspaper *København*, 28 June 1896.

40 *Social-Demokraten*, 2 May 1897.

41 *Politiken*, 13 March 1897. See also Pontoppidan, 1993.

42 *Social-Demokraten*, 2 November 1897.

43 *Illustreret Tidende*, 12 August 1894, p. 589.

Archives, correspondence and newspaper articles:

Sources include documents in Copenhagen City Archives, Carl Jacobsen's Correspondence Archive, and articles from the following Danish newspapers:

Berlingske Tidende
Dannebrog
Fædrelandet
Illustreret Tidende
København
Politiken
Social-Demokraten
Stubbekjøbing Avis

Bibliography

Ambt, Charles: "Om Planer til Byers Udvidelse og Bebyggelse", *Den Tekniske Forenings Tidsskrift*, Year 12, 1888–1889.

Bang, Herman: *Stuk*. Copenhagen: Det Danske Sprog- og Litteraturselskab, Borgen, 1987 (1887).

Bonderup, Gerda: "Kolera i 1800-tallet – med særlig henblik på Danmark", *Tidsskrift for Forskning i Sygdom og Samfund*, Year 5, No. 8 (2008), pp. 35–48.

Bramsen, Bo (ed.): *København – før, nu og aldrig*, Vol. 9. Copenhagen: Fogtdal, 1998.

Bønnelycke, Emil: *Asfaltens Sange*. Copenhagen: Gyldendal, 1918.

Christensen, Villads: *København i Kristian den Ottendes og Frederik den Syvendes Tid 1840–1857*. Copenhagen: Gads Forlag, 1912.

Haugsted, Ida: *Københavns Rådhus*. Copenhagen: Copenhagen City Council, 1996.

Holm, Axel, and Kjeld Johansen: *København 1840–1940 – Det københavnske Bysamfund og Kommunens Økonomi*. Copenhagen: Nyt Nordisk Forlag, 1940.

Hübertz, J.R.: *Beretning om Cholera-Epidemien i Kjøbenhavn, 12 Juni–1 October 1853*. Copenhagen: Bianco Luno, 1855.

Hyldtoft, Ole: *Københavns industrialisering 1840–1914*. Herning: Systime, 1984.

Jacobsen, Carl: *Ny Carlsberg Glyptoteks Tilblivelse*. Copenhagen: Ny Carlsberg, 1906.

Jensen, Chr. Axel: "Loven om Bygningsfredning", *Fortid og Nutid*, Vol. 2, 1919, pp. 205–214.

Jensen, Nicolai Falberg: "Den nordiske Industri-, Landbrugs- og Kunstudstilling i København 1888 – en introduktion til arkivet og dets anvendelsesmuligheder", *Erhvervshistorisk Årbog*, Year 64, No. 1 (2015), pp. 52–98.

Jørgensen, Caspar: "Affolkning og citydannelse i det indre København 1855–1985", *Fabrik og Bolig*, No. 2, 1987, pp. 3–17.

Jørgensen, Caspar: *Aspekter af citydannelsen i København – En analyse af samspillet mellem funktionsskift og kommercielle bygninger i det indre København ca. 1870–1911*. Unpublished MA dissertation, University of Copenhagen, 1986.

Jørgensen, Caspar, Tim Knudsen and Anders Møller: "Charles Ambt og gadeplanlægningen i Vestervold kvarter", *Historiske Meddelelser om København*, 1989, pp. 85–107.

Knudsen, Tim: *Storbyen støbes – København mellem kaos og byplan 1840–1917*. Copenhagen: Akademisk Forlag, 1988.

Lauring, Kåre: *Københavnerliv 1857–1939*, Copenhagen: Gyldendal, 2010.

Meldahl, Ferdinand, and P. Johansen: *Det kongelige Akademi for de skjønne Kunster 1700–1904*. Copenhagen: Hagerups Boghandel, 1904.

Morgen, Mogens A., and Jannie Rosenberg Bendsen: *Fredet – Bygningsfredning i Danmark 1918–2018*. Copenhagen: Strandberg Publishing, 2018.

Mortensen, Mette Tapdrup: "Et skjul for al slags elendighed – Peder Madsens Gang i 1870'erne", *Historiske Meddelelser om København*, No. 97, 2004, pp. 52–76.

Parby, Jakob Ingemann: *Den grænseløse by*. Copenhagen: Gads Forlag, 2022.

Pedersen, Merete Bøge: *Den reglementerede prostitution i København fra 1874 til 1906 – En undersøgelse af prostitutionsmiljøet og de prostitueredes livsvilkår*. Copenhagen: Museum Tusculanum Press, 2000.

Pedersen, Merete Bøge: *Prostitutionen og Grundloven – Regulering af og debat om prostitution i Danmark i perioden ca. 1860–1906*. Copenhagen: Museum Tusculanum Press, 2007.

Pontoppidan, Henrik: *Enetaler*. Copenhagen: Aschehoug, 1993. Originally published in the newspaper *Politiken*, Spring 1897.

Skyggebjerg, Louise Karlskov: *Industri på udstilling*. Aarhus: Aarhus University Press, 2017.

Thelle, Mikkel: *Rådhuspladsen 1900 – Det moderne Københavns brændpunkt*. Copenhagen: Gyldendal, 2015.

Toftgaard, Jens: *Citydannelse, butiksstrøg og byidealer – Dannelsen af centrale byrum i Odense samt Aarhus og Aalborg 1870–1970*. PhD thesis, University of Southern Denmark, 2012.

Ulrik, F.F.: "Kan Peder Madsens Gang betragtes som et Sygdoms Focus her i Staden?" *Særtryk af Hygiejniske Meddelelser*, Year 7, No. 1 (1871).

Wagner, Michael F.: *Det polytekniske gennembrud – Romantikkens teknologiske konstruktion 1780–1850*. Aarhus: Aarhus Universitetsforlag, 1999.

Willerslev, Richard: *Sådan boede vi – Arbejdernes boligforhold i København omkring 1880*. Copenhagen: Akademisk Forlag, 1979.

Zerlang, Martin: *Herman Bangs København*. Copenhagen: Politikens Forlag, 2007.

Østergaard, Jan Stubbe: "Glyptoteket og omverdenen i Carl Jacobsens tid – Den udadvendte virksomhed 1882–1914", in: Flemming Friborg and Anne Marie Nielsen (eds.): *Ny Carlsberg Glyptotek i tiden*. Copenhagen: Ny Carlsberg Glyptotek, 2006, pp. 125–135.

Sophia Kalkau

Entranced

It's almost impossible. Close your eyes, choose a gallery. But it's the sum of them all, of all galleries I protest – and close my eyes. I go through the glass door, count seven black stone steps and sink onto a wooden bench in the Winter Garden. The air is warm and slightly humid, the sound of hushed voices and clinking of coffee cups mingling with the trickling of the fountain. I tilt my head back and look up into the huge glass dome with its hint of pink rising above me – and close my eyes. When I open them again, I'm in the circular Egyptian gallery, a rotunda with golden walls and a jade-green terrazzo floor with breathtaking mosaics. I stand under the centre of the dome above and turn on my own axis. Shining mosaic tiles gleam in the floor rosette. Along the walls are black plinths supporting kings, gods, goddesses and others of rank, plus a bronze cat – a coffin for a mummified feline. The works entrance me ...

How did I get here? I know – past the fountain, then up the steps to the Roman limestone lions and fiery red Central Hall with its high green marble panels, colonnades and coffered glass ceiling. Up the stairs to the left flanked by two sphinxes, through the strict symmetry of the long axial Egyptian gallery with its dusty green walls, reddish-brown terrazzo floors and three white marble steps at the end.

I squeeze my eyes shut. I had forgotten the column. I stand slightly stunned at the top of the white marble steps to the rotunda and bite my lip. Straight ahead stands a tall palm column from a temple in Kawa right in the middle of the room. This means I can't see the innermost parts of the beautiful terrazzo floor's rosette. I also can't stand in the middle and turn around under the dome – the best spot in the room. I don't remember when the column was put there, but I do remember the rotunda without it. I turn my back on the temple column, divided between the work of art and the space it's in and look up into the dome. I try to keep the mesh of wires holding the lamp rack in place out of my line of vision as I look at the stucco decorations. In vain. I count the eighteen black plinths along the wall instead. They stand on a black ring of terrazzo on the jade-green floor. Around the edges of the ring are ivory-coloured mosaic tiles, and in front of each of the entrances a fine bronze grating. From the rotunda I look into the gallery with azure walls and works from Nubia, and from there one gallery after the other, like pearls on a string – one dark green, one yellow ochre, one red ochre, then a lighter green one leading into a new rotunda with dark red walls and yet another exquisite floor. Each gallery a unique version of the other.

I return to the large Egyptian gallery and savour the proportions of the space, the fine barrel-vaulted glass ceiling, the daylight pouring in from above. There is an entrance to the small Egyptian gallery with the finest small sculptures and artefacts displayed in glass vitrines, and opposite that the descent into the underworld of tomb models, mummies and sarcophagi. I sit on one of the leather-upholstered chairs and admire the blooming papyrus ornamentation in the reddish-brown terrazzo floor, the large cooling fans of plants. I love this motif and the strict symmetry of its mirroring, staggering and repetition. It covers almost the entire floor. It makes me want to dance, to glide with the light across stalks and papyrus buds, lifting my foot high above peacock tails, fans and almond eyes. I could sail around the entire bel étage without once lifting my eyes from the beauty of its floors.

The works here are from a time when art was a magical instrument, the text on the wall of the Egyptian gallery tells me. It still is, for some of us. I read on. These sculptures were not created for the human eye but to perform their magic in the darkness of walled-up tombs. Yet here they are, standing before me in full daylight. Magnificent works of art in sandstone, greywacke and basalt. Porous, dense and hard stone that absorbs the light in places and in others gently reflects it. I actually came to look at the architecture – the proportions of the galleries, the ornamentation, the interior design. But it's the sculptures that draw my gaze, connecting us with invisible threads. I register my breathing, my chest, my body. My senses are open. I am quiet, I listen, I hear. I feel wonderfully present. I have never been hypnotised but imagine this entranced state to be comparable. The works speak across time and space. They speak of the world order, power and glory, death and the hereafter. And I hear them. I breathe lightly and heavily at the same time, to the pit of my stomach. In some kind of wondrous way I perpetuate their secret. Before I leave I stand for a long time before the scribe Gebu, royal bearer of the seal. I take another look at the soft limestone reliefs with their magical hieroglyphs and wishes for the afterlife of the dead. From a time when they knew that what was written came true. Sometimes it still does.

Peter Thule Kristensen

HANDED-DOWN FORMS IN NEW BUILDINGS

Historicism in the Age of Dahlerup and Kampmann

For the architects and art patrons of the 19th century history was inescapable in the creation of anything new or understanding their own age. As Danish architect Vilhelm Klein, the leading Danish contemporary writer on architecture and a recurring insider's voice in this article, wrote:

> "The style of a building only emerges when one (temporarily) adheres to the forms that have been handed down to us, adapting these to new and different purposes so they become something else entirely. If one's approach is solely rational, the only effect of forcing development will be affectation."[1]

History was a constant starting point for architects in the 19th century, even when designing buildings with new functions such as museums, railway stations, hospitals and industrial complexes. Partly because like Klein in the citation above they subscribed to the idea of a natural development in which the architecture of history was automatically transformed and gradually condensed into the style of a new era.

This way of thinking did not, however, mean that architects did not question the usefulness of historical heritage. On the contrary, this was a period of heated debates on the correct historical style for a specific project, and many architects regretted that their generation had not managed to define a contemporary style of its own. Hack Kampmann, the architect behind the Glyptotek's extension, asked himself with a touch of melancholy:

> "Is it the right thing to do, turning endlessly to the past and admiring its achievements and creations? I concede there is plenty to look at, but in doing so one should not overlook the time in which one lives. Of what use is it to be wise about the past yet unable to find one's own front door?"[2]

In the following I take a closer look at the mindset of historicism and some of its dilemmas. Using examples I then go on to show that despite having a shared view of history, historicist architecture was also a site of conflict: conflict between a national and more cosmopolitan approach, between an eclectic and orthodox style, and between a focus on technology and atmosphere.

The Historicist Mindset

Renaissance architects and artists were not interested in history as such but in reusing the heritage of the Mediterranean culture of ancient Rome and Greece, which they considered to be exemplary.[3] Over a long period, from the late 15th century to the end of the 18th century, European architects almost always based their work on classical antiquity, including the ancient Roman architectural theorist Vitruvius's treatise *De Architectura* and the five classical orders (Tuscan, Doric, Ionic, Corinthian and Composite) in which the profiles and three-part construction of columns — pedestal,

Sketch by Vilhelm Dahlerup depicting
an architect who has "returned from his
travels" with his head full of historical
inspiration.

Hack Kampmann's Central Hall at the
Glyptotek shows that the heritage of
Mediterranean antiquity was still very
much alive in the 20th century.

pillar and capital – constituted a form of architectural DNA. Styles using this ancient vocabulary in an unorthodox or dynamic way – later to be called Mannerism or the Baroque by art historians – did emerge. Even here, however, the classical orders continued to be the point of departure. From the mid 18th century this system was challenged. One such challenge came when architectural historian and archaeologist Johann Joachim Winckelmann's measurements of ancient temples revealed that the proportions used during the Renaissance did not match those of classical antiquity.[4] Artists and architects influenced by incipient Romanticism had also started to rediscover the potential of the Gothic, a style that had previously been looked upon with disdain. With the emergence of Romanticism around 1800 the architectural repertoire expanded and was supplemented by new aesthetic ideals permitting the use of elements such as heavy contrasts, asymmetry, fragmentation, abstraction and obscure symbols.[5]

Historicism, which developed during the 19th century, was the child of the Enlightenment's anti-authoritarianism and Romanticism's expanded view of art. From the Enlightenment, historicist architects inherited the idea of the

Prussian architect Karl Friedrich Schinkel's Altes Museum in Berlin from 1823–1830 was one of the first purpose-built museums. Typologically Schinkel combines the Roman Pantheon of the museum's central rotunda with a reinterpretation of the Greek colonnade in the row of columns facing the city.

196

natural progress of history, a faith in science and technology and a belief that in-depth historical research could bring new and profound insights to art and architecture. From Romanticism came an interest in atmosphere, artistic individualism and eclecticism, sometimes combining elements from different epochs and realms in a single work. This dual heritage gave historicism a strangely inherent conflict, which can be seen to live on today.[6]

Historicism also embraced the idea that artists played a role in a historical and rational development. Whereas the architects of the Renaissance had looked back to antiquity and 18th-century architects saw themselves as having perfected its heritage in an improved modern form of classicism, from the 1830s onwards many started to see their own era as transient, a step on the way to some kind of utopian future.[7] Vilhelm Klein, who could find the presence of many different styles at once difficult, was nonetheless hopeful "that the seemingly confused agglomeration is part of a certain rational progression and that it will also lead to a certain goal. What this could be, however, can only be sensed, and certainly not identified by the generation as yet in its midst".[8] As early as 1835 the prominent Prussian historicist Karl Friedrich Schinkel remarked that he found himself "trapped in a large labyrinth" as a result of his lifelong investigation of "the vast, immeasurable treasure of forms already brought into the world by the creation of buildings over centuries of development by very different nations".[9]

A way out of Klein's agglomeration and Schinkel's labyrinth presented itself with the new concept of style in art history, which started to become an independent discipline in the mid 19th century and developed a systematic catalogue of 'turnkey' categories linking styles to specific historical epochs. In 1860, for example, Swiss art historian Jacob Burckhardt (1818–1897) established the idea of the Italian Renaissance as a continuous, turbulent epoch marking the beginning of a new humanist form of modernity.[10] According to Klein, style was "the product of a large number of intellectual and material factors" that could limit the number of random possibilities for design.[11] It did not solve the problem of finding a contemporary style that fit new programmes and technologies, but it did give some indication of what such a style should be capable of. The sections below chart the ways this work of developing a new, contemporary style played out in Denmark.

National Versus Imported Architecture

In 1844 the influential Danish art historian N.L. Høyen (1798–1870) argued that art should have local origins:

> "The history of Scandinavia, built on the foundations of the fundamental characteristics of the country and its people, is from whence the art we have imported fully grown from beyond our borders is to be born again in our midst".[12]

With these words Høyen, who was otherwise sceptical about the quality of Danish building culture, sparked a discussion that was to dominate 19th-century architecture in Denmark. The versatile architect Michael Gottlieb Bindesbøll, who had based Thorvaldsen's Museum (1839–1848) on classical antiquity, may have been the first. In the 1850s he designed a house in Old Norse style and another in the style of a Danish farmhouse.[13] He was also one of the first in Denmark to experiment with Gothic architecture. He was awarded a gold medal for a Gothic cathedral project he designed in 1833, a style he continued in his work with churches.[14] Michael Gottlieb Bindesbøll was followed by others, creating a movement that the architecture historian Knud Millech (1890–1980) and architect Kay Fisker (1893–1965) called the Herholdt school (named after Danish architect Johan Daniel Herholdt) or free historicism. The architects of this school worked with regional sources of inspiration in brick, a material familiar from Danish medieval architecture. This style, which according to Millech and Fisker also included buildings designed by Hack Kampmann, positioned itself in opposition to what they called 'the Europeans' including architects like Vilhelm Dahlerup.[15]

Johan Daniel Herholdt (1818–1902) was the architect behind the University Library in Copenhagen (1855–1861). It was inspired by the medieval architecture of Northern Italy, but he also used bricks, carved details and cast-iron constructions, adhering to their inherent logic and the tried and tested methods of craftmanship. Herholdt was to have a major influence on a later generation of architects, including Henning Wolff (1828–1880), H.B. Storck (1839–1922) and Hans J. Holm (1835–1916). They also worked with visible brickwork to painterly, textural effect, as well as bold details from different historical epochs, as in Holm's late magnum opus, the

Johan Daniel Herholdt: University Library
in Copenhagen, 1855–1861. The library
is a good example of a historicist building
using modern cast-iron construction
elements and a materiality inspired by,
for example, medieval masonry.

Royal Danish Library (1898–1906). Holm was appointed professor at the architecture school of the Royal Danish Academy of Fine Arts, where he had his students measure and map historical Danish architecture. These students included Martin Nyrop, Martin Borch (1852–1937) and Hack Kampmann, who later became exponents of National Romantic architecture with buildings like Nyrop's Copenhagen City Hall (1892–1905), Borch's St. Andrew's Church in Copenhagen (1898–1901) and Kampmann's Custom House in Aarhus (1895–1897). Many such works were built at almost the same time as Dahlerup's Glyptotek, and like the museum were examples of new types of building for a new era. Yet despite their penchant for expressive, voluminous brick structures and the fact that both styles shared details referring to historical architecture, there were also differences between them. "It is first and foremost about making the whole good," as Martin Borch wrote, "for even the best, most brilliant details cannot save a building with a poor disposition. The opposite is true of a successful whole, where if one manages to create such a thing one can make do with little or no detail at all."[16]

Around the 1870s a new style inspired by Renaissance Revival architecture on the continent emerged in Denmark.[17] The Danish architects dubbed 'the Europeans' were associated with the powerful figure of Ferdinand Meldahl.[18] In 1864 he was appointed professor at the academy instead of Herholdt, who he held in high regard. Like Herholdt, Meldahl had worked with medieval-style brick architecture in the past.[19] It is not always possible to make a clear distinction between architects working in the two styles, and it perhaps makes more sense to use the term Neo-Renaissance as in other countries. Neo-Renaissance architecture is usually reminiscent of the urban architecture of cities like Paris, Berlin and Vienna, which made it a natural extension of Copenhagen's expansion after the demolition of the city's ramparts in the 1850s. Inspiration from the Renaissance can, for example, be seen in the use of horizontal cornices and mouldings, pilasters, half and whole columns or ashlar lesenes (vertical pilasters without a capital but with horizontal joints), all elements encountered in Italian Renaissance architecture. Vilhelm Klein – again – was one of the advocates of Neo-Renaissance architecture, which he described in the following way:

Hack Kampmann: Custom House in Aarhus, 1895–1897. The building is an example of the National Romantic movement's enthusiasm for sculptural brickwork and solid craftmanship.

"Two things characterise the Italian Renaissance. The most conspicuous is its development of an entirely new system of forms, such as the cornice on Palazzo Riccardi, the lesenes on Palazzo Ruccelai, the square windows, etc. The other is the introduction of more elegance, both in details and the overall distribution of elements of the façade."[20]

For Klein and others among his contemporaries the Renaissance represented a broad yet flexible set of principles of form, and a number of Vilhelm Dahlerup's buildings in Copenhagen, such as the Port Authority building (1868), Hotel d'Angleterre (1873–1875), the Royal Theatre (1872–1874), the National Gallery of Denmark (1889–1896) and then the Glyptotek, are also obviously inspired by Renaissance architecture.

Architects like Vilhelm Klein and Ferdinand Meldahl drew on the Italian Renaissance but also the French Renaissance or Louvre style with its typical pavilion-like division of buildings crowned by distinctive, high mansard roofs, or a variation on the Renaissance from the Low Countries and Denmark, such as the Christian IV

Vilhelm Dahlerup and Ove Petersen: Royal Danish Theatre in Copenhagen, 1872–1874. A typical building for Dahlerup and theatre architecture at the time, inspired by the Italian Renaissance when the proscenium theatre was developed. Renaissance features include the loggia with arches and the emphasis on horizontal divisions.

or Rosenborg style. This style became popular in the 1850s, especially after a fire at Frederiksborg Castle in 1859 and its subsequent reconstruction. In 1863 Christian Hansen (1803–1883), who had worked in Greece for many years, introduced Byzantine-inspired brick architecture to Denmark with Copenhagen Municipal Hospital, a style that was to dominate many of the period's large, functional institutional buildings.[21] Later, in the early 20th century, the Baroque had a brief revival in the form of heavy brick buildings with dynamic forms and voluminous tiled roofs.

With the Christian IV style Millech's 'Europeans', who included Herholdt and others who shared his views, were also inspired by continental architecture and drew on medieval picturesque references that were not necessarily Danish. A more useful distinction between the two styles could perhaps be based on whether

the architecture referred primarily to the Middle Ages and the vernacular building culture of different regions with a focus on craftmanship, which was the case for Herholdt, Holm, Kampmann and Nyrop, or whether it operated with a more classicist paradigm, which was the case for Meldahl, Klein and Dahlerup.

Similar divisions recurred in the 20th century with a classicist revival between the 1910s and 1920s represented by the late works of Hack Kampmann and the school that emerged with P.V. Jensen-Klint (1853–1930). Jensen-Klint did not care for Neoclassicism, turning instead to vernacular buildings and medieval architecture as sources of inspiration. Danish architect Kay Fisker actually used his texts on architecture to legitimise his own buildings, which he located in a national, functional tradition and the Herholdt school, as opposed to the competing international functionalism movement of the same period.[22] The writing of history is rarely neutral.

Eclectic Individualism Versus Stylistic Orthodoxy

During Dahlerup and Kampmann's careers there were discussions as to whether architects should adhere to one style at a time, or could take a more eclectic approach referencing different periods and regions in the same project in a more individualistic manner. Despite his use of the Renaissance, Vilhelm Dahlerup was an example of an eclectic architect. This drew criticism from the more orthodox Vilhelm Klein: "Dahlerup is more of a decorator

With Copenhagen Municipal Hospital from 1858–1863 Christian Hansen introduced Byzantine-inspired architecture to the Danish capital. The hospital was also an example of rational institutional architecture comprised of pavilions connected by wide passages.

than an architect, which is why he places so much importance on enforcing his decorative whims."[23] According to Klein, this was also reflected in the architecture of the Glyptotek, which he described as Dahlerup's most "meaningless" project:

> "The exterior is a hotchpotch of 4–6 different buildings that have nothing to do with each other; there is not a single consistent moulding. On the front a large arcade parades, borne by polished granite columns, but it is nothing more than a screen in front of a fence, and seeing it as framing the statues that were to be displayed under the arches is equally ridiculous since the frames relate in no way whatsoever to that which they are meant to frame."[24]

Klein found the interior equally unsatisfactory:

> "Dahlerup's original plan was for a small building, like Bramante's chapel at San Pietro in Montorio in the middle of the courtyard, but this feeble-minded idea was thwarted by Mayor Hansen and Judge Kock, to Dahlerup's great regret."[25]

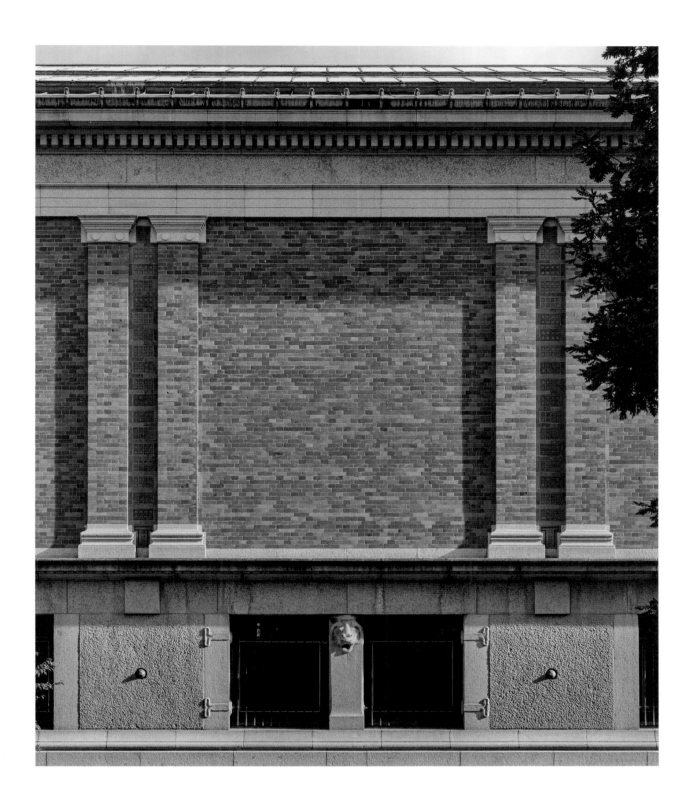

Despite being critical of the Glyptotek, Vilhelm Klein had more respect for Hack Kampmann's extension to the museum, although he disapproved of Kampmann's "meagre lesenes" on the façades. These were the brick pilasters between the base and beam of the extension's façades, which Klein intimated Kampmann had been forced to include by the client.

Dahlerup's small, circular temple was later realised in the Glyptotek's domed Winter Garden. This kind of eclecticism, in which a composition is comprised of multiple disparate elements, did not harmonise with the concept of beauty the Italian Renaissance architect Alberti defined as "harmony of all the parts [...] fitted together with such proportion and connection that nothing could be added, diminished, or altered for the worse".[26] This Renaissance ideal of a unified whole could be one basis for Klein's critique – together with the belief that adhering to one style at a time gave a more consistent result.

Hack Kampmann could also be eclectic and difficult to confine to any specific school or style. Klein again:

> "[Kampmann], unlike so many others, does not have a particular hobbyhorse in his stable. It would perhaps be better if he had something of the sort. There is almost always something of interest in what he does, but he dashes all over the place, making it difficult to actually see him."[27]

Klein is, however, slightly more charitable about Kampmann's extension to the Glyptotek than Dahlerup's main building:

> "In the original proposal for the extension to the Glyptotek the outer surfaces were entirely smooth, which was not too bad, except he could have chosen something more in keeping with the old building. Since, however, the committee made demands of this nature, he could not avoid decorating the surfaces with some meagre lesenes, which were neither here nor there."[28]

Kampmann's use of various references fell roughly into phases. At the beginning of his career his breakthrough work, Viborg Archive (1889–1891), showed him to be an exponent of National Romanticism, inspired by architects like Herholdt, Holm and Nyrop. This was followed by projects like Villa Kampen in Aarhus (1906) and Carl Jacobsen's villa on the site of the New Carlsberg brewery (1890–1905). Around 1910 Kampmann can be seen to be increasingly influenced by the Neo-Baroque, for example with Custom House in Horsens (1911–1913). After this there was another shift where Kampmann – possibly inspired by his work on the Glyptotek

(1900–1906) and a new generation at the drawing office – started to work with a purer form of classicism, culminating in clearly defined projects such as Viborg Grammar School (1915–1926), Randers State School (1918–1926) and Copenhagen Police Headquarters (1919–1924). These projects were inspired by architecture from around 1800, including C.F. Hansen's (1756–1845) simple classicism that enjoyed a renaissance after the brewer Carl Jacobsen's failed attempt to add a Baroque spire to Hansen's Copenhagen Cathedral in 1910.[29] Klein's 1908 appraisal of Kampmann above could be a sign of this coming change, and the fact that the extension to the Glyptotek with all its pre-existing parameters was to mirror the collection of antiquities pointed in a different direction than Kampmann's earlier works.

The eclecticism that can be traced in the architecture of both Dahlerup and Kampmann was, however, perhaps not as ill-considered as Vilhelm Klein seemed to think. It can also be seen as an attempt to create a modern form of architecture through the juxtaposition of historical forms and motifs with different associations: a kind of architectural mind map marshalling the entire arsenal of historical forms to make the function and content of the building clear and create a new kind of unified, artistic whole. Danish art historian Mirjam Gelfer-Jørgensen captures perfectly the complexity of the period in her book on the Danish Arts and Crafts movement around 1900. She emphasises two interconnected trajectories: the search for a unique national style by individual countries, and the search for an individual style by contemporary artists, both of which were driven by the ambition to unite arts, crafts and architecture in a synthesis or *Gesamtkunstwerk*.[30]

Compared to the galleries of Vilhelm Dahlerup, Hack Kampmann's galleries were more abstract with clearer distinctions between individual elements, such as door frames, skirting boards and ceilings. The materials used by Kampmann were also easier to identify.

Technology Versus Atmosphere and Craftmanship

The historicists' hunt for a new, modern style coincided with the Industrial Revolution's introduction of mass production and new technologies that created cast-iron constructions, rail and steamship transportation, and cities on an unprecedented scale.[31] The Industrial Revolution also restructured society, and Denmark went from being a feudal society to one divided by class. The up-and-coming industrial bourgeoisie of Carl Jacobsen owned the new means of production but aspired to a 'classical' style like that of the aristocracy and royals of the past. They were often disparagingly described as social climbers looking for redolent architecture (as was Meldahl), a stucco 'illusion' devoid of respect for authenticity, genuine materials, social justice or the demands of a new age. On the other hand, the recycling of historical references in industrial culture by historicists can also be seen as an attempt to establish a shared horizon, making a world in the throes of vast and rapid change familiar and providing a cultural fixed point for a new bourgeois public sphere – an attempt to create a collective culture. If using genuine materials is the ideal, it might seem 'fake' to use stucco to cast the sandstone ornamentation of former times in cement and zinc. From a different perspective, however, it can be seen as an attempt to reconcile a familiar universe with the technologies of a new age. The picture is more complex than it first appears, and Carl Jacobsen's mother and father, J.C. Jacobsen and Laura Jacobsen, for example, were both visionary and socially engaged. In their family villa in the grounds of the Carlsberg brewery in Valby the couple combined the late classicism emerging from Danish Biedermeier culture with the latest technology. They had ultra-modern

central heating and conservatories with cast-iron constructions inspired by London's Crystal Palace built for the Great Exhibition in 1851.[32] This kind of combination would later be judged inconsistent by modernists, but it was a key characteristic of historicism.

During Dahlerup and Kampmann's lifetime we encounter two strategies regarding the use of technology. In Dahlerup's Winter Garden at the Glyptotek from 1906 we are witness to an attempt to use cast iron to create a historical form, in this instance a domed building. Dahlerup originally wanted to build a brick dome, but due to the cost had to make do with glass and iron. This he tried to make less industrial in appearance by covering the upper ribs of the dome in copper and using yellowish brown not white glass[33] but had to abandon his dream of covering the supporting columns in black, white, blue and red majolica faience.[34] It was a strategy that adapted the technology of a new age to fit the style of a historical era. The brewer J.C. Jacobsen used a similar strategy in his conservatory in Valby, which was built in the shape of a three-nave basilica.

Kampmann presents a more complex picture. He was originally influenced by architects such as Herholdt, Holm and the National Romantics, who also incorporated visible cast-iron constructions in buildings like Herholdt's University Library or Martin Nyrop's large, glass-covered hall at Copenhagen City Hall. In both cases the new constructions were autonomous structural elements, but at the same time both architects wanted to revitalise traditional crafts to counter the mass production of industrial culture. In Hack Kampmann's extension to the Glyptotek, the skylights of a new era in the galleries and Central Hall are plain and simple, made on the terms of the technology that made them possible, whereas the patterned floors and variations on stucco ornamentation on the ceilings testify to the skill of traditional craftsmen. In his use of materials Hack Kampmann also distinguished more clearly between the different elements of the interior than Dahlerup.

The Duality of Historicism

For the architects of historicism, historical references were an integral part of designs inscribed in a narrative of progressive development. Classical Rome and Greece were, however, no longer the sole frame of reference, which could contribute to an overwhelming confusion of possibilities.

Historicist architects and their clients wanted to connect new cast-iron technology to historical styles of architecture. Here, for example, we see the home of the brewer J.C. Jacobsen and Laura Jacobsen in Valby. They built several conservatories. They called this hybrid between a modern greenhouse and an ancient Roman peristyle 'Pompeii'.

This photograph of the museum attic reveals some of the modern construction techniques and materials hidden behind the historicist façade of Dahlerup's building.

Kampmann's gallery for the Glyptotek's
Antiquities Collection is classically simple
in style and devoid of ornamentation.
Apart from the cornice between the wall
and the barrel vaulting it could have been
built today. The floor is not original.

Art history's new concept of style created a system for the many expressive forms, but for many historicists it also served to underline the absence of a modern style of their own.

The search for historical forms that could connect to a new age and make sense in terms of new kinds of buildings manifested itself in opposing strategies. The desire to create a nationally rooted architecture by architects like Hack Kampmann led to the proliferation of an eclectic use of medieval references and vernacular building cultures, not all of which were Danish, whereas the Renaissance Revival architecture, of which Vilhelm Dahlerup was an exponent, drew to a larger extent on a classicist and shared European frame of reference. Both Hack Kampmann and Vilhelm Dahlerup used historical material in an eclectic manner that met with criticism from more stylistically orthodox architects like Vilhelm Klein. In relationship to the technological breakthroughs of industrialism, architects tried to both adapt new construction methods and materials to historical forms to render them in a more autonomous style. In other cases, attempts to relaunch traditional crafts or focus on atmosphere can be seen as a reaction against industrial culture. Historicist architecture is thus characterised by duality. Eclectic individualism and new technologies stand alongside the belief in a rational process of development and history being the basis for all design.

In the wake of World War I the old world order collapsed in large parts of Europe, taking historicism with it. From the 1920s onwards a new generation of architects had an explicit 'anti-historical' approach, focusing instead on the new technologies and needs of industrial societies.[35] Yet they shared the 19th-century belief in progress, and the idea that certain epochs were connected to certain styles. For Danish architects like Kay Fisker, however, history remained a source of inspiration, and from the 1960s onwards postmodernists revisited historical architecture as part of their critique of modernism, inspired by architects like Robert Venturi (1925–2018) and his 1966 book *Complexity and Contradiction in Architecture*.[36] Today some architects use historical references as a corrective to market forces and growth ideology. According to the English architectural practice Caruso St John: "Anything that can contribute to the fragile continuities between the contemporary situation and past architectures is worth the effort. It is only by understanding and reflecting on the past that architecture can continue to be a relevant social and artistic discipline."[37] Historicism's endeavour to create continuity is not lost but expressed in new ways – using new technologies and methods of design.

Notes

1. Vilhelm Klein, "Blade af Vrøvlets Historie" (1905–1906), in Jørgensen and Kristensen, 2019, p. 315.
2. Letter from Hack Kampmann in Mantova, 8 June 1885. Cited from Dirckinck-Holmfeld, Gehl and Soldbro, 2017, p. 8.
3. See, for example, Peter Thule Kristensen, "Vilhelm Klein og historien om arkitekternes brug af historien", in Jørgensen and Kristensen, 2019, pp. 449–472.
4. See Bisky, 2000; Winckelmann, 1762.
5. See also Svane, 2003.
6. See also Hvattum, 2004.
7. Gumbrecht, 1978.
8. Klein, 1877, p. 201.
9. Schinkel, 1979, p. 150.
10. Burckhardt, 1860. Published in English as *The Civilization of the Renaissance in Italy*, most recently translated by Peter Murray. London: Penguin Classics, 2004.
11. Klein, 1894, p. 179.
12. N.L. Høyen, "Om Betingelserne for en skandinavisk National-konsts Udvikling" (1844), in Høyen, 1871, p. 360.
13. See Kristensen, 2013.
14. Ibid. in the chapter "Guddommelig gotik", pp. 176–199.
15. The two styles were introduced in Millech and Fisker, 1951. The distinction between the two is also partially maintained in, for example, Sommer, 2009, whereas Harald Langberg sees a more gradual development, with first the Middle Ages then the Renaissance becoming the focus of architects' attention. See Langberg, 1978.
16. Martin Borch is quoted in Millech and Fisker, 1951, p. 224.
17. See, for example, Milde, 1981, or Bligaard, 2008, Vol. 1, pp. 217–218.
18. Millech and Fisker, 1951.
19. Madsen, 1983, pp. 123–124.
20. Vilhelm Klein, "Architektportraiter" (1906 addendum), republished in Jørgensen and Kristensen, 2019, p. 273.
21. See, for example, Haugsted, 2009.
22. Millech and Fisker, 1951.
23. Vilhelm Klein, "Architektportraiter" (1896), republished in Jørgensen and Kristensen, 2019, p. 230.
24. Ibid., p. 233.
25. Ibid., p. 234.
26. *De re aedificatoria* (VI.2) here cited after Alberti, 1988.
27. Vilhelm Klein, "Architektportraiter" (1908 addendum), republished in Jørgensen and Kristensen, 2019, p. 289.
28. Ibid., p. 289.
29. On classicism in the early 20th century, see Andersson, Jørgensen et al., 1982.
30. Gelfer-Jørgensen, 2020.
31. See, for example, Loyer, 1983.
32. Kristensen, 2021, pp. 77–113.
33. Bruun, 1907, pp. 86–87.
34. Ibid., p. 88.
35. Forty, 2000, pp. 198–199.
36. Venturi, 1966.
37. Caruso, 2004, in Per (ed.), 2005, p. 114.

Bibliography

Alberti, Leon Battista: *On the Art of Building in Ten Books*, translated from *De re aedificatoria* by Joseph Rykwert, Neil Leach and Robert Tavernor. Cambridge, MA: MIT Press, 1988.

Andersson, Henrik O., Lisbet Balslev Jørgensen et al.: *Nordisk klassicism*. Helsinki: Suomen Rakennustaiteen Museo, 1982.

Bisky, Jens: *Poesie der Baukunst – Architekturästhetik von Winckelmann bis Boisserée*. Weimar: Hermann Böhlaus Nachfolger, 2000.

Bligaard, Mette: *Frederiksborgs genrejsning – Historicisme i teori og praksis*, Vols. 1–2. Copenhagen: Forlaget Vandkunsten, 2008.

Brunner, Otto (ed.): *Geschichtliche Grundbegriffe*, Vol. 4. Stuttgart: Klett-Cotta, 1978.

Bruun, Andreas: *Jens Vilhelm Dahlerups Liv og Virksomhed*. Copenhagen: H. Hagerups Boghandel, 1907.

Burckhardt, Jacob: *Die Kultur der Renaissance in Italien*. Basel, 1860.

Caruso, Adam, "Traditions" (2004), in: Aurora Fernández Per (ed.): *As Built – Caruso St John Architects*. Vitoria-Gasteiz: a+t ediciones, 2005.

Dirckinck-Holmfeld, Kim, Elisabeth Gehl and Louise Kampmann Soldbro: *Hack Kampmann del 2 – En individualist i en brydningstid*. Nykøbing Sj.: Bogværket, 2017.

Forty, Adrian: *Words and Buildings – A Vocabulary of Modern Architecture*. London: Thames & Hudson, 2000.

Gelfer-Jørgensen, Mirjam: *Kunstarternes forbrødring. Skønvirke – en kalejdoskopisk periode*. Copenhagen: Strandberg Publishing, 2020.

Gumbrecht, Hans Ulrich: "Modern, Modernität, Moderne" in Otto Brunner (ed.), *Geschichtliche Grundbegriffe*, Vol. 4. Stuttgart: Klett-Cotta, 1978.

Haugsted, Ida: *Arkitekten Christian Hansen*. Nykøbing Sj.: Bogværket, 2009.

Haugsted, Ida: *Nye tider – Historicisme i København*. Copenhagen: Nyt Nordisk Forlag Arnold Busck, 2003.

Hvattum, Mari: *Gottfried Semper and the Problem of Historicism.* Cambridge: Cambridge University Press, 2004.

Høyen, N.L.: *Niels Laurits Høyens Skrifter*, Vol. 1. Copenhagen, 1871.

Jørgensen, Mette Lund, and Peter Thule Kristensen: *Klein – Arkitekten Vilhelm Kleins skrifter og historicismen i Danmark.* Copenhagen: Arkitektens Forlag, 2019.

Klein, Vilhelm: "Bygningskunsten og de tekniske Kunster", in: André Lütken (ed.): *Opfindelsernes Bog – En Oversigt over Menneskets kulturhistoriske Udvikling og Fremskridt paa Videnskabens, Kunstens, Industriens og Handelens Omraader fra tidligste Tid til vore Dage*, Vol. 1. Copenhagen, 1877.

Klein, Vilhelm: "Det danske Kunstindustrimuseums Opgaver", *Tidsskrift for Kunstindustri*, 1894.

Kristensen, Peter Thule: *Gottlieb Bindesbøll – Denmark's First Modern Architect.* Copenhagen: Danish Architectural Press, 2013.

Kristensen, Peter Thule: "Microcosm at Valby Bakke – Architectural History and J.C. Jacobsen's Villa", in: *Will, Works and Values – J.C. Jacobsen's Villa at Carlsberg.* By Birgitte Possing et al. (eds.): Copenhagen: Strandberg Publishing, 2021.

Langberg, Harald: *Danmarks Bygningskultur – En historisk oversigt*, Vol. 2 (1955). Aarhus: Fonden til Udgivelse af Arkitekturværker, 1978.

Loyer, François: *Architecture of the Industrial Age, 1789–1914.* Geneva: Skira, 1983.

Madsen, Hans Helge: *Meldahls rædselsprogram – F. Meldahl, arkitekt og politiker 1827–1908.* Copenhagen: Nyt Nordisk Forlag Arnold Busck, 1983.

Milde, Kurt: *Neorenaissance in der deutschen Architektur des 19. Jahrhunderts.* Dresden: VEB Verlag der Kunst, 1981.

Millech, Knud, and Kay Fisker: *Danske arkitekturstrømninger 1850–1950.* Copenhagen: Østifternes Kreditforening, 1951.

Schinkel, Karl Friedrich: *Lebenswerk – Das Architektonische Lehrbuch.* Munich: Deutscher Kunstverlag, 1979.

Sommer, Anne-Louise (ed.): *Den danske arkitektur.* Copenhagen: Gyldendal, 2009.

Svane, Marie-Louise: *Formationer i europæisk romantik.* Copenhagen: Museum Tusculanum Press, 2003.

Venturi, Robert: *Complexity and Contradiction in Architecture.* New York: Museum of Modern Art, 1966.

Will, Works and Values – J.C. Jacobsen's Villa at Carlsberg. By Birgitte Possing et al. (eds.): Copenhagen: Strandberg Publishing, 2021.

Winckelmann, Johann: *Anmerkungen über die Baukunst der Alten.* Leipzig: Johann Gottfried Dyck, 1762.

Sif Itona Westerberg

The Central Hall

I have a clear bodily memory of my first visits to museums as a child: the silence, the veneration, the galleries devoid of people with display cases full of relics that landed in my body as a tingling vibration, a heightened awareness, a sense of calm and the call of another time. I grew up with mythological stories borrowed on tape and listened to again and again until they were worn out and the sound distorted. Stories of heroes and gods, revenge, desire, feasts and transformation – a doorway opening onto another world. To this very day something strange happens inside me when I move between the potsherds, sarcophagi and sculptures at the Glyptotek. It is if something in my flesh simultaneously tightens and releases, as if time stands still, as if my mind is filled by senses rather than words. My inner voice falls silent when all the exhibits start to speak at once. The tingling vibration is back.

As soon as I step into the Glyptotek there is always one place that pulls me towards it: the Central Hall, the heart of the museum with colonnades reminiscent of a Greek temple or Roman forum. I am propelled towards the hall's furthest left corner, where two Dionysian theatre masks as over-dimensioned in size as in twisted theatricality create a sense of masquerade and identity games still inescapable today, thousands of years later. I love the interweaving of different periods on this very spot. Love the stackable chairs, the theatre masks, and the grand piano that can be rolled back and forth depending on whether it is in use. It is my favourite corner of the Glyptotek – a box room, a clash, a dance with baggage and dreams.

The main character in the Central Hall is its red colour. It is as if the pigments time and culture have erased from the white marble sculptures in the museum stream down these deep red walls, evidence of a drama long past so basic and fundamentally human that it continues to play out and always will. I want to get between the layers of umbra, red, chalk and salt and like a time traveller allow myself to be transported back to the past. Not only to the time the Central Hall was built but to ancient feasts, rituals and ceremonies where Greek colonnades and cold hard marble sculptures formed the backdrop for celebrations we will never fully understand or be part of. If walls could talk, I would love to hear what the red walls of the Central Hall have to say. Maybe it is precisely a concentration of all the events that have taken place in here that makes the colour so deep and compelling.

In this building, built to preserve, study and learn from our shared past, the Central Hall so often provides the setting for lectures, music, theatre, tributes and gatherings that are to catapult us into the future. A future of new movements, new directions, and new forms of artistic expression.

When a pile of queer bodies writhes in playful, identity-exploratory performance art on top of the covered mosaic floor in the centre of the Central Hall – asking and insisting that we remember our innate ability and desire to play with gender and sexuality – it is as if the Greek god Dionysus is looking on in approval from the hollow eyes of the masks. We have come full circle, cycles repeat, and the concept of time becomes wonderfully mutable.

I think the tingling feeling is reinforced by the presence of ruins, by the astonishing and strange act of being able to touch (although you are probably not allowed to) stones that were hewn during times we have not experienced ourselves. Like letting my fingers trace the grooves of a rock carving and feeling a stirring in my belly, imagining a portal in time and space that connects my hands to the hands that carved the rock thousands of years before I even existed. As if the tactility creates a glimpse of connectedness just before the portal closes again and stone goes back to being stone. All that is left are the rigid expressions, the stoical calm, the unseeing eyes carved in marble, songs about heroes and gods and raped women. We have ruins, relics, fragments, stories; we have speculations, endings and rational hypotheses. But we can never travel back in time. We have to keep dancing forward, and where better to do that than in the Central Hall?

Birgitte Kleis

BEHIND THE FAÇADE

Construction Innovations and Inventions at the Glyptotek

Vilhelm Dahlerup's Building

The red and pink brick façades of Vilhelm Dahlerup's building rise from its granite plinth full of details in moulded brick, terracotta and sandstone. There are pillars, pilasters and cornices made of different types of granite and limestone. Originally slate, the curved copper roof above the main wing and vestibule at the front has large skylights. More skylights are to be found along the roof ridges of the side wings.

The exterior of the building was constructed using traditional materials, but the load-bearing construction behind the façade was based on ground-breaking technical solutions. This article examines the most important of these in Vilhelm Dahlerup and Hack Kampmann's buildings and the museum complex they built uniting old and new methods and materials during a pioneering period for construction technology.

A Firm Footing for Concrete Foundations

Dahlerup drew up a building plan in which he divided the planned construction into stages, from the excavation and foundations to details of the brickwork, roofing and carpentry. He was particularly thorough in his description of digging and pouring the foundations. Building just a few hundred metres from Kalvebod Wharf he must have been aware of the high groundwater levels. Boring had established that the terrain under the planned main wing was "under 11 feet of water," and that the two side wings were "under 9 and 7 feet of water" respectively.[1] In metric measurements, this would mean digging almost 3.5 metres to lay the foundations of the main wing, and 2.8 and 2.2 metres for the two planned side wings. Dahlerup foresaw that the high level of groundwater would make it necessary to continuously pump water out of the earth trenches immediately before pouring the foundations.[2]

When digging the basement, the street line was established as the baseline. Since the terrain itself was circa 45 centimetres below the street line, the basement had to be dug 2 feet (62.7 centimetres) deeper. This made the level of the basement floor circa 107 centimetres below the street line. The entire area within the perimeter of the building was to be dug as a basement. Dahlerup noted that the excavated earth was to be deposited nearby so it could be used on either side of the concrete foundations in a layer 6 inches (15 centimetres) thick and as deep as the foundations. The earth around the foundations was then to be thoroughly stamped down and watered to ensure maximum stability.[3]

A Recipe for Concrete

Concrete had existed since the Roman Empire, but using concrete to pour foundations was relatively new in Denmark. It was not, however, unprecedented. The National Bank of Denmark, for example, had been built on concrete foundations in 1866.[4] Despite this Dahlerup felt he had to provide both a recipe for the concrete and instructions on how to use it for the foundations.

The concrete was to be made of one part cement, four parts gravel and eight parts crushed stones, all of which were to be precisely measured prior to the mixing of each batch. The sand and cement were to be mixed first then poured over a 5–7-centimetre-thick layer of crushed stones. This was then to be watered and shovelled back and forth a total of six times. If necessary the concrete was to be sprinkled with a watering can to achieve a consistency "like thick, hard porridge and never so wet that it approaches gruel".[5]

Once the concrete had been mixed, the foundations had to be poured as quickly as possible. A 15–20-centimetre-thick layer was to be laid, and each layer was to be vibrated and levelled before the next layer could be added. The concrete was to be poured between movable wooden shuttering boards that could not be removed until twenty-four hours later. If it was not possible to pour an entire foundation in a day, 'steps' were hammered into the semi-dried concrete before the next section was poured. This made the joins between sections stronger.[6]

Bricks and Mortar, Terracotta and Stone

Dahlerup's instructions for the construction process stipulated that the cast pillars of the foundations in the basement were to be connected by brick-built arches made of large hard-fired bricks measuring 2⁵⁄₁₂ by 4½ by 9½ inches (6.13 by 11.93 by 24.63 centimetres), dimensions he stipulated should apply everywhere bricks were used apart from the façades.

Dahlerup's brick specifications were based on what Danish brickworks could supply. The size of bricks was not yet standardised and varied from factory to factory. The size of bricks used in Denmark has changed throughout history, from

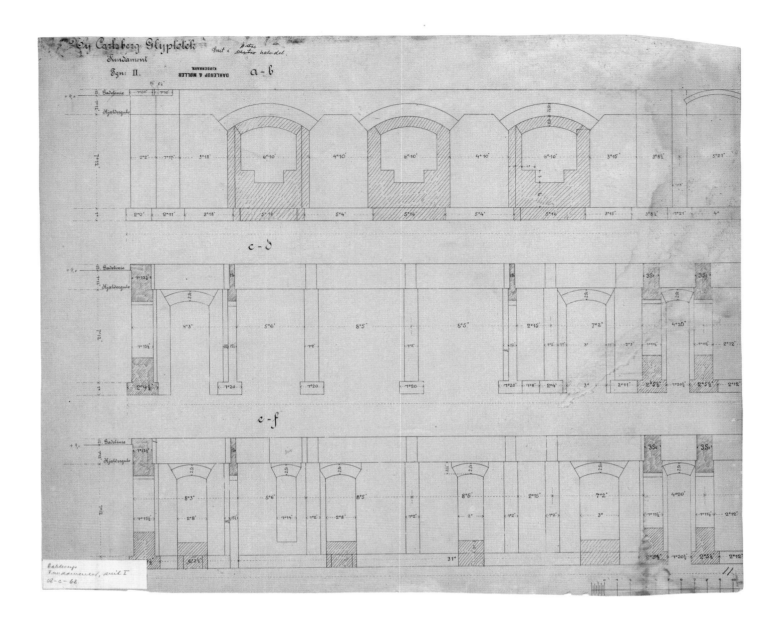

Vilhelm Dahlerup: The Glyptotek, Copenhagen, undated. Longitudinal section of the east side of the foundations with the foundation dimensions, street line and basement floor marked. The base of the foundations was to be poured to a width of 140–150 centimetres. The remaining brick-built foundations were to be three bricks wide.

Vilhelm Dahlerup: The Glyptotek, undated. Dahlerup wrote instructions for many of the craftsmen who worked on his building, but the masons were given drawings of the façades indicating the dates Dahlerup expected various stages of the brickwork to be complete.

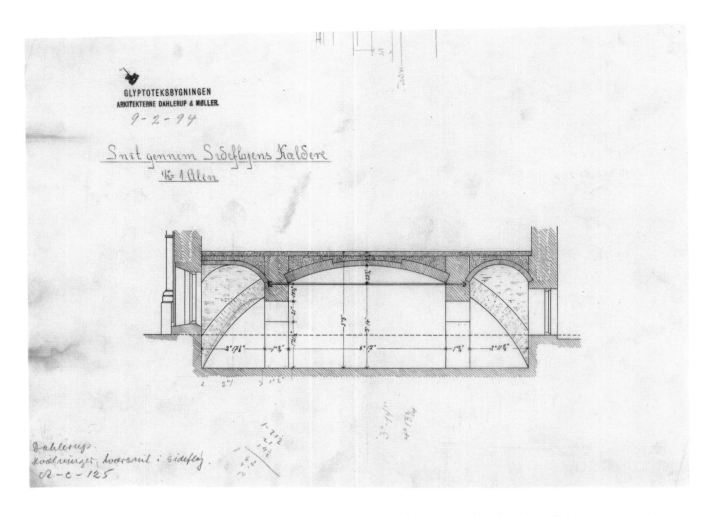

Vilhelm Dahlerup: The Glyptotek, Copenhagen, 1894. Cross-section of the foundations and vaulted arch in the basement showing the position of cast ties and cinders on top of the bricked arches to make a screed coat for the concrete floor above. The floor-to-floor height from the basement to the ground floor was 3.9 metres.

the large bricks of the Middle Ages measuring 8.5 by 13 by 27.5 centimetres to the narrow Flensburg bricks of the Renaissance measuring 4.5 by 10 by 22 centimetres. Not until 1896 did the Danish Architectural Association, the Association of Engineers, the Mason's Guild and the Association of Brickmakers agree on a standard size of 22.8 by 10.8 by 5.5 centimetres, which is still the standard size of bricks in Denmark today.[7]

The bricks were to be laid with a machine-mixed lime mortar containing a minimum of eight per cent hydrated lime mixed with sharp pit gravel or sharp sand. For the load-bearing vaulted arches in the basement – serving as abutments for iron girders – and the brick back wall a stronger mortar consisting of three parts lime mortar and one part cement mortar was used. Builders were fined if the composition of the mortar did not meet the stipulated standards on inspection.[8]

Many kinds of brick were needed to create the details of the façades, first and foremost the machine-made bricks used to build the façade walls. These bricks had a pinkish hue and – measuring 27/12 by 48/12 by 98/12 inches (6.56 by 11.85 by 24.55 centimetres) – were marginally different in size to the bricks used on the back wall. The

Vilhelm Dahlerup: The Glyptotek, Copenhagen. The wall on both sides of the main entrance is decorated with three large terracotta panels. The terracotta tiles are mounted diagonally with no visible joins.

masons must have had to think long and hard to figure out the thickness of the mortar and calculate the position of the bond between the back wall and façades. The bricks of the façades were laid in cross bond and there were strict instructions for the masons' work:

> "The brickwork on all street façades is to be laid for pointing, work that is to be done with extreme care. Each course of bricks is to be precisely spaced with the divisions marked on the course preceding it. The header joints are to follow each other vertically, and the façade bricks to be carefully sorted. Only entirely flawless bricks are to be used [...] all mortar joints inside and out are to be scraped to a depth of 3/8″ immediately after the bricks have been laid. [...] All joints in the street façades are to be pointed precisely with gelded joints according to the instructions of the architects and example in the constructed model."[9]

The decoration of the main wing's façade included three large sections of diagonal terracotta tiles on either side of the main entrance. Once the production of terracotta bricks became industrialised in the 1850s it became widely used across Europe and the US, especially in historicist buildings. Terracotta tiles were made by pouring clay into plaster casting moulds that were the negative of the desired ornamentation. These were then dried and fired at a constantly high temperature to ensure an even colour.[10] It was a method that made a high level of detail possible.

Decks between the Floors – *Système Monier* and *Rabitz-Methode*

Looking at the sectional view of the vaulted arches in the basement beneath the main wing it emerges that the ceilings above the porter's lodge in the north-east corner of the building were not supported by brick vaulted arches like the rest of the basement, but were constructed of reinforced concrete made using the Monier method. There was also a note in the third section of the invitation to tender stipulating that the decks between the floors of the building were to be made using *Système Monier*, which gives some indication of the role technical breakthroughs and new inventions played in Dahlerup's historicist building. The Monier system was named after the French gardener Joseph Monier (1823–1906),

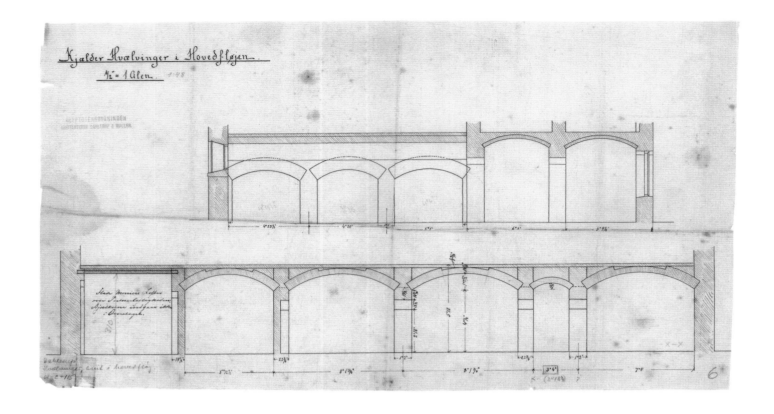

Vilhelm Dahlerup: The Glyptotek, Copenhagen, 1894. Cross-section of the main wing showing that the floor deck above the porter's lodge in the north-east corner of the basement was a flat poured concrete construction. It was made using the Monier reinforced concrete system, making it possible to reduce its height. The notes say that the steel girders were to be paid for separately and not included in the estimate.

who started out experimenting with reinforced concrete flowerpots, a method he patented in 1867. After this he developed a range of reinforced concrete construction systems, including reinforced concrete panels for the façades of buildings in 1869 and reinforced concrete beams in 1878. Even though Monier was not the first to develop reinforced concrete construction elements, he was the first to realise how strong the combination of the compressive strength of concrete and tensile strength of steel made constructions. The method also optimised the use of materials, making it possible to reduce the dimensions of the supports for decks between floors, for example.[11]

In Dahlerup's building all the floors above basement level, the barrel vaulting above the vestibule and the arched ceilings of the staircases were made using this system. First an abutment was carved in the outer and partition walls. Iron girders were then laid across these, and a 4-inch (10-centimetre) layer of concrete was poured. The concrete was then covered with a 2.5-centimetre layer of plaster before the mosaic and terrazzo floor was laid.

On the ground floor a layer of cinders was laid on top of the upper side of the basement

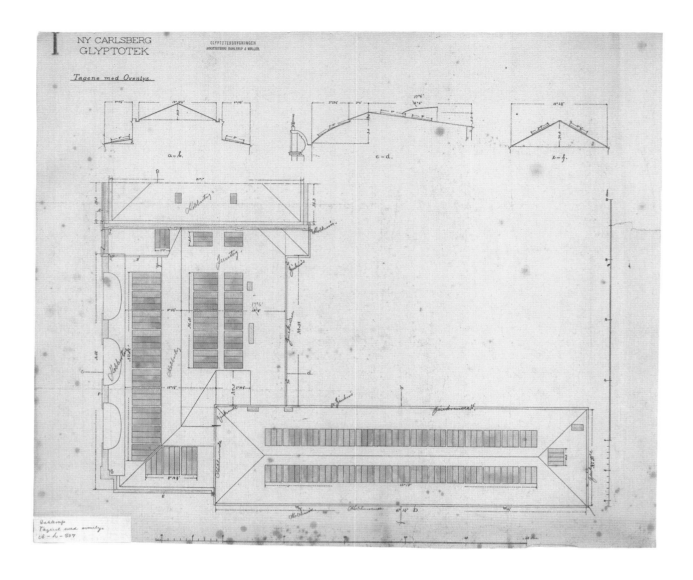

vaults to make the floor more even before the concrete was poured.

All the interior walls up to a height of 12 feet (3.7 metres) were first plastered with mortar made of one part cement mortar and two parts lime mortar. This was then scoured and polished until perfectly smooth. The barrel-vaulted skylit galleries of the main wing and arched ceilings above the vestibule and staircases required the installation of an extra inner ceiling structure before the coffering and ornamentation could be carried out. These were built using a relatively new method of making thin inner walls and ceilings called the Rabitz method. Named after its German inventor Carl Rabitz, the method involved installing a plaster base for a layer of lime-gypsum plaster 5 centimetres below the suspended ceiling. It was a method that spread alongside the development of the use of steel in construction materials.[12]

Vilhelm Dahlerup: The Glyptotek, Copenhagen, undated. Cross-sections of the roof profiles on the vestibule, main wing and side wing, and below plans for the skylights. The notes say that the roofs facing the street were to be clad with copper, and those facing the courtyard with steel. The drainpipes and guttering facing the street were also to be made of copper, whereas those facing the courtyard were to be made of zinc.

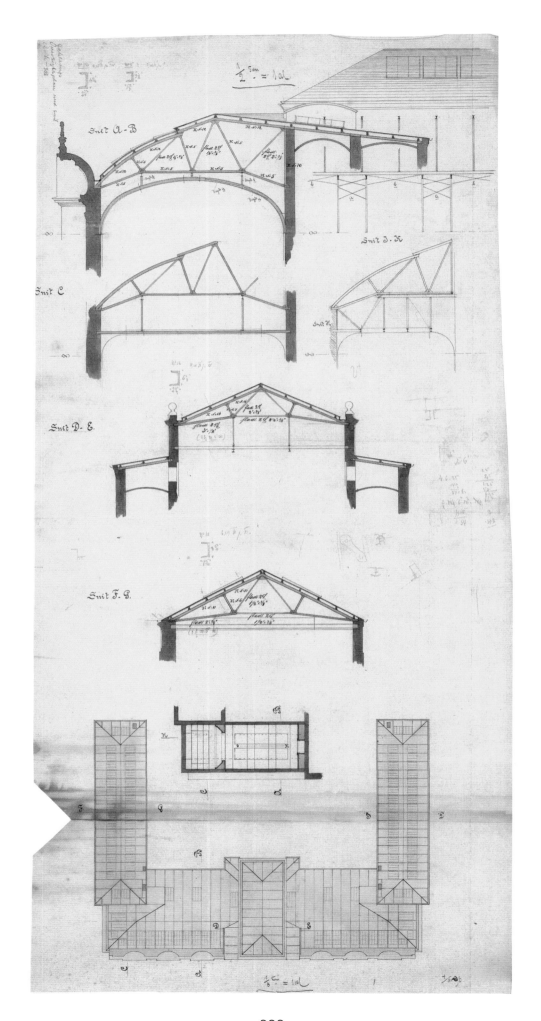

Vilhelm Dahlerup: The Glyptotek, Copenhagen. The photograph shows the asymmetrical construction of the roof above the main wing with steel trusses connected longitudinally by roofing purlins. The top of the barrel-vaulted skylight can be seen at the bottom of the photograph.

Vilhelm Dahlerup: The Glyptotek, Copenhagen, undated. Plan and cross-sections of load-bearing steel roof constructions.

A Roof Construction of Steel, Wood and Copper

Below the copper roofs of Dahlerup's building at the Glyptotek there was another hidden construction, also the product of the age of industrial breakthroughs it was born of. It was not a traditional wooden structure, but a load-bearing construction made of trusses with geometries adapted to the shape of the outer roof. The trusses were made of I-beam girders and joists, with wooden purlins running lengthwise supporting the underlay, fireproofing and roof cladding. The joints of the truss struts were bolted or riveted together with gusset plates. The entire roof construction supported the plaster and skylights in the gallery ceilings, in some places with thin steel rods and in others suspended directly from the trusses.[13] The glass panels captured dust and dirt from the roof construction at the same time as allowing daylight to filter down into the galleries.

The choice of steel for the roof construction was probably based on a new method for its production developed by the English engineer Henry Bessemer (1813–1898) in 1856. Bessemer's method made it possible to manufacture steel without using fuel, resulting in steel products of a superior quality that could be produced faster, cheaper and in far greater quantities than in the past. Within a decade the method had revolutionised steel production.[14]

Today all the roofs at the Glyptotek have copper cladding, but in the invitation to tender Dahlerup's instructions for the roofs were as follows:

> "All roofs are to be made of steel with wooden roofing purlins. On the flatter roofs this is to be covered by 1¼″ of fire cladding then copper sheeting. All the steeper roofs are to have slate roofs on laths. [...] The large arched sections of the main façade and the half dome are to be clad with copper plates with folded edges."[15]

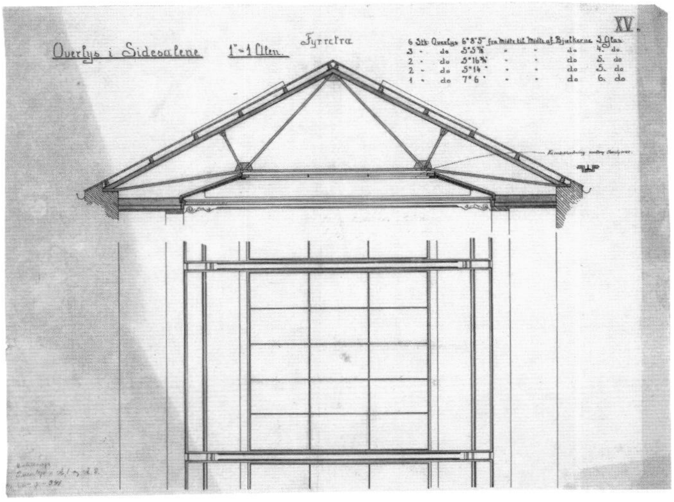

The roofs of the two side wings with rows of skylights were originally clad with slate, whereas the arched part of the roof on the main wing and the roof above the vestibule had cooper cladding with saddle joints.

Glass Roofing and Skylights

"The skylights are to be mounted in wooden frames of 2″ planks and have steel and zinc bars; the glass is to be pinstriped below and plain on the top, ¼″ thick and held in place by putty." This is all Dahlerup had to say about glass at the museum in the tender documents of March 1891. With the invitation to submit tenders five years later, however, the different types of glass to be used in the building were described in more detail.

The suspended arched skylights above the galleries in the main wing Dahlerup described as "pinstriped" were to be made of corrugated glass ⅛ inch (3 millimetres) thick. Corrugated glass was made with small waves or folds running lengthwise along the curved glass, making it considerably stronger than standard glass. In the galleries on the first floor of the side wings on the other hand, the glass panels were to be horizontal and made of glass that was ¼ inch thick. According to the bid list the glass was to be chequered glass. The woven structure of the glass made it translucent so the roof structure above was only faintly visible.[16]

The glazier Thorvald Peter August Duvier (1860–1928) won part of the tender to make glass for the Glyptotek.[17] He was a leading figure in the field, a manufacturer of glass mosaics as well as

Vilhelm Dahlerup: The Glyptotek, Copenhagen, undated. Plan, cross-section, and a list with the number and size of glass panes required for the skylights and glass roofs on the first floor of the side wings. The drawing also indicates that the load-bearing structure for the glass ceilings was to be made of pine.

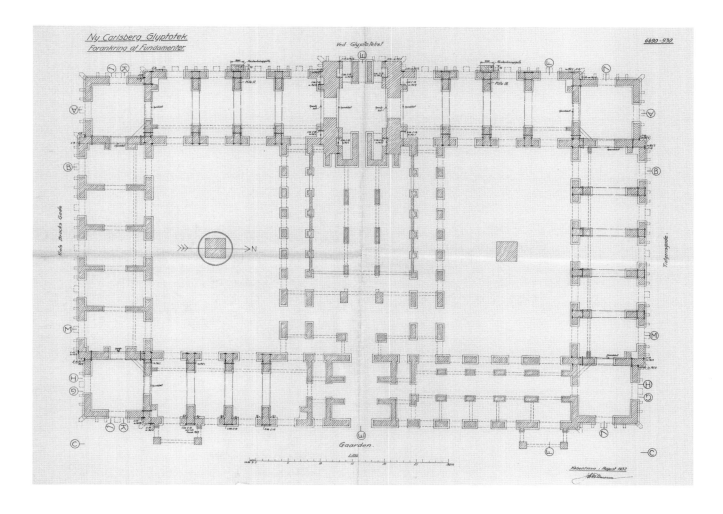

Hack Kampmann: The Glyptotek, Copenhagen, undated. Plan for anchoring the foundations. Twenty years after Kampmann's building was completed the foundations under the south-west corner of the building had to be reinforced with steel clamps and concrete buttresses to prevent them collapsing.

a glazier who had reintroduced stained glass to Denmark. Before being commissioned to deliver and install glass at the Glyptotek, he had completed several assignments for J.C. Jacobsen at his Carlsberg brewery.[18]

Hack Kampmann's Building

There had not been any quantum leaps in technology during the nine years that passed between the construction of Dahlerup and Kampmann's buildings. There was a lot of similarity in their construction methods and execution, although Kampmann had a more traditional approach than Dahlerup, a pioneer when it came to new technology.

Kampmann also drew inspiration from history, but found elsewhere than Dahlerup. He based his building on classical architecture but chose simple materials sourced in Denmark or elsewhere in Scandinavia – the magnificent exception being the many kinds of Italian marble with different colours and patterns in the Central Hall. As in Dahlerup's building, Kampmann's brick walls rose above a large granite plinth with high steps at the base. The plinth was made of granite from Bornholm and Norway, whereas

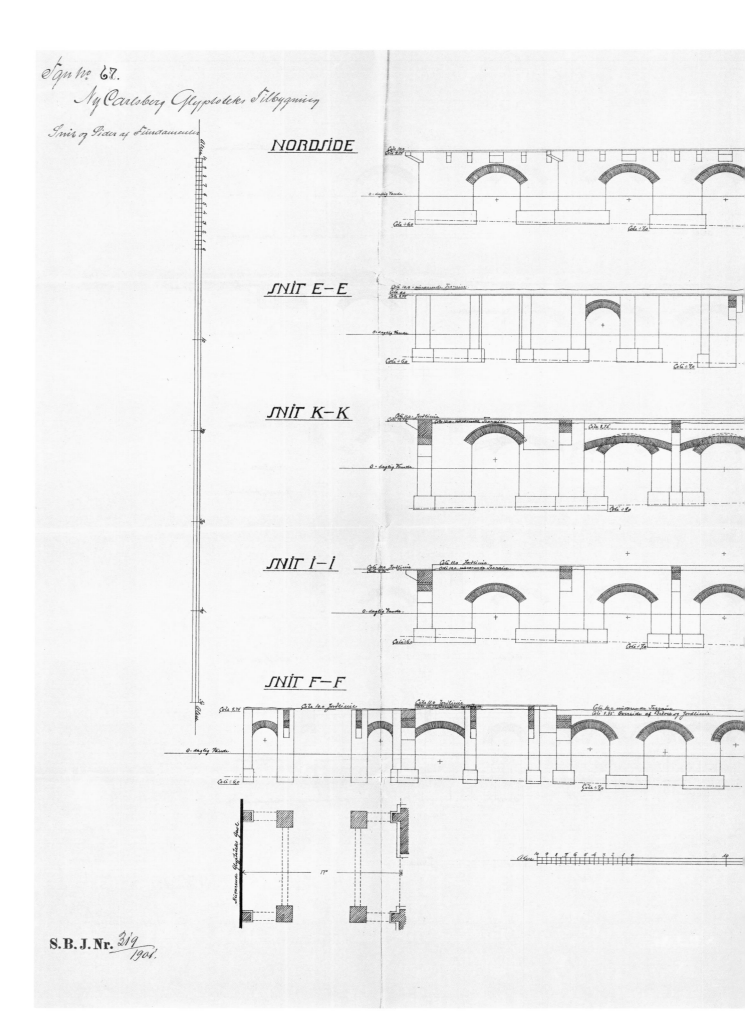

Tgn Nr. 67.

Ny Carlsberg Glyptoteks Tilbygning

Snit og Plan af Fundamentet

NORDSIDE

SNIT E–E

SNIT K–K

SNIT I–I

SNIT F–F

S. B. J. Nr. 319
1901.

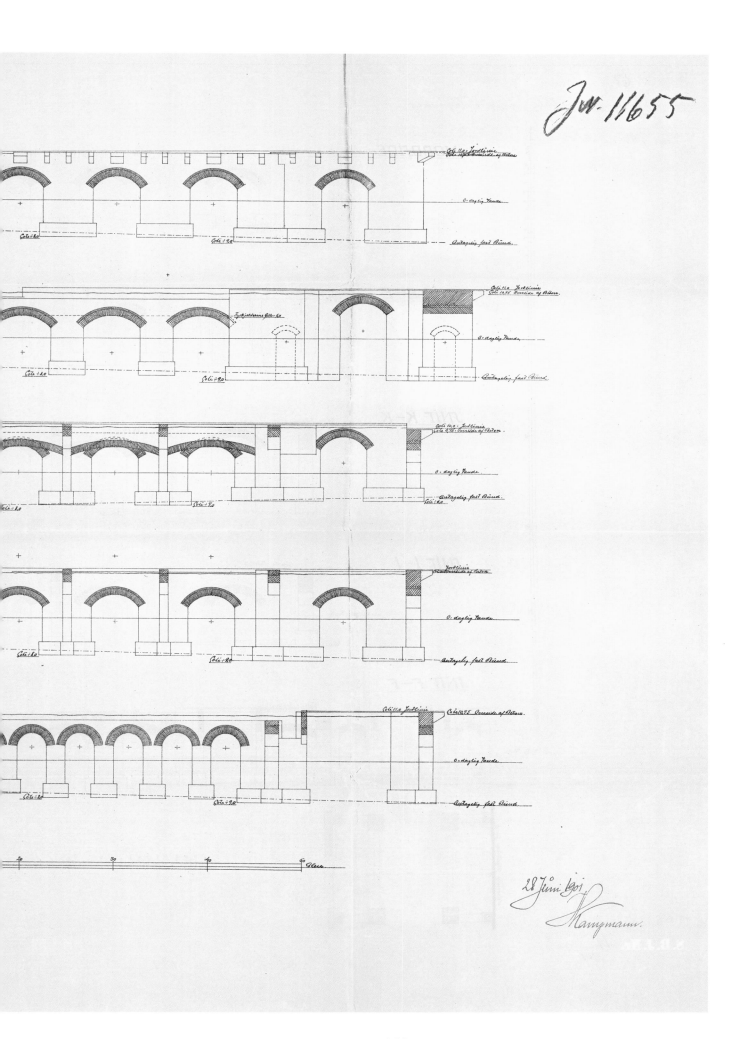

28 Juni 1901
Kampmann.

233

the cornice and step pyramid were made of light-coloured Norwegian granite.

The roofs were clad with copper, and vast skylights occupied most of the surface on every wing except the one facing Tietgensgade. Kampmann's roofs were flatter than Dahlerup's – a pitch of circa twenty-two versus twenty-seven degrees – so they were scarcely visible from the street. What was visible were the four lanterns on the corners of the building giving passers-by a hint that daylight could penetrate the hidden depths of the building below.

Kampmann optimised designs and technical solutions throughout his building, not least its roof construction.

A Firm Footing and *Système Hennebique*

The base of the foundations was dug even deeper for Kampmann's building than Dahlerup's, extending 16–18 feet (10–11 metres) below ground level before reaching a firm footing for the building.[19] The plan for laying the foundations also shows a stronger structure with foundations up to a metre wide. These were not simple trench foundations but a kind of T-shaped pad foundation, possibly to strengthen it sideways.[20]

Hack Kampmann: The Glyptotek, Copenhagen, undated. Plan of the roof construction showing the main sections and skylights. The sections above the Central Hall are around twice as close together as those in the wings to the east, west and north because they span most almost twice the distance. The wing to the (south-)west has a load-bearing cross-partition and no skylights.

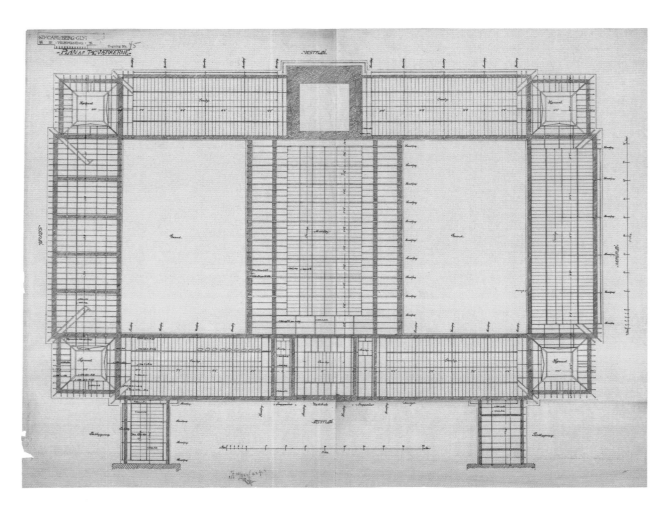

The floor division above the boiler room under the Central Hall was to be made of steel girders with concrete between them: "The floor division between the boiler room and colonnade is to be a *Hennebique* construction."[21] The name came from Frenchman François Hennebique (1842–1921), who patented nothing less than a world sensation in 1892: reinforced concrete.[22] Reinforced concrete – steel embedded in concrete – was able to absorb tensile forces, making it ideal for beams and concrete slabs. This revolutionised construction at the time, and reinforced concrete is still part of almost every load-bearing construction today. In 1902 Kampmann's inclusion of *Système Hennebique* in the technical requirements for his building at the Glyptotek marked the first time the method was used for a load-bearing construction in Denmark. It worked and was therefore also used for the foundations of the Winter Garden built around the same time. All the other floor decks were built with traditional brick arches. The floor decks above the galleries on the ground floor were relatively flat cross vaults.

The tactile quality of the brickwork shows that these bricks were hand-moulded and not the machine-made bricks so popular at the time. They were also a different format and size to those used to build Dahlerup's building and laid with butt joints only ⅛ inch (3 millimetres) thick. The brick façade was scoured with a powerful abrasive comprised of silicon and carbide – silicon carbide – synthetically produced in the US.[23] The walls were not, however, hosed down to remove the remains of mortar once the bricks had been laid.[24]

Kampmann never explained why this abrasion of the brickwork was necessary or even a good idea, but it could be that he wanted to make a more homogeneous surface out of the hand-moulded bricks in order to accentuate the monumentality of the masonry.

Roof and Skylights

There is a world of difference between the ground-floor landscape of heavy, brick arches and exploring the possibilities of steel in the roof. This testifies to Kampmann's understanding of what different materials, be they bricks or steel, could create architecturally in relationship to their physical capacities.

In Kampmann's building the entire load-bearing roof construction was made of steel, or rather of steel bolted to a cast-iron base resting

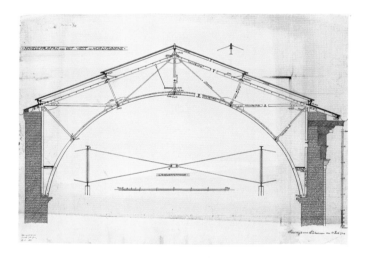

Hack Kampmann: The Glyptotek, Copenhagen, 1903. Cross-section of the main roof truss used above the east, west and north wings. The load-bearing steel construction looks almost delicate compared to the solid brickwork it rests on, clearly demonstrating the excellent properties of steel for load-bearing constructions. The drawing also shows longitudinal bracing straps comprised of four round iron bars connected in the centre by a strap tightener.

on the wall below it. Under the heading *Beregning af Jærntagene* ('Calculation of Steel Roofs')[25] in the instructions accompanying Kampmann's drawings, the main trusses in the three skylit wings were to be positioned with 20½ feet (6.35 metres) between them.[26] The construction was a pitched roof supported by three longitudinal I-beams: the ridge beam and two others sharing the load of the long glass skylight on either side of it. Suspended from and bolted to these were lattice girders made of double mirrored angle beams joined by ¾-inch rivets to make T-beams. This steel construction was thinner and more elegant than Dahlerup's construction from ten years before, possible partly due to the use of struts and ties made of round steel bars that minimised the dimensions of the main rafters and secondary construction. Unlike Dahlerup's building the construction was also supported lengthwise by four circular round steel bar ties bolted together with a gusset plate in the centre of each main span. This complex new construction method was virtually untried in Denmark. Kampmann's notes on drawings of the roof also provide instructions for making the final decisions on how to build it on site:

> "The details of the rafter sections above the east, west and north wings [...] and the precise direction of the struts will have to be decided when marking off the entire roof."[27]

The skylights in the pitched roof had copper glazing bars. When it came to glass, a review

Hack Kampmann: The Glyptotek, Copenhagen, undated. Detailed drawing of the joints in the steel construction of the roof indicating their number and position as well as the dimensions of the bolts and rivets.

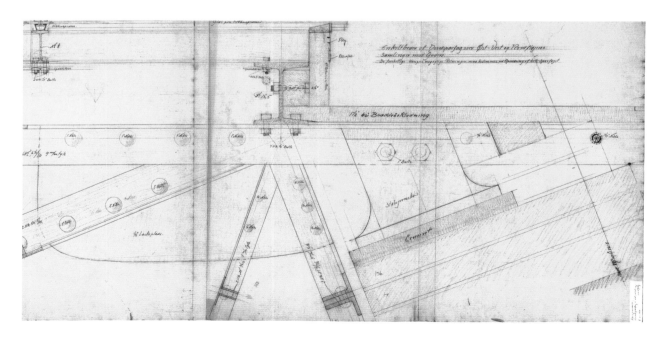

of the building published in the architectural journal *Architekten* in 1906 described the glass roofs as "covered with hammered glass and copper".[28] This must have seemed strange to the lay reader, since glass is probably the only material used in the construction that could not survive being "hammered". The textured glass in question was what was known as cathedral glass. Cathedral glass is made by pouring molten glass through steel rollers with embossed patterns to create a textured surface.[29] The curved glass of the barrel-vaulted suspended skylights was also rolled glass embossed lengthwise with an undulating pattern.

The four lanterns above the corner galleries are the only places where the construction of steel, copper and glass can really be seen from the street. The construction seems almost too slight to bear the weight of the copper calotte on the roof. The dimensions of load-bearing steel structures in the corners are only slightly greater than the bars between the individual panes of glass, and the cross bracing of the lanterns is provided by thin, almost invisible ties mounted in the upper corners and gathered in the centre by the lowest steel strap.

Hack Kampmann: The Glyptotek, Copenhagen. As when first built, the load-bearing roof construction is an ingenious system of steel profiles and ties supporting both the roof and the barrel-vaulted skylight.

The Central Hall

The meeting or rather clash between antiquity and modernity is most pronounced in the Central Hall with its profusion of polished Italian marble in shades of yellow, green and red, fluted marble columns and vast roof of steel and glass.[30] Kampmann created the illusion of the twenty-six marble columns and pillars bearing the main load of the glass roof. This, however, is only true in the context of the entire construction, where the columns support the longitudinal beams and therefore also help support the bottom copper-clad part of the roof. In reality, however, the main steel rafters run across the hall from outer wall to outer wall, connected at the ridge of the glass roof by finely decorated metal fittings bolted to the rafters. The steel rafters thus support the entire glass roof without a ridge or tie beam. According to the archived drawings the main rafters were to be 10 feet and 2½ inches (3.73 metres) apart, resulting in nine sections or lights. Each section is divided by two thin longitudinal steel roofing purlins per section, then again by four bars. This meant 15 panes of cathedral glass per window per section, giving a total of 270 panes of glass.

Hack Kampmann: The Glyptotek, Copenhagen, undated. Lantern cross-section. The circular ceiling has a flatter curve than the copper calotte above it. A single pencil line from each of the upper corners to the top of the sloping glazing bars indicates that Kampmann might have considered installing more cross-bracing.

According to the calculations the greatest technical challenge with the roof was anchoring the steel rafters securely enough in the outer walls so they could withstand an upward gust and prevent the glass roof from tipping upwards.[31]

The Winter Garden

The Winter Garden had been on the drawing board since Dahlerup drew his first sketches for the Glyptotek in 1888, but was not built until Kampmann's building was under construction. Even then it had to wait until the four walls that were to form the base for the glass roof and dome had been built. The position of the dome was determined by the point of intersection of the axes running through the museum, but instead of being in the centre of the large Winter Garden it was moved towards the original courtyard façade in the main wing. This brought it closer to the front of the museum, making it more visible in the city and sending an important signal that the Glyptotek was now complete. The glass dome was – and still is – the only one of its kind in Denmark.

Iron and Steel

In spring 1904 work could begin, starting with digging the foundations and driving piles (reinforced concrete posts) into the ground. The Hennebique method was used again for the vertical pile foundations, reportedly the first time this method was used in Denmark.[32] According to the on-site architect running the project, Osvald Rosendahl Langballe (1859–1930), they anticipated having to dig 20 feet before finding a firm footing for the foundations.[33]

The steel construction was projected by Vilhelm Dahlerup and the mechanical engineer P.C. Henriksen from the Danish engineering works and iron foundry Borch & Henriksen. He sent Langballe the project specifications in November 1903. The project was divided into two parts: the construction of the dome and supporting columns, and the glazed roofing in the rest of the Winter Garden. The dome had an interior diameter of 15.7 metres and an interior height of 29.5 metres and was to be supported by twelve cast-iron columns. Eight of these provided direct support, and the four forming the corners of a square circumscribing the circular dome provided additional indirect support.[34] At a height of 50 feet (15.5 metres) the columns had to be cast in three sections, which were then assembled with bolts and arched flanges. The solid baseplates on the columns, which were to transfer the load to the foundations, were also cast iron with holes for bolts. The columns were left as they were, devoid of ornamentation as if fresh out of the casting mould. The square capitals of the columns on the other hand had leaf-decorated bars of steel that supported the upper construction of parallel girders.[35] That the columns had an industrial appearance – which we might consider visual honesty or integrity today – was not to Dahlerup's liking. He wanted to cover them with black-and-white and blue-and-red glazed ceramic tiles, a wish that was not granted. He had to make do with covering the baseplates with plaster. This has since been removed, presumably to prevent corrosion.[36]

The columns underpinned the arched girders supporting the glazed roof of the rest of the Winter Garden. The girders rested partly on the surrounding walls and partly on the columns. An octagon made of eight girders with a double diagonal cross in each triangular section was attached above this. Then came the tambour supporting the sixteen steel rafters that formed the dome. There were three thinner rafters between each main rafter, and the resulting sixty-four rafters were connected horizontally to fourteen round tapered steel beams.[37] All the joints were connected by steel gusset plates distributing the load between various parts of the construction. Inside the dome itself the fittings were steel cross bracing, and at the top the load was absorbed by a steel fitting that also underpinned the copper-clad lantern and flagpole that were to crown the dome.

Rendle's Patent Glazing

Instead of using putty to secure the panes of glass in the traditional manner, they were attached to the load-bearing construction using Rendle's Patent Systems of Glazing.[38] Known as patent glazing, the method involved glazing with a slight overlap between the upper and lower panes, which were then attached to the glazing bar below using steel profiles that created a tight seal without putty. The method was invented then patented in England in 1882 by W.E. Rendle. In 1893 it was also patented in the US, where it was used in the glazed roofs of stations and factories. In 1904 the glass dome of the Glyptotek brought the system to Denmark. After lengthy negotiations with an English engineering company, the Danish firm Wienberg & Son sent an estimate for glazing the dome of the Winter Garden to Langballe.[39]

The pillars in the Winter Garden are 15.5 metres high and had to be cast in three sections. They were made of modern steel but their capitals are more like those of ancient columns. The pillars are visibly bolted together.

The system made it possible to glaze the curved dome with small panes of glass that were not themselves curved. This cost less but maintained the illusion of a large unbroken glass dome.

Construction Technology a Century Ago
As charted above, the building technology involved in the construction of the Glyptotek was far-sighted and forward-thinking. Dahlerup's and Kampmann's buildings included a series of innovative techniques and new inventions. Construction materials were sourced in the Nordic countries and Europe, and the principles of construction informed by a visionary approach and knowledge of technical advances in England, the US and France.

Other techniques built on centuries of experience. Taken together, the two tell the story of developments in building technology that were surprisingly innovative and formed by combining methods old and new. Which unlike the museum architecture itself is perhaps not surprising. Both buildings were constructed in the wake of the first Industrial Revolution, when production methods and technology were advancing in leaps and bounds. Here over a century later the building technology at the Glyptotek tells the story of a unique building in Copenhagen, but also the broader story of a key century in the history of construction and industrialisation.

Notes

1 Dahlerup & Møller, 21 March 1891.
2 Ibid.
3 Ibid.
4 Pontoppidan, Spile and Skyggebjerg, 2021, p. 13.
5 Dahlerup & Møller, 21 March 1891.
6 Ibid.
7 Rasmussen, 1937, p. 55.
8 *Beskrivelse over samt særlige Betingelser for Udførelsen af Murerarbejdet ved Ny Carlsberg Glyptoteksbygning*, section 5, undated, unpublished.
9 Ibid.
10 Vadstrup, 2006.
11 Chisholm, 1911, pp. 835–840.
12 Suenson, 1954, p. 80.
13 Olesen, 1985.
14 www.denstoredanske.lex.dk/ Bessemer-proces
15 Dahlerup & Møller, 21 March 1891.
16 Duvier, 18 January 1896.
17 Letter to Langballe, 9 September 1897.
18 www.skovgaard.ktdk.dk/ personer/august-duvier
19 "Musæumsbygningen for antik Kunst", 1906, p. 412.
20 This was not, however, enough. In 1937 the foundations under the façade facing the museum garden were anchored with steel clamps attached to concrete buttresses. Building Inspector for the 1st District, 24 June 1937.
21 Kampmann, 22 May 1902, pp. 1–3.
22 www.britannica. com/biography/ François-Hennebique
23 "Musæumsbygningen for antik Kunst", 1906, p. 413.
24 www.denstoredanske.lex.dk/ karborundum
25 The calculation was made by architect Theodor Andreas Hirth (1862–1925), a contemporary specialist in such calculations.
26 Kampmann, 22 May 1902, p. 5.
27 Sectional view of the roof construction, detail. Glyptotek Drawing Archive, undated.
28 "Musæumsbygningen for antik Kunst", 1906, p. 413.
29 www.villumwindowcollection. com
30 "Musæumsbygningen for antik Kunst", 1906, p. 415.
31 Kampmann, 22 May 1902, p. 3.
32 "Musæumsbygningen for antik Kunst", 1906, p. 410.
33 "Glyptothekets Kuppelbygning – Arbejdet paabegyndes", 26 April 1906.
34 "Musæumsbygningen for antik Kunst", 1906, p. 407.
35 Ibid.
36 Olesen, 1985.
37 Henriksen, 1903, p. 3.
38 *The British Trade Journal*, April 1882, p. 248.
39 Wienberg & Søn, 10 May 1904.

Sources and Bibliography

Unpublished Sources

The Glyptotek Archive

Beskrivelse over samt særlige Betingelser for Udførelsen af Murerarbejdet ved Ny Carlsberg Glyptoteksbygning ('Specifications and Special Conditions for Masonry at the New Carlsberg Glyptotek'), undated.

Central index of architectural drawings, register XXVIII, Ny Carlsberg Glyptotek.

Dahlerup & Møller: *Beskrivelse over Arbeider ved Opførelsen af Ny Carlsberg Glyptotheksbygning i Henhold til de fremlagte Tegninger* ('Stages of the Construction of the New Carlsberg Glyptotek with Reference to the Appended Plans'), 21 March 1891.

Duvier, August: *Tilbudsliste for Glarmesterarbeidet til Ny Carlsberg Glyptoteksbygning* ('Tender for Glazing at the New Carlsberg Glyptotek'). Presented at the submission of tenders on 18 January 1896.

Forslag til Program for Opvarmnings og Ventilationsanlæget til Ny Carlsberg Glypthotek ('Proposal for Heating and Ventilation Installations at the New Carlsberg Glyptotek'), undated.

Letter to Architect Langballe: *Liste over håndværkere, der arbejdede på Glyptoteksbygningen* ('List of Craftsmen Who Worked on the Glyptotek Museum Building'), signed F.V. Hansen, 9 September 1897.

Ramsing, Christian: Letter to Museum Curator Oppermann, 17 August 1897.

Wienberg & Søn: Letter to O.R. Langballe, 10 May 1904.

Copenhagen City Council's Building Department Archive.

Building Inspector of the 1st District: Letter to Engineer Johannes Møllmann for the New Carlsberg Glyptotek, 24 June 1937.

Crone & Koch Engineers: *Byggeandragende vedrørende ventilationsanlæg* ('Planning Application for Ventilation System'), 22 March 1994.

Henriksen, P. Chr.: *Beskrivelse af Konstruktion af Tag- og Kuppeloverdækningen i Ny Carlsberg Glyptotek* ('Description of the Roof and Dome Covering at the New Carlsberg Glyptotek'), 6 November 1903.

Kampmann, Hack: *Ny Carlsberg Glyptoteks Tilbygning. Beskrivelse til Tegningerne* ('Annotated Drawings for the Extension to the New Carlsberg Glyptotek'), 22 May 1902.

Publications

British Trade Journal, April 1882.

Chisholm, Hugh: "Concrete (material)", in: *Encyclopedia Britannica*, 11th edition, Vol. 6. Cambridge University Press, 1911.

"Glyptothekets Kuppelbygning – Arbejdet paabegyndes", *Dannebrog*, 26 April 1906.

Jacobsen, Carl: *Ny Carlsberg Glyptoteks Tilblivelse*. Copenhagen: Ny Carlsberg, 1906.

Johansen, Flemming: "Ombygning og nybygning – Fire års byggeaktivitet i Glyptoteket", *Meddelelser fra Ny Carlsberg Glyptotek*, 1996.

"Musæumsbygningen for antik Kunst", *Architekten – Meddelelser fra Akademisk Architektforening*, Year 8, No. 38, 1906.

Olesen, Lene: "Vinterhaven", in: *Informationsark*, No. 15, Ny Carlsberg Glyptotek, 1985.

Pontoppidan, Grethe, Sanne Spile and Louise Karlskov Skyggebjerg: "Betons historie", in: *Betonhåndbogen*. PLACE: Danish Concrete Society, 2021.

Rasmussen, D.: *Husbygning*. Odense: Andelsbogtrykkeriet, 1937.

Suenson, E.: *Betontekniske Fagudtryk*. Copenhagen: Danish Society of Engineers/Teknisk Forlag, 1954.

Vadstrup, Søren: *Materialer til bygningsbevaring*. PLACE: Danish Centre for the Restoration of Built Heritage, 2006.

Wanscher, Vilhelm: "Glyptotheket", *Architekten – Meddelelser fra Akademisk Architektforening*, Year 9, No. 3 (1906).

Østergaard, Jan Stubbe: "*Semper Ardens* – Facaden af Hack Kampmanns bygning til Glyptotekets antikke samling", *AIGIS, supplementum*, No. 1, May 2011.

Websites

www.bygningsbevaring.dk
www.britannica.com/biography/ François-Hennebique
www.danmarkshistorien.lex.dk
www.denstoredanske.lex.dk/ Bessemer-proces
www.denstoredanske.lex.dk/ karborundum
www.skovgaard.ktdk.dk/personer/ august-duvier
www.villumwindowcollection.com

LIDT DET KVN BAADER AT MESTEREN HVSET OPBYGGER
BYGGER EI HERREN MED HAM OG DETS GRVNDVOLD BETRYGGER
⚓ MENNESKENS HAAB ⚓
HØRER EI HERREN HANS RAAB   BLIVER TIL FLYGTIGE SKYGGER

**Anne Jonstrup Simonsen
and Kristina Lindholdt**

STRIVING FOR PERFECTION

Architectural Paint Research at the Glyptotek

The regeneration of Vilhelm Dahlerup's colour scheme shows how the colours alternated from gallery to gallery. The untinted colours of the mineral pigments on the walls are finely attuned to the ornamentation of the floors and ceilings.

Throughout the history of the Glyptotek the colours of its galleries have played a central role for the architecture and works of art alike. The walls have been repainted many times in many different colours over the 125 years or more since the museum opened in 1897. The colour and type of paint used at the Glyptotek reflect contemporary trends and tastes and tells the story of technological developments in the 20th century. Over the years the colour scheme has moved away from the colours that originally greeted visitors to Vilhelm Dahlerup and Hack Kampmann's buildings. Only now do we have the knowledge we need to appreciate the rich array of colours on display when the buildings were inaugurated in 1897 and 1906 respectively.

In 2021 the Glyptotek decided to initiate extensive investigations to uncover the original colours of the walls in the two buildings to provide a more detailed picture not only of the different colours of paint used in the interior but also of the history of the museum building. The main goal of the subsequent architectural paint research was to uncover and document the colours Carl Jacobsen collaborated with Vilhelm Dahlerup and Hack Kampmann in choosing. Both architects left an indelible mark on the architecture, but posterity has erased the distinctiveness of their original colour schemes and choice of materials. When the architectural paint research began, the Glyptotek's galleries had a relatively homogenous colour scheme. The investigation showed that not long passed before the original differences between the colour schemes in the two buildings were erased. Visitors to the museum were therefore no longer presented with the styles and ideals of two different architects: Dahlerup's polychrome earthen colours in rich oil-based paints and Kampmann's clear contrasting colour scheme in matt distemper. On the contrary, Dahlerup's bold alternating colours have taken over both buildings and become synonymous with the Glyptotek.

Even though the transition from one building to the other is still marked by a change in the style of architecture, the difference between them was originally made more evident by the original colour schemes and the tactility of the materials used. Since then, changing periods and ideals have resulted in this contrast being toned down.

This article covers the results of architectural paint research conducted at the Glyptotek by the Copenhagen conservation company

Kampmann's small galleries were painted their current colours in 2014 and show that over the years Dahlerup's historicist colour scheme also spread to Kampmann's galleries.

Københavns Konservator in 2021. In conjunction with archival research, uncovering and analysing layers of paint can help identify the period when the individual layers were painted. What follows includes examples charting the complex nature of the research and the many different sources that have been key to answering the questions that arose during it.[1] The investigation was able to provide detailed insight into the original choice of colours at the Glyptotek, as well as the colours it was painted over the years that followed.

Colours at the Glyptotek in the 20th Century

Changes to colour schemes and the painting of walls are rarely recorded in the archives. This is also true at the Glyptotek, where changes in the colour scheme did not start to be documented until the end of the 20th century, and for Dahlerup's building not until 2006. This absence of documentation underlines the lack of importance attached to changes in the colours of the walls. Due to the results of architectural paint research, however, some of these gaps in knowledge can now be filled. Numerous different layers of paint were uncovered in Dahlerup's building, from the oldest oil-based paints to the most recent acrylic paints. Changes to the colour scheme were probably made in connection with special exhibitions or new presentations of works in the museum's collection. They were thus made with a focus on the artworks on display rather than the architecture surrounding them.

A good example of a colour scheme based on the art exhibited occurred in 1978, when a professor of perceptual psychology was hired to design a colour scheme for Kampmann's building. The colours were inspired by Mediterranean nature – yellow ochre sand, olive-green vegetation, terracotta red, sky blue – and aimed at harmonising with the colours of the sculptures.[2] This was not that far removed from Kampmann's original idea of the building mirroring its contents, but the end result was very different to the original colour scheme.

The latest colour scheme in Kampmann's building was based on more accurate knowledge of the original colour of the walls at the Glyptotek. In connection with the reinstallation of the Antiquities Collection in 2006 the museum investigated the paint layers in Kampmann's building. Some of the colours that came to light inspired the design of a new colour scheme painted with industrial paints. Here too the boundaries between the wall colours in the two buildings was blurred: Kampmann's building had a Dahlerup-inspired scheme, with each gallery painted an alternating bold colour, and Dahlerup's building was then painted in colours that continued the project in Kampmann's building.[3]

Vilhelm Dahlerup's Colours and Materials

Vilhelm Dahlerup's architecture was rooted in historicism, something manifested in both his building design and palette of colours. The layers of paint uncovered show a palette of red, yellow, blue, green and brown, all traditional mineral pigments typical of the architecture of the late 19th century. These natural pigments can be divided into two categories: organic pigments (from plants), and inorganic or mineral pigments. Mineral pigments are also called earth pigments, since they were traditionally extracted from the earth. It is the iron compounds of the minerals, also called iron oxides, that result in red, yellow, brown, grey, blue-grey and green colours. At the end of the 19th century mineral pigments were primarily used in dark saturated oil-based paints.[4]

Dahlerup's use of colour was a finely calibrated element of the overall architectural experience. In Galleries 35–37 the investigation uncovered a colour scheme with two Prussian-blue galleries on either side of a red oxide gallery originally called the Empress Hall. The layers are oil-based paint, which means the walls originally had a dense colour and silk matt sheen akin to that of the polished mosaic and terrazzo floors. The dense, saturated colours created a contrast to the light ceiling of a room united by recurring architectural elements – cornices, pilasters, architraves – which were painted a light warm grey colour and polished to resemble natural stone, unlike the white colour they have today.

This particular colour scheme is documented in colour in one of Dahlerup's proposals for the Glyptotek. The decoration of the galleries today does not match that in the drawing, but Dahlerup had apparently already decided on a red-and-blue colour scheme. The drawing also clearly demonstrates that Dahlerup's work with Carl Jacobsen was an ongoing process, and that the style he was to follow at the Glyptotek was pretty much given. Whilst not an exact copy the Empress Hall in the drawing, for example, is heavily inspired by the Empress Hall at the first

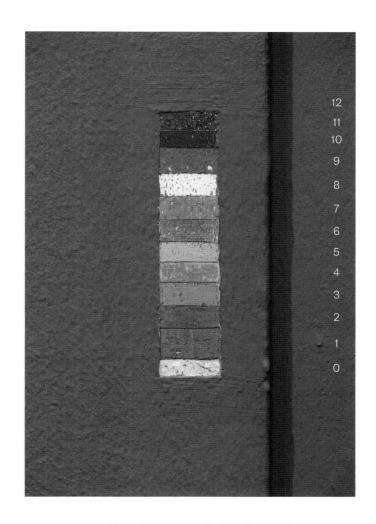

The paint stratigraphy in Gallery 44 shows the number of times the walls in Dahlerup's building were repainted. The oldest layer of paint is a dark olive green.

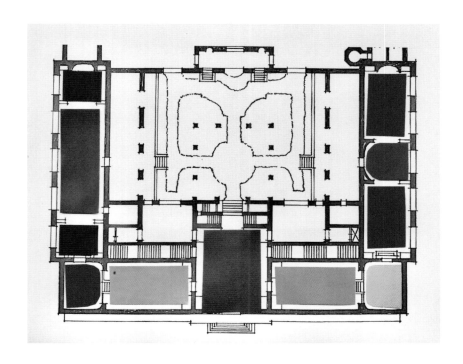

This plan with the original colours on the ground floor of Vilhelm Dahlerup's building shows the architect's passion for mineral pigments and changing the colour from gallery to gallery.

The cornices and ceilings in Dahlerup's
hand-coloured elevation drawing were
changed, but not the red and blue colour
of the walls, which are a perfect match for
those discovered on the walls of Galleries
35 and 36.

CLTNDIOK CHBINSK NUSIPLCH NICALNMH TBIANODAM

275

Photograph of the Empress Hall at
Carl Jacobsen's first Glyptotek in Valby,
the model for the interior of Gallery 36.

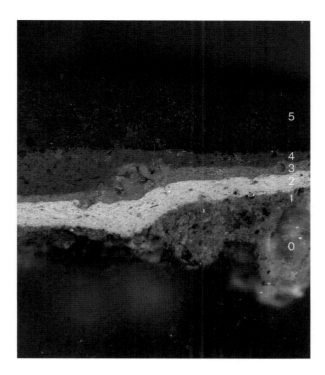

From the bottom up this cross-section of paint from the apse in Gallery 45 has a layer of plaster (0), then a layer of brownish yellow paint absorbed by the plaster (1). Above this come more recent layers of yellow, red and blue paint (2–5).

Glyptotek in Valby and shares the same shape, colour scheme and sculptures planned for exhibition here.

The Riddle of the Apse

In the apse of Gallery 45 architectural paint research uncovered some interesting deviations from the rest of the colour scheme, discoveries that underline the importance of such investigations being supplemented by archival research. The walls of the apse are decorated with low relief ornamentation, now the same colour as the other walls in the gallery. When the Glyptotek first opened, however, one reviewer praised the dark colours of the walls, which he wrote "create a tranquil and flattering background for the white sculptures". He was otherwise critical of Dahlerup's work, particularly of "the brutal blue colour of the apse behind the figure of Christ".[5] The blue is presumably the same colour still seen at the top of the apse but not on its walls. Yet instead of being able to confirm that the oldest layer of paint was blue, while conducting the architectural paint research a brown ochre colour was discovered on the ornamentation, background and architrave. The low dado was a reddish grey colour, corresponding to the colour of the stone bases of the columns on either side of the apse. The surface of the layer of paint was unusually coarse and slightly powdery.

Closer examination of the apse provided a basis for identifying the colour it was originally painted as well as the subsequent chronology. Uncovering a larger area on the edge of the relief revealed the traces of drips of golden-brown paint, paint that could have been so thin or carelessly applied that it went over the edges. The cross-section revealed five layers of paint, the oldest of which was also a golden-brown colour. The plaster could have been pigmented, or a thin colour wash absorbed by the plaster may have been used. The traces of drips of paint support the latter, which means the apse was probably a monochrome golden-brown colour with a rough surface made to resemble stone like the wall reliefs in the Winter Garden. This is supported by the dado being the same colour as the stone column bases: a visual synthesis between genuine and imitation materials. After the golden-brown layer there was a series of industrial paints in pale yellow, red oxide, cardinal purple and ultramarine. But why had only

277

The colour scheme in Gallery 45 is a
partial reconstruction of the original.
Architectural paint research on the apse
behind the figure of Christ could not
tell us what the apse originally looked
like so the museum chose to paint
it in colours that harmonise with the
gallery's ornamentation.

a single layer of old paint been preserved? The explanation probably lies in the fact that at some point between 1937 and 1951 the apse in the gallery was boarded up.[6] If the first year is correct, then it looks as if the original yellow ochre colour of the apse had not been repainted for around forty years prior to this.

The apse was not reopened until 1983, when it is highly likely the relief was repainted with inspiration from the original colour, hence the layer of yellow paint. In a photograph from 1998 the apse is yellow,[7] so it had been repainted before then. From 1998 onwards there were two undatable periods when the niche was red before being painted ultramarine in 2006.

Hack Kampmann's Colours and Materials

Hack Kampmann's classicist building was to bridge the eclecticism of Vilhelm Dahlerup's main building and the Antiquities Collection it was to house which Carl Jacobsen wanted to see reflected in the interior. Kampmann allowed the surfaces of materials to come to the fore, and architectural paint research has shown that as a man of his time he was willing to experiment with materials. In the early 20th century many European architects, including Hack Kampmann, started to move away from the multiple architectural styles of historicism, rejecting its imitation and eclectic ornamentation in favour of an emphasis on genuine materials and authenticity. Paints were to retain the pure colour of pigments, wood was to be treated in ways that enhanced its natural patterns and colour, and plaster ceilings were to be painted with white distemper to retain the appearance of the material they were made of.

Whereas there is little to document Dahlerup's choice of colours, archival material on Kampmann's colour scheme does exist. This material includes the architect's own sketches and notes, as well as interviews, contemporary reviews, and correspondence between Kampmann and Carl Jacobsen. Such sources and the results of the architectural paint research show that Kampmann had clear plans for the colour scheme of his interior and that these plans were by and large carried out.

In the small galleries (Galleries 5 and 14–17) Kampmann wanted each gallery to alternate between bright shades of yellow, green, red and

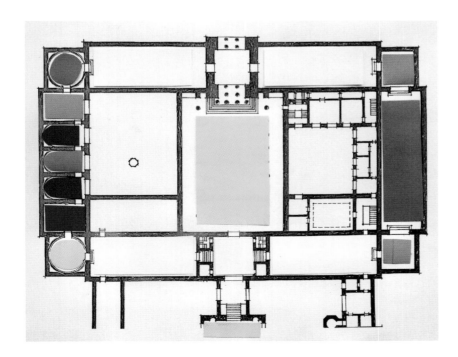

The floor plan shows Kampmann's use of vibrant colours. The galleries on the long sides of the building are painted the same colour, whereas the colours in the small galleries changes.

279

blue. The galleries were predominantly painted with distemper, which unlike oil-based paint retains the natural colour of pigments. With the exception of a single gallery painted a green-earth colour, the larger galleries in Kampmann's building retained the white of the plaster.

Gallery 5 – The Red Room

Gallery 5 is a good example of the interplay between the architecture of the interior and the colours, ornamentation and sculptures in Kampmann's building. It is also a prime example of the complexities of architectural paint research. On one of the floor plans the colours of what is now Gallery 5 have been labelled by hand as black (for the floor), lily of the valley, then blue and green along the walls. On an elevation drawing of the same gallery the walls are dark red.

The first time the layers in Gallery 5 were uncovered it looked as if the oldest layer of paint was dark green, but there were also fragmentary traces of red on the surface of the plaster. This is not a colour usually found in ordinary coats of plaster, and further investigation of the built-in plaster radiator covers confirmed the presence of a thick layer of red oxide distemper. The matt

Kampmann's hand-coloured drawing labelled "Lily of the Valley Hall" shows a gallery with barrel vaulting, stucco lily-of-the-valley decorations and Anne Marie Carl-Nielsen's painted copy of the ancient Greek sculpture *Typhon* mounted on the end wall.

280

Uncovering the layers of paint on the wall and radiator in Gallery 5. Only the microscopic grains of red pigment in the paint stratigraphy indicate that the oldest layer of paint might not have been dark green. The red distemper on the radiator cover, on the other hand, was well preserved.

surface of distemper is almost velvety, but it is also highly porous and sensitive to wear and tear, stains and damp. Before being repainted, a wall painted with distemper has to be either washed down or sealed. In Gallery 5 the walls were obviously more thoroughly washed down than the radiator covers. This was an unintended gift for a conservator: the preserved remnants of red distemper on the radiator cover confirmed the original red colour scheme in the gallery.

The Central Hall – An Ancient Forum

The only place at the Glyptotek where Kampmann deviated from the contemporary principle of using local materials was in the Central Hall, where the floor, wall coverings and columns are dark-veined marble in green, yellow and white. In Kampmann's elevation drawings the Central Hall is always yellow, and in a newspaper article on the opening in 1906 it is described as follows: "Up to a height of six feet the walls are covered with rare Verde Antico marble. Above this they are rendered with yellow fresco."[8] Investigation of the upper walls confirmed the presence of a layer of light yellow ochre embedded in the plaster rather than on top of it, followed by another

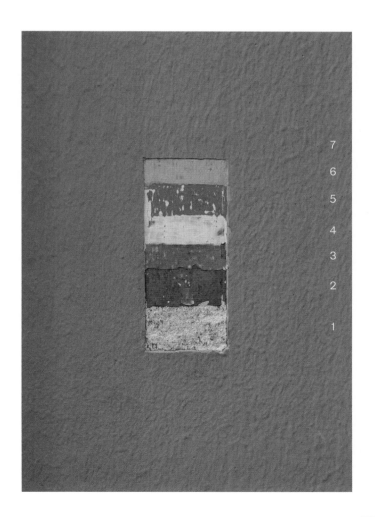

layer of yellow ochre distemper. Fresco is the technique of painting pigments mixed with water on freshly applied wet plaster. As the plaster sets the pigments set too, creating a sealed, hard-wearing and highly durable surface. If lime is used as a binder for pigments they can also be applied a secco on plaster that has been allowed to dry and set. Both methods require the application of thin layers: each layer can only contain a certain amount of pigment, plus the colour becomes lighter as it dries.[9] That the pigment has been absorbed by the plaster indicates that the yellow ochre colour on the walls was indeed applied using the fresco technique.

After one or more periods painted a yellow ochre colour, a white primer was applied before the walls were painted their current red colour using an abstract marbling technique. The 1968 edition of the museum's yearbook reports that a restoration and repainting of the Central Hall in 1967 was funded by the New Carlsberg Foundation.[10]

The same year a colour photograph was taken of a Central Hall with red upper walls. Since architectural paint research only uncovered one layer of red paint, we can only surmise

The paint stratigraphy and cross-section in the Central Hall show a layer of plaster (0) pigmented an almost yellow ochre colour (1). It is possible that the fresco technique that had only recently reached Denmark gave surprising results. The following layer of distemper is the same yellow ochre colour (2), which could have been a layer to enhance the colour or from when the wall was repainted at a later date. The cross-section also shows a white layer (3) under the current layer of marbling.

that the Central Hall has not been repainted since it was painted red in 1967. Even though the walls have been red for almost half the lifetime of the building, it still represents a departure from Kampmann's colour scheme, in which the yellow walls may have had structure but were presumably monochrome, providing a contrast to the variegated surfaces throughout the rest of the hall. The investigation also revealed that the yellow ochre colour can be seen to trace the central axis running through the building: yellow ochre frames the reliefs in the Winter Garden, and the traces of older layers of yellow ochre paint have been found on the walls of the landing, on the edging and interlacing ornamentation of the stairwell and vestibule, in the Central Hall and finally on the coffered ceiling.

White Walls – Archival Research, Analysis and Interpretation

The Glyptotek is proof that Hack Kampmann worked consciously with tactility and colour, but also the absence of colour. For many visitors, the museum is probably synonymous with colourful walls providing a contrast to the white sculptures, and archive material shows that Carl Jacobsen

In Hack Kampmann's drawings of the Central Hall the walls are the same yellow ochre colour as the paint uncovered during architectural paint research at the museum.

The red marbling on the walls has become emblematic of the Central Hall, but the walls were not actually painted red until after 1967.

was convinced that ancient sculptures should have a colourful backdrop. But Kampmann had other ideas. On a layout plan Kampmann has written "white" as the colour of the walls in Galleries 1 and 6, and newspaper articles on the opening of Kampmann's building indicate that there were several white galleries.[11] Several sources indicate that this was not an unproblematic choice. In the minutes of a meeting of the board of the Glyptotek in 1905 Carl Jacobsen describes how he and Kampmann had originally agreed on a dramatic, alternating colour scheme but that Kampmann had changed his mind and now wanted white walls everywhere. Carl Jacobsen did not agree, but allowed a couple of white galleries as an experiment. A trip to Germany, however, reinforced his conviction that strong colours were the right choice.[12] A 1906 interview with Kampmann made it clear that the conflict had not been resolved:

"I have aimed for subtle colours on the walls and have generally tried to avoid anything too dramatic. My client, on the other hand, loves grandiosity, anything that can astonish and overwhelm the masses, so he and

This photograph taken in 1920 indicates
that at least one of the galleries was still
white then.

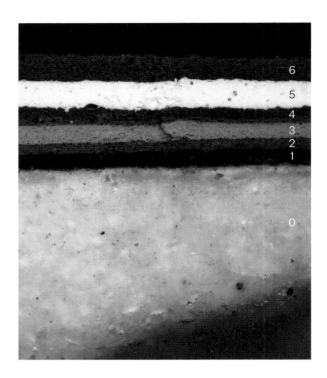

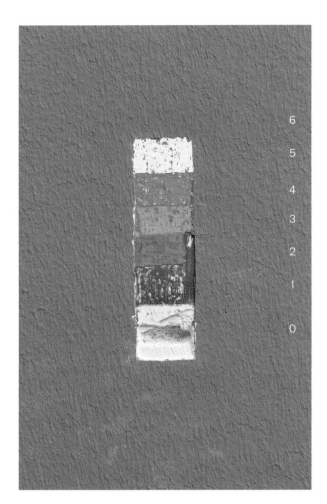

I have not always fully concurred on all the particulars. The white walls in the long galleries are very much against Jacobsen's wishes. Yet I do believe most connoisseurs would consider me to be right."[13]

With or without Carl Jacobsen's blessing. A photograph from the same year shows the trial installation of a colour background for the sculptures in one of the white galleries. The walls were not, however, repainted immediately because in another photograph of Gallery 10 from 1920 the walls are still white. Perhaps Carl Jacobsen learnt to appreciate the effect of white walls after all.

What can architectural paint research tell us about the white walls? An average of eight layers of paint were uncovered on the walls of Galleries 1, 6, 10 and 12, all of them bright intense colours. At first glance the oldest layer in all four galleries is a shade of dark green, although on closer examination the ground layer was discovered to be a bright white fine-grained substance entirely unlike the plaster in the other galleries. This white ground was seven to eight millimetres thick and comprised of two layers: first a five-to-six-millimetre-thick layer with a coarse

This cross-section and paint stratigraphy from Gallery 10 illustrate the very finely grained compacted material with a smooth surface uncovered on the walls of Galleries 1, 6, 10 and 12 (0). This can be compared to the large particles in an ordinary coat of plaster on page 282. After this comes a series of layers of paint, most of them green (1–6).

surface then a circa two-millimetre layer with a smooth polished surface. These atypical base layers indicate that the first time the gallery walls were covered was not with colour paint but a fine, polished plaster.

In the early stages of designing his building at the Glyptotek Kampmann worked on plastering the façade with red, white or yellowish plaster.[14] This was rejected by Carl Jacobsen due to the Danish climate and city pollution. Until now the police headquarters in Copenhagen (1919–1924) was thought to be the first building where Kampmann, in collaboration with fellow architects Hans Jørgen Kampmann (1889–1966), Holger Jacobsen (1876–1960), Anton Frederiksen (1884–1967) and Aage Rafn (1890–1953), used coloured stucco lustro on door surrounds and plinths, but architectural paint research indicates that Kampmann was already thinking of having stucco lustro walls at the Glyptotek, and if it could not be done outside then it would have to be done inside. This is supported by a letter from Carl Jacobsen to Kampmann dated 9 June 1904, where Carl Jacobsen complains about the surface of the interior walls:

> "I simply cannot allow this kind of plaster to be used in these rooms. It is far too coarse and looks unfinished. [...] Whilst there may be buildings in the now so popular rustic style where such a finish would be in harmony with concrete or the contents of the building, it is not elegant enough for the Glyptotek. We are patricians not plebeians!"[15]

After which he suggests using fine, polished marble-based plaster or at a pinch lime plaster. That Carl Jacobsen had his own way in terms of the walls is underlined in a letter dated 16 June 1905 in which he reacts to budget and deadline issues: "I also think we should abandon any idea of marble plaster, since this would represent a sizeable saving."[16]

Cement plaster had thus been replaced by marble plaster but was now in danger of being axed entirely. Architectural paint research, however, shows that Carl Jacobsen and Kampmann found a solution that met both Carl Jacobsen's uncompromising demands about the quality of materials and Kampmann's aesthetic standards.

There are two types of surface treatment of walls that can explain the stucco lustro Carl

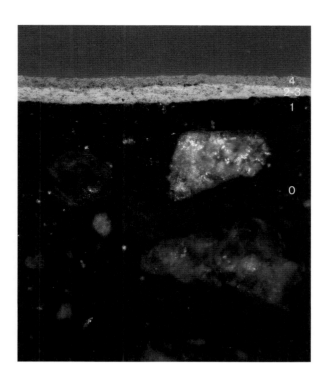

The architraves in Kampmann's small galleries were also made of fine polished plaster. This cross-section shows the same finely grained material as that on the walls of Galleries 1, 6, 10, and 12, here with dark grey pigment.

287

Jacobsen refers to in his letter: stucco lustro and stucco marble, or scagliola.[17] Stucco lustro is a lime-rich plaster mixed with marble dust. It is applied in thin layers then after the last coat has been applied the surface is polished, compacting the layers and making the wall hard and glossy. After polishing the plaster can be painted using the fresco technique. Monochrome stucco lustro walls can be a challenge since variations in the pressure applied during polishing can result in differences in the depth of colour.

Stucco marble is plaster mixed with lime to a clay-like consistency. Pigments are added and mixed into the plaster, which is then cut into slices and applied to the wall. These are scraped and polished until the surface is smooth and even. Once dry, the now hard walls can be sanded and polished. This process is repeated many times with increasingly fine sandpaper. The end result is a high-gloss wall.

Analysis of the white surface confirmed the presence of a high level of plaster and a small amount of lime. Based on the plaster content and the smooth surface discovered in the stratigraphy, it was probably monochrome stucco marble applied in two layers then sanded and polished.

The discovery of stucco marble on the walls led to an investigation of the doorways in the smaller galleries of the Antiquities Collection (Galleries 5 and 14–17). Whereas the other wings have doorways of highly polished stone, these small galleries now have profiled plaster doorways that have been painted black. These are similar to those at Copenhagen's police headquarters, and the stratigraphy showed that they were made of the same finely grained material but with grey pigment. Whether the surface was monochrome or marbled can only be established if a larger area is uncovered.

The Future of Colours at the Glyptotek

Architectural paint research has provided a far more detailed picture of two of Denmark's most noteworthy architects' attitudes to colours and materials. Vilhelm Dahlerup's saturated earthen colours are the choice of an architect deeply rooted in historicism. The colours are carefully matched to the elements of each gallery, and the way the colours alternate from gallery to gallery reflects his willingness to create a magnificent, vibrant temple for Carl and Ottilia Jacobsen's collection of French and Danish art. We will never know who deserves most credit for the colour scheme,

Vilhelm Dahlerup or Carl Jacobsen. In some instances Dahlerup followed a colour scheme developed in collaboration with the colour-loving brewer, although correspondence between the two men indicates that this was a far from frictionless process, and one in which Carl Jacobsen had the last word. Despite this there are clear instances where Kampmann prevailed. Architectural paint research has documented a contemporary colour scheme in bright contrasting colours and the use of fresco and the natural colours of materials, but also white plastered walls that seem surprisingly modern, pointing as they do towards an incipient functionalism.

There remains much to be discovered about colours at the Glyptotek. The ceilings, cornices and decorative elements, for example, have yet to be investigated, but the results to date only serve to underline the important role played by each individual element, including colour, in the original interior.

The desire to know more about the architectural history of colour schemes marks a paradigm shift in recent years in terms of how the interiors and exteriors of buildings are viewed. Architectural paint research has been used to restore the original interiors of a number of Danish museums, including Øregaard Museum, the Museum of Copenhagen, and the Natural History Museum of Denmark (the former Geological Museum and College of Advanced Technology buildings). Perhaps this increase in interest reflects a growing appreciation of architecture as a synthesis of forms, colours and materials. The unwillingness to embrace colour of recent decades has been replaced by a more positive view and the realisation that the original colours of interiors can easily cater to contemporary needs – also as a backdrop for modern exhibits and works of art.

The first steps at the Glyptotek have now been taken. The walls on the ground and first floors of Dahlerup's building have been restored and repainted based on architectural paint research conducted so far. The colours are based on the uncovered original colours but have been adapted to other colours and ornamentation in the galleries that have been changed since 1897. Another difference is that industrial paints have been used instead of oil-based paints.

Restoring an original colour scheme is no easy matter. First and foremost, perceptions change. As a client it is important to acknowledge that architecture is a work of art in and of itself, not a stage set to be changed according to the building's contents, which can pose a challenge for museums with changing temporary exhibitions.

The first hurdle in reconstructing the original walls and ceilings in Dahlerup's building at the Glyptotek would be materials. Using original materials and methods is far more demanding and costly today than in the past, and certainly more expensive and time-consuming than a quick paint job with modern acrylic paint. Professional painters also have to provide guarantees that make restoration virtually impossible: painted surfaces are to be maintenance-free and washable, neither of which apply to many older materials. Durability takes precedence over aesthetics and authenticity, as a result of which many have to prioritise such practical considerations instead of using materials rich in aesthetic qualities, such as handmade paints with authentic pigments that create depth, lustre and life. Work on the restoration of colour schemes therefore has to be accompanied by a change of attitude in relationship to maintenance, an acceptance of patina, and an understanding of the different qualities and properties of different types of paint.

At the Glyptotek Kampmann's white walls pose a further challenge because the walls were not simply white. They were polished and vibrant and in subtle interaction with the sculptures, floors and matt ceilings. For precisely this reason, a coat of white paint would not be able to recreate the same effect. Only a complete stratigraphy would be able to provide an accurate basis for achieving the desired result.

Architectural paint research has generated new knowledge about the colourful history of the Glyptotek – and also raised new questions. The results have hopefully contributed to the museum having an informed basis and options for future restoration. Regardless of which option is chosen, it is our hope that the investigation has shown the value of using the right techniques and materials rather than settling for second best. Complex restorations are based on thorough historical research on the architecture and building in question, and it can be difficult to accommodate competing demands for functionality, aesthetics and authenticity. Here we can perhaps find succour in Carl Jacobsen's uncompromising attitude when it comes to choosing the right materials: "We are patricians not plebeians!"

The colour scheme in Galleries 35, 36 and 37 is a reconstruction of the original. Returning the galleries to their original colours has created more harmony between the ceiling decorations, walls and mosaic and terrazzo floors. The niche at the far end of the photograph has yet to be restored and is still a greenish blue colour.

Architectural Paint Research

Architectural paint research is a cross-disciplinary scientific field based on three core elements: uncovering layers of paint, analysing a cross-section of paint layers, and archival research.

Paint Stratigraphy

To expose the layers of paint the conservator conducts a stratigraphy of the painted surface. Using a scalpel or solvent, each layer is exposed in chronological order, the oldest layer at the bottom and the most recent at the top. This produces a visual history of the paint colours in the area under investigation. A paint stratigraphy cannot, however, stand alone. The results require a high degree of analysis and interpretation. It can be difficult, for example, to ascertain whether a layer is an extra coat of the same paint to ensure an even surface, a new coat applied years later to freshen up a wall's appearance, or the base coat for a new colour. Some of the paint layers could also have been sanded away or washed down before the wall was repainted and are therefore partially or wholly missing. Layers of paint can also have yellowed with age or changed in other ways.

Cross-Section of Paint Layers

For a cross-section a small sample is taken from the painted surface. This is then cast in clear plastic and finely polished. This creates a cross-section of all the layers of paint to be examined under a microscope to reveal layers not visible to the naked eye. The components of the paint can also be seen: grains of pigment and the binding material. The latter can, for example, be chalk, lime, oil or more recently acrylic.

Layers of dirt or discolouration can also be identified under the microscope, but a cross-section also has pitfalls. Under the microscope the layers of paint are under intense light, making the individual pigments visible. The layer of paint 'dissolves' into its constituent parts, which makes it difficult to assess the impact their combination had on the overall appearance. The cross-sections are also very small and only able to tell us what the paint looked like in the precise area where the sample was taken. They can therefore never stand alone.

Archival Research

Once the layers of paint have been uncovered, the conservator will try to date them, partly through their knowledge of the styles and materials of different periods and partly through archival research.

Relevant archival material for such research can include drawings and elevations by the architect or evaluations made in connection with insuring a building. Later it could be building surveys, planning permission applications, or bills and accounts documenting the materials purchased during construction. Occasionally there are colour elevations, but more often than not colours are omitted and the picture has to be pieced together from uncovered layers of paint, cross-sections and any documentation that exists.

Notes

1 We would like to express our gratitude to Claus Grønne at the New Carlsberg Foundation for his extensive and invaluable assistance in tracing the archival sources used in the architectural paint research and this article.
2 See Johansen, 1978, pp. 7–16.
3 See Moltesen and Østergaard, 2006, p. 213.
4 See Bregnhøi, 2017, pp. 101–102.
5 Article on the Glyptotek's interior, *Dannebrog*, 4 May 1897.
6 See Friborg, 1998, p. 76.
7 Ibid.
8 Article on the inauguration of the Winter Garden and Central Hall, *Social-Demokraten*, 23 June 1906.
9 See Mogensen, 2022, p. 60.
10 See *Meddelelser fra Ny Carlsberg Glyptotek*. Copenhagen: Ny Carlsberg Glyptotek, 1968, p. 95.
11 "The rooms are painted different colours, yellow and white, red and black, but the main colour is white" (*Kristeligt Dagblad*, 27 June 1906), and: "The architect accompanies us through the 'Roman gallery' and the 'Renaissance Gallery'. The walls are plain white so as not to distract any attention from the works of art – the only decoration is a stucco frieze running under the ceiling." (*Ekstra Bladet*, 28 May 1906).
12 Ibid.
13 *Politiken*, 27 June 1906.
14 There is no consensus on the colour in the archives; see Bender, 2014, p. 474; Dirckinck-Holmfeld, Gehl and Soldbro, 2021, p. 116; Friborg, 1998, p. 79.
15 Letter from Carl Jacobsen to Hack Kampmann, 9 June 1904. Carl Jacobsen's Correspondence Archive.
16 Letter from Carl Jacobsen to Hack Kampmann, 16 June 1905. Carl Jacobsen's Correspondence Archive.
17 We would like to thank Peter Funder for the explanation below.

Bibliography

Anonymous: "Glyptoteket 1. april 1967- 31. marts 1968", *Meddelelser fra Ny Carlsberg Glyptotek*. Copenhagen: Ny Carlsberg Glyptotek, 1968, p. 95.

Bender, Johan: *Arkitekt Hack Kampmann*. Copenhagen: Forlaget Klematis, 2014.

Bregnhøi, Line: *Det malede rum – Materialer, teknikker og dekorationer 1790–1900*. Copenhagen: Gads Forlag, 2017 (2010).

Dirckinck-Holmfeld, Kim, Elisabeth Gehl and Marie Louise Kampmann Soldbro: *Hack Kampmann del 2 – En individualist i en brydningstid*. Nykøbing Sj.: Bogværket, 2017.

Friborg, Flemming: "Carl Jacobsens helligdomme", in: Flemming Friborg, Anne Marie Nielsen and Sylvester Roepstorff: *Carl Jacobsens helligdomme*. Copenhagen: Ny Carlsberg Glyptotek, 1998.

Johansen, Martin: "Nye farver", *Meddelelser fra Ny Carlsberg Glyptotek*, Year 35, 1978, pp. 7–16.

Mogensen, Johanne Bornemann: *Malet – Maling, farver og teknik i 1900-tallets arkitektur*. Copenhagen: Gads Forlag, 2022.

Moltesen, Mette and Jan Stubbe Østergaard: "Kunst, kronologi og kontekst – nyopstillingen af Glyptotekets antikke skulpturer", in: Flemming Friborg and Anne Marie Nielsen (eds.): *Ny Carlsberg Glyptotek i tiden*. Copenhagen: Ny Carlsberg Glyptotek, 2006, pp. 204–213.

Mogens A. Morgen

Eyes at the Glyptotek

The Mummies

In the belly of the Glyptotek, deep beneath the earth, lie the mummies. Taken from the sanctity of their graves they lie in state, waiting for those who descend the dimly lit stairs to the dark chamber below the museum. Striding down the passage generates a sense of suspense: you are about to enter the heart of the pyramid, the mummies' crypt. The same thrill of fear you experienced as a child sent down to the dingy depths of the cellar, where all sorts of horrors could lurk. The dim lighting makes for a dramatic descent, like being the first explorer ever to penetrate the walls of the tomb.

The Light

In the Winter Garden above you encounter the all-enveloping light so characteristic of the Glyptotek, which was originally a daylight-hours museum that closed when the sun set in the winter months. The light-filled existence of the museum lives on in architect Henning Larsen's extension. The terms of the architecture competition included artificial light for the museum's painting collection, but the main architectural attraction is a broad stairway bathed in daylight,

Nekhet-kawis sarkofag
Sedment, ca. 2050 f.Kr.

Sarcophagus of Nekhet-kawi
Sedment, c. 2050 B.C.

which like an alley in a southern mountain village winds around a monolithic box housing the museum's special exhibitions. A single statue placed on the ascent to the roof terrace transforms the alley into an imposing sculpture passage with the play of shadows from the recessed walls and bars of the skylight above adding character to the space. Echoing Egyptian architecture and the collection of mummies below, the light, lustrous, polished stucco walls of the box slope slightly inwards. The Carrara marble of the stairs amplifies the natural light to a dazzling whiteness, creating a counterpoint to the darkness of the steps leading down to the mummies. The staircases leading up towards the light and down into the dark have the same contours, gradient and broad gliding steps, but the staircase going down is lined with dark Portuguese granite, making the descent to the mummies a singularly dark passage, the antithesis of the luminous light of the rest of the complex.

The Eyes

Down in the tomb lie the sarcophagi that once held corpses wrapped in layer upon layer of cloth. In the wall niches stand four stone sarcophagi and at the end of the chamber three open mummy cases lifted from their natural horizontal position to stand upright, bringing them to life as a species of *homo erectus* visitors can meet at eye level. Life did not end with death for the Egyptians. The soul lived on as long as the body existed, which is why they embalmed their dead. There is life in the tomb! You feel it in the piercing gaze at the back of your head as you face the vertical mummy cases. It is a gaze that comes from several directions in a chamber where alert eyes follow your every move.

These eyes belong to the faces of some very lifelike mummy portraits laid on top of the mummies' faces, as well as some fragments on thin wooden boards at the opposite end of the chamber. They are lifelike portraits of the people wrapped inside the mummies, skilfully painted in a portrait tradition with a surprisingly realistic depiction of clothing, jewellery and hairstyles. The faces are those of younger people, which may have been painted while they were still alive. But their youthfulness could also be because many died at a young age. Ancient Egyptians did not live as long as people do today. The faces are realistic, the heads slightly turned, and even though the portraits are anonymous historians can often recognise the work of an individual artist from their personal hallmarks. As a viewer the large watchful eyes of the mummy portraits mean you too feel watched. They regard you quizzically, brought to life by the exchange of gazes. And as you leave the chamber to ascend into the light again you are followed by the vigilant gaze of large eyes from around 2500 BCE painted directly onto Nekhetkawi's yellow sarcophagus.

The Senses

It is difficult to think of any other building in Denmark where the architectural narrative embraces you more as a sensing, living being between life and death than at the Glyptotek. From the darkness of the crypt, you are whirled up – as with the spiralling Malwiya Minaret of the Great Mosque of Samarra, the tower of Copenhagen's Church of Our Saviour, or the coiling path inside the city's Round Tower turned inside out – to the light of the heavens on the roof terrace. Moving through the Glyptotek you are uniquely aware of the *raison d'être* of architecture: to create spaces for human beings and human existence. It is a powerfully sensory experience also manifested in Danish architect Vilhelm Dahlerup's Winter Garden, where the lushness of the plants is overwhelming, where you are bathed in light, where water trickles into the pool of *The Water Mother*, and where the mosaic floors undulate beneath your feet, as if the foundations were shifting. The air here vibrates in your nostrils with the smell of damp earth, as if to prepare you for the rank odour you might discover on entering the mummy chamber's soulful morgue – or the fresh air you can inhale on the roof terrace where the crowns of oaks sway above the museum garden.

**Ida Carnera and
Vibeke Cristofoli**

FROM FRIULI
TO COPENHAGEN

The Mosaic Floors
of Hack Kampmann's
Building

As a visitor to the Glyptotek you are bombarded by art, culture and sensory impressions, by French paintings, Egyptian mummies and the marble bodies of ancient sculptures. But the museum also has other, less explored works of art equally worth a visit: the mosaic and terrazzo floors traversed by thousands of feet for more than a century. The floors are interesting not only due to their beauty, variety and the ideas behind them, but also because of the story of the people who created them.

It is the story of the development of a specialised craft in the small villages of north-east Italy and how the skills of villagers here became sought-after not only in their native Italy but in the US, by the tzar of Russia, and in numerous European cities like Copenhagen. When building the Glyptotek Carl Jacobsen refused to compromise on quality, also when it came to the floors. Which is why he insisted that a group of master craftsmen travel from northern Italy to Denmark to create the floors of his museum. In doing so Carl Jacobsen created a unique connection between Denmark and Italy in the 1880s that exists to this day. How this connection across 1,500 kilometres between the master craftsmen

of the north-eastern Italian district of Friuli and Copenhagen came into being is the subject of what follows.

The mosaicists of Friuli made the floors for Vilhelm Dahlerup's building (1897) and Hack Kampmann's building (1906) at the Glyptotek of hand-cut marble mosaics surrounded by terrazzo. This article provides insight into the migration history and craft of the master mosaicists. Its main focus is the floors in Hack Kampmann's building, which represented a new departure in the way mosaics were made.

The Friulian Craft

The forces of nature were what created the basis for the emergence of a unique craft in the Italian district of Friuli. Villages like Arba, Colle, Fanna, Sequals and Solimbergo all lie at the foot of the Carnic Prealps about 120 kilometres from Venice at the edge of the River Tagliamento and the River Meduna. The relationship between the people living here and the rivers is where we find the lifeblood of their craft.

Before dams existed the winter thaw would swell the rivers and flood the meagre crops of local people. Under the intense heat of the summer

With its rich supply of stone and proximity to
Venice the Tagliamento is one of the rivers in
Friuli that created the basis for the region's
strong mosaic tradition. The river is 178
kilometres long and one of the few in Europe
to have retained its original morphology of
intertwining streams.

Group portrait of the Friulian mosaicists
in Gallery 36 of the Glyptotek during
the construction of Dahlerup's building
in 1896. In the middle of the second row
Vincenzo Odorico and at the right
end Andrea Carnera, both from Sequals.

sun the wide riverbeds dried out, creating vast deposits of stone of different colours, sizes and qualities the Friulians called *claps*. The population of the area gathered these stones and used them to form where they lived by building dams, walls and houses. A solid tradition for stone carving emerged in the small village communities, passed down from father to son at a very early age.

Migrating to Venice

In the 16th century many Friulian stone carvers migrated to Venice to find work. Venice was a centre for the mosaic tradition Venetians had been taught by Byzantine mosaic masters travelling around the Mediterranean. In Venice the stone carvers from Friuli developed and refined their craft to include mosaics. An eminent example is the Bianchini family, who decorated large parts of the interior of St Mark's Basilica in Venice with mosaics in the 16th century. Many Friulians started their own mosaic and terrazzo businesses in Venice, transporting stones from the Meduna and Tagliamento to the city. During the dry season this was done by horse-drawn carts travelling along the riverbanks, and when the rivers rose again, boats were used to transport the stone.

Students at Scuola Mosaicisti del Friuli in 1922–1924 (left) and 1927 (right), which started in the village of Sequals. It opened officially in the town of Spilimbergo in 1922, where it is now an international mosaic academy attended by students from all over the world.

The yellow and pale green stone they used came from the Meduna, and the black and red stone from the Tagliamento.

It was during this period that the craftsmen developed the stone floors they called *terrazzo alla veneziana* seen in so many of Venice's public and private palaces. And whilst the name included the city they were made in, the stone came from the rivers of Friuli and the hands that made them came from the same place. The title of *terrazziere* or master terrazzo maker was officially recognised by the Republic of Venice's Il Consiglio dei Dieci ('The Council of Ten') in 1582 when the craftsmen formed of their own guild. The Friulians soon became known for their diligence and precision – qualities also demonstrated by the men who came to Copenhagen to make mosaic and terrazzo floors at the Glyptotek.

New Horizons

The second half of the 19th century was a period of political tumult in Northern Italy, and many Friulian mosaic and terrazzo makers who had previously migrated within Italy started to emigrate abroad, their skills their only resource. They often took their wife and children with them,

hoping to settle permanently where working conditions were good. One of these men was the master mosaicist Gian Domenico Facchina (1826–1903) from the village of Sequals in Friuli. He was a pioneer of modern mosaics. After working on the restoration of buildings such as St Mark's Basilica in Venice he travelled to France.[1] Here he met the French architect Charles Garnier (1825–1898) who had spent years trying to find the right experts to create mosaics for the planned Opéra Garnier in Paris (inaugurated in 1875). Facchina and his team only had a few months to make all the mosaics at the opera house, including the 300-square-metre vaulted ceiling of the foyer covered entirely in mosaic. Facchina recruited mosaicists in the village he came from and brought them to Paris where they introduced a new revolutionary 'reverse' technique called *la tecnica a rovescio*, which elevated the quality of the work at the same time as reducing costs.

In *la tecnica a rovescio* coloured mosaic tiles were placed face down on pieces of sticky paper of a workable size. These were applied to the wet plaster surface, then the paper was removed with water. Key to the method's success was the invisibility of the joins between one

In 1875 master mosaicist Gian Domenico Facchina, who invented the reverse mosaic technique, and his team of fellow Friulians created the mosaics at Opéra Garnier in Paris. It was the first time mosaics were used in this way in a French public building. The project became a European model for mosaic art and won Facchina international acclaim. He was also awarded France's Ordre national de la Légion d'honneur.

section and the next. The result was exceptional, and Opéra Garnier became the gold standard for modern mosaic art in France and made mosaics fashionable. Facchina patented the method in Paris in 1858.

New Connections

In 1878 the World's Fair *L'Exposition Universelle* was held in Paris, a major event for the dissemination of inventions, techniques and materials from around the world. The façades of several of the national stands were decorated with Italian mosaics, and the public and professionals alike responded with enthusiasm.[2] Carl Jacobsen visited the fair with Vilhelm Dahlerup. He was inspired by the beauty of the mosaics and would have had the opportunity to meet the master mosaicists from Friuli at the fair.

We do not know whether he actually spoke to them at the time, but they had documented contact in 1885 when Carl Jacobsen wanted to order mosaic and terrazzo floors for the first Glyptotek at his home in Valby.[3] Carl Jacobsen contacted the Friulian-run Odorico mosaic company's headquarters in Frankfurt. The company, where master mosaicist Vincenzo Odorico (1859–1950) worked, had created custom-made mosaic floors in Copenhagen for the family of the Russian tzar two years previously. Vincenzo Odorico was born in Sequals in Friuli, but left the village at an early age to work in his family's construction company, Johann Odorico in Frankfurt. The company was named after the founding member of the family, Giovanni Odorico,[4] and specialised in the traditional mosaic and terrazzo techniques of his native Friuli, work that took the master mosaicists to Russia to make mosaic floors for the Russian tzar. Vincenzo Odorico was one of them, working first in St Petersburg, then at the palaces of the Kremlin in Moscow. Here he met the future Tzar Nicholas II (1868–1918) who was the same age as Vincenzo and the young men became friends.[5] Nicholas II was the son of Alexander III (1845–1894) and his wife, the Danish princess Dagmar, who became Tzarina of Russia under the Russian name Marija Fjodorovna (1847–1928). When Alexander III agreed to build the Russian Orthodox church in Copenhagen (Alexander Nevsky Church), a long-held wish of his wife, it was the mosaic and terrazzo makers of Friuli he hired to make the floors. Their journey from Russia to Copenhagen was on foot, walking beside wooden horse-drawn

After Vincenzo Odorico and his Friulian team had made mosaics at the palaces of St Petersburg and the Kremlin the Russian tzar hired them again to make mosaic floors for the Russian Orthodox church in Copenhagen. Building the church was a long-held wish for the Danish princess Dagmar, who married Tzar Alexander III of Russia and took the Russian name Marija Fjodorovna as tzarina. The church was the Friulian mosaicists' first project in Denmark.

carts full of tools and materials on a trip said to
have taken eight weeks.[6]

Whilst they first came to Denmark to work
on the Russian church in the early 1880s, it was
Carl Jacobsen and his many building projects
that helped make it possible for the mosaic and
terrazzo masters of Friuli to start their own businesses and settle in Denmark.[7]

Written correspondence between Carl
Jacobsen and the Johann Odorico company
prior to the construction of the Glyptotek in Valby
shows that he was highly involved and engaged in
his building projects and had very specific ideas
about the colours and design of the floors. Their
correspondence also shows that he was interested in getting a good deal. In 1885 he received
an estimate for 100 square metres of terrazzo
and mosaic flooring, presumably calculated on
the basis of what the Friulians had been paid to
make the floors at Alexander Nevsky Church in
Copenhagen for Tzar Alexander III.[8] Carl Jacobsen replied to the offer by saying he expected a
sizeable discount for a considerably larger area of
over 300 square metres. We do not know whether
Carl Jacobsen ever got his discount.

The collaboration between Carl Jacobsen
and the mosaic and terrazzo specialists of Friuli
resulted in mosaic floors being a central feature
of the buildings Carl Jacobsen built over the coming years: the first Glyptotek in Valby (1885), the
Church of Jesus (1891) and Vilhelm Dahlerup's
and Hack Kampmann's buildings at the Glyptotek
(1897 and 1906).

The Mosaic and Terrazzo Floors in Kampmann's Building

"In this way Kampmann, artistic genius that he
is, has gone through life with his eyes open, dis-
covering beauty and connections where others
have not."[9] This praise for Hack Kampmann was
published in the illustrated weekly *Hver 8. Dag* in
1906. Kampmann had never restricted himself to
a specific architectural style and the floors of his
building at the Glyptotek represented yet another
new departure. Whereas in the past it had been
customary to use the standard patterns listed
in the catalogues of mosaic companies, Kampmann made his own designs for the gallery floors
of the new Glyptotek building, elevating them
to an entirely new level. Studying Kampmann's
drawings it is obvious that he was an exception-
ally analytical, meticulous and creative architect,
something also demonstrated in the cornucopia

Hack Kampmann designed all the floors at
the Glyptotek himself. Some of the floors
refer to the art intended for the gallery,
others were decorated with Nordic plants
and flowers, and others again symbolised
the professional and private life of the
brewer Carl Jacobsen. This is Kampmann's floor plan for the mosaics. Gallery
4 in the bottom left corner, for example,
was to house the ancient Egyptian art
mirrored in the mosaic floor with its
elegant symmetrical pattern of the lotus
flowers thought to be a symbol of Upper
Egypt at the time.

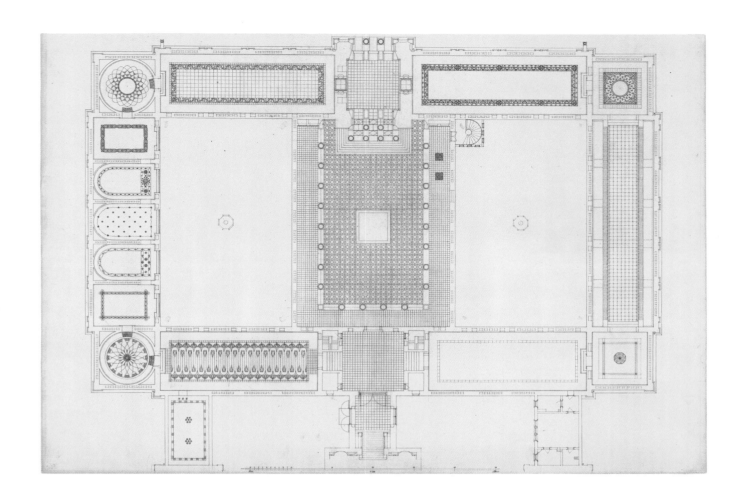

Hack Kampmann's rose design for the mosaic in Gallery 16, probably a dog rose (*Rosa canina*). The mosaic itself was made by Friulian mosaicists but Kampmann included mosaic tiles in the design from the very beginning. They became an integral part of his thinking. Even though the mosaic rose looks simple, making it required cutting a lot of tiles in different shapes and sizes, some of them very challenging.

307

Making the mosaic floor in Kampmann's Central Hall. The upper photograph shows the original ancient Roman mosaic *Europe and the Bull* being carefully lowered into the Roman pool in the middle of the marble floor. When filled with water, the pool reflected the architectural opulence of the hall.

of designs in his sketches for the museum's floors. The floors were not only to be beautiful and functional but like the mosaics of the Byzantines also full of references and symbols. Kampmann was probably also inspired by the many trips abroad he had taken since receiving a two-year travel bursary to Italy as a young architect.

He drew every single floor in the building, each of them with its own distinctive design. Some of the floors refer to the works of art planned for the gallery in question and others to the professional and private life of Carl Jacobsen. The designs included Nordic plants and flowers clearly inspired by the decorative arts of Art Nouveau. Kampmann's sketches show the sensitivity with which he studied plants, drawing them from various angles and experimenting with different watercolour combinations. It is as if Kampmann wanted to capture the essence of each plant focusing on his own interpretation rather than detailed accuracy. Drawing and sketching can encompass a wealth of detail, whereas mosaics encourage architects to simplify their ideas.

Kampmann's sketches show how he even started to include small mosaic tiles (*le tessere*) in his drawings. He began, in other words, to think in stone, coming a step closer to the nature of the material and the art of mosaic making itself. The sketches also show Kampmann's interest in floors as an architectural element. Instead of merely being a surface beneath people's feet, they become a way to frame and elevate the works of art above them. In Kampmann's building the mosaic and terrazzo floors interact with their surroundings without drawing attention from the artworks. They are part of an integral whole, of the connection between the artworks on display and the architecture. Walking through the galleries the patterns on the floors lead naturally through the museum, from galleries that are small and intimate through those that are elegant and round then into larger rectangular galleries. Each floor seems carefully thought through, harmonising with the proportions, colours, artworks, natural light and motifs in the stucco relief ornamentation on the ceilings of each gallery. Every floor is different, a work of art itself.

Despite the detailed nature of Kampmann's drawings, they still needed to be interpreted to translate into mosaic floors by cutting huge, heavy blocks of marble into small tiles of the precise shape and colour needed to make the individual pieces coalesce into what Kampmann

had sketched and drawn. In addition to technical expertise, this demonstrates the virtues of mosaic art: precision, meticulousness and a strong aesthetic sense. Making mosaics was a new craft for Danish workers, but it was in the blood of Friulians. The floors of Kampmann's building were created by seventeen Friulian mosaicists led by Vincenzo Odorico. During a visit to the Glyptotek in 1905, one year before Hackmann's building was completed, a newspaper journalist from *Nestved Tidende* described the Friulian mosaicists as follows:

> "It is amusing to observe them. One gets the impression that it is not every Southern European who cannot be bothered to work. Their hauling of heavy blocks of marble and sacks of tiles defies any accusation of idleness. And they have a sure hand. They cleave the marble with a powerful blow of the hammer as precise as any machine. And at such a pace. There is an unimaginable bustle and hurry behind the mysterious fence. [...] Building, cutting and casting, a treat to see."[10]

Floors Framing Art
Visiting the Glyptotek is a poetic experience: being greeted by the plants and flowers in the lush Winter Garden, then continuing to the galleries of Kampmann's building and finding the motifs of nature again in the flowers and plants that bring life to the stone floors. In general the gallery walls are plain, painted in dense earthen colours. This makes the floors and ceiling stand out, complementing each other.

Gallery 4 is particularly noteworthy for several reasons. First and foremost because the round gallery is a prime example of the design of the mosaic floors and stucco work on the ceiling corresponding to the art on display: floors that have an Egyptian plant theme to match the exhibits from Egypt,[11] and works of art that are also in dialogue with the motifs of the floor. Small Egyptian sculptures are raised on dark pedestals that merge discretely with the dark band of terrazzo framing the perimeter of the gallery. Sixteen lotus plants fan out from the centre. At the time the lotus flower was believed to be an early symbol of Upper Egypt, and those here seem to nod to the Egyptian sculptures in an exchange that accentuates both. As in nature there is a lightness to the gallery's lotus plants and their organic forms and movements in a sea of green terrazzo. This lightness is underlined by a single row of sand-coloured marble tiles in different shades. The lotus plants create an elegant round form mirroring the overall dome-shaped architecture of the gallery. Exploring the floor something else appears, something more easily seen by studying Kampmann's floor plan, because seen from above the sixteen lotus plants form a large lotus flower. This motif is mirrored when looking up at the stucco reliefs on the ceiling. Kampmann's integration of every element of his interior flourishes in Gallery 4 and the floor plays a significant role in that.

Floor Motifs at the Glyptotek

Nordic flowers and plants adorn the floors of the museum's five small galleries (Galleries 5 and 14–17). It is also here that the influence of Art Nouveau is most strongly felt. The flowers occasionally float in isolation, but more often they are intertwined, weaving between each other as they would in nature, the lightness of their petals carved in heavy marble. One small gallery leads naturally to the next. Each one is different, but at the same time they feel connected.

The mosaic roses on the floor in Gallery 16 float gracefully and elegantly, their clear light colours appearing beneath and between pedestals with Roman busts amidst the green terrazzo surrounding them.[12] Zooming in on one of the roses reveals how masterfully crafted the composition is and how skilful the cutting of the tiles. The stigma in the centre is made of a small round tile, a challenge to cut on this scale by hand. From here narrow rectangular tiles extend as stamens towards the almost square tiles that form the anthers. The innermost parts of the flower are made of burnt-orange marble, a colour accentuated by the black terrazzo surrounding it. The heart of the flower is encircled by five petals (each with an incision at the tip) unfurling in different directions in sand-coloured marble that harmonises with the ancient busts in the gallery. Whilst the roses in the middle float freely, those closest to the walls are connected by a meandering mosaic stem with sharp thorns also seen in the reliefs on the ceiling.

The floor in Gallery 12 has mosaics of hop vines and the floor in Gallery 13 ears of barley, both basic ingredients in Carl Jacobsen's brewery business and thereby key to the creation of the Glyptotek. The floor of Gallery 13 has a

In Gallery 16 small roses in light marble mosaic tiles emerge from the green terrazzo floor as if to greet the Roman busts above them. The orange and sand-coloured tiles of the mosaic harmonise with the colour of the walls and the ancient sculptures.

The marble mosaic hop vines in Gallery 14 symbolising Carl Jacobsen's brewing business.

A light, elegant mosaic pattern with ears of barley on the floor of Gallery 13. The same motif is repeated in the ceiling reliefs and is another symbol of Carl Jacobsen's brewing business.

sophisticated symmetrical circular pattern. In the centre of the gallery a large circle of black terrazzo merges with the pedestal and statue it forms the foundation for. From this hard black core a light delicate pattern unfolds, beginning with a circular mosaic band with eighteen small identical corncockle flowers placed with perfect symmetry.[13] The reddish colour of the corncockles harmonises with the colour of the walls. Despite its prettiness, the corncockle is actually a poisonous weed. Almost extinct today, in the past it was a major source of frustration when harvesting crops. From this band of mosaic an elegant pattern of intertwined ears of barley sweeps across the floor, again in thin lines of sand-coloured marble mosaic tiles surrounded by green terrazzo. Finally, there is a discrete narrow band of mosaic tiles around the edge of the gallery, a feature Friulian mosaicists often used to accentuate the proportions of a room.

Whereas the floors of Galleries 12 and 13 relate to Carl Jacobsen's professional life, Gallery 10 brings us closer to the private sphere of the brewer. Here the floor is decorated with thistles, his wife Ottilia's favourite flower and the national flower of her native Scotland.[14] Perhaps in keeping with the personal nature of the theme, the floor here also has a domestic element: a long 'carpet' of light terrazzo framed by a metre-wide border in the same soft colours as the marble decorating the large rectangular gallery. The border has an exquisitely crafted pattern of alternating green and red thistles nestling between sand-coloured mosaic tiles that follow the swaying of the thistle heads. Despite being made of hard shining stone, the mosaics create the impression of something soft and tactile, inviting us to touch the small smooth tiles of the 'carpet trim'. Which we can, because the floors at the Glyptotek are one of the few things visitors cannot avoid physical contact with as they walk through the museum. The Italian term for mosaic is *la pittura per l'eternità* ('a painting for eternity'), which seems particularly appropriate here. Despite being walked on every day, mosaics can adorn a surface without falling into disrepair or fading in colour. More than a century later visitors to the Glyptotek still walk across the museum's original mosaic 'carpet'.

A Key Combination of Factors

A number of factors combined to make the floors of Kampmann's building exceptional. The builder was a wealthy man who was passionate about art – and Italy – and refused to compromise on aesthetics or quality. That the floors also refer to the personal life of Carl Jacobsen make them no less interesting or unusual. In addition to which, Carl Jacobsen allied himself with Hack Kampmann, one of Denmark's best architects of the period, who challenged the usual way of making and using mosaic and terrazzo floors. The floors were custom-made with a sense of creative freedom and flair, forming part of an integral whole in a manner unprecedented in Denmark. It took skilled master craftsmen to translate Kampmann's drawings into finished floors, and there was only one group of Northern Italian specialists in mosaics and terrazzo who were up to the task. Their expertise and skills were in high demand, bringing them from small villages in Italy via Russia to Copenhagen where Carl Jacobsen played a key role in helping their businesses flourish. Like a mosaic where each individual tile contributes to the whole, Carl Jacobsen, Hack Kampmann and the Friulian mosaicists all contributed to the creation of the Glyptotek's sublime floors.

The Subsequent Danish-Italian Connection

When the Italian king Victor Emmanuel III (1869–1947) visited Denmark in 1922 he discovered a strong Italian community held together by lively social and cultural associations. To mark the sixth centenary of the death of Italian poet Dante Alighieri (1265–1321) Victor Emmanuel III participated in the ceremonial laying of the foundation stone for Dante's Column in front of the Glyptotek. He visited the Glyptotek not once but twice, enthusiastically declaring it to be a "connecting link between Danish and Italian culture".[15] His only apparent regret was that the cultural heritage of Italy was more impoverished after Carl Jacobsen had taken so many beautiful works of art from his country to Denmark.[16]

In the early 1920s there were around 150 Italians living in Copenhagen, most of them master mosaicists from Friuli. Vincenzo Odorico's family firm was the most prominent, but there were also others, including the Friulian master mosaicist Andrea Carnera (1874–1946), who set up his own mosaic and terrazzo company after working on the floors at the Glyptotek. Only a few years after opening his business he was awarded a gold diploma by the Italian mosaic federation

The thistle mosaic in Gallery 10.

315 Kaupmann
819, galvatauille,
2. f — 211

Kampmann's watercolour of a thistle,
presumably the common thistle *Cirsium
vulgare*, designed for the floor of Gallery
10. The thistle was the favourite flower of
Ottilia Jacobsen, wife of Carl Jacobsen.
It is also the national flower of her native
Scotland.

The marble mosaic and terrazzo
mistletoe in Gallery 14.

Federazione Mosaicisti di Venezia. Connections with the villages of Friuli were carefully nurtured especially during the summer holidays. This is when the many branches of the Friulian families who had emigrated to Europe met in their home district, the birthplace of mosaics. It was on holiday in a Friulian village, for example, that Andrea Carnera met his future wife, French-based Ida Odorico (1881–1941), the daughter of another emigrant master mosaicist who had made his mark with the mosaics he created for Opéra Garnier in Paris. During Victor Emmanuel III's visit to Denmark in 1922, Andrea Carnera with Ida Odorico Carnera at his side was awarded the royal order Il Cancelliere dell'Ordine della Corona d'Italia for his contribution to Italian culture in Copenhagen. Numerous master mosaicists from Friuli have contributed to the beautification of Copenhagen since, including the Odorico family, the Carnera family and the Cristofoli family.

Anyone wanting to explore the contribution Friulians have made to the beauty of Copenhagen only has to look down at the city's floors: the floors in the hallways of luxury apartments, Frederik's Church (1894), Copenhagen City Hall (1905), the Royal Library (1906), Christiansborg Palace (1928) and the Hirschsprung Collection (1911) to name but a few. More recently the Friulian master mosaicist Umberto Londero left his indelible mark on both Henning Larsen's extension to the Glyptotek (1996), where he built the staircases and installed the marble floors, and his granite paving of Amager Square crossed by thousands of feet of every single day. The Friulians' landmark meeting with Carl Jacobsen brought beauty and a rich heritage of culture, art and craftsmanship not only to the Glyptotek but also to the city of Copenhagen.

Terrazzo

"A polychrome carpet with a stone soul, cool in the summer and easy to clean".[17] This simple yet accurate definition of terrazzo was made by the Italian art critic Gillo Dorfles (1910–2018) during a visit to the international mosaic academy Scuola Mosaicisti del Friuli in 2009.

Terrazzo (a derivation of the word *terra* for earth) is a hard floor. Its appearance changes depending on the type of marble or granite crushed and mixed with a binding agent, originally made of slaked lime and later cement. Terrazzo is applied on top of a screed coat in a layer one to two centimetres thick. The crushed stones in terrazzo can include marble of various kinds and sizes which are spread using sieves with different sized holes. The crushed marble is then rolled into the wet mixture until it is on a level with the other crushed stones. Once the terrazzo has hardened it is sanded and polished. In the past this was a done by hand, which was the case at the Glyptotek. This arduous task is now performed by electric sanders.

During the rhythmical, manual sanding of terrazzo the Friulian mosaicists sang a ditty: "What a beautiful job to be a terrazzo master. Eye focused, knee bent, smoothing the moist mass to make terrazzo. But once the work is done, a flowering meadow appears."[18]

Mosaic

Making mosaics is more specialised than making terrazzo. The technique involves placing small tiles of one or more materials next to each other to create a design on a surface made of mortar or another binder. A wide range of materials can be used to make mosaics. Stone, glass, wood, metal and ceramics – even feathers and straw – have all been used.

Originally the small tiles the master mosaicists from Friuli used in stone mosaics had to be cut on site with a scalpel then placed in a binding material according to a drawn design. The drawing had to be full size so small holes could be made in the paper and charcoal dust be sprinkled on the surface beneath to trace the motif on the floor. When terrazzo and mosaics are combined, the mosaics are made first. The terrazzo is then cast around them. The result is the kind of beautiful mosaics surrounded by terrazzo seen at the Glyptotek.

Students working on mosaics at Scuola Mosaicisti del Friuli in Spilimbergo in the 1960s. Tiles in many colours are cut by hand then placed on the surface with pinpoint accuracy using a scalpel.

Students at Scuola Mosaicisti del Friuli making mosaic floors at the school in Spilimbergo in 1934–1935.

Notes

1. Comune di Sequals: http://www.comune.sequals.pn.it/it/vivere-il-comune-26435/luoghi-26444/personaggi-illustri-26466
2. Caillarec and Martin-Adam, 2009, pp. 19–20.
3. Letter from Carl Jacobsen to Johann Odorico, 11 December 1885. Carl Jacobsen's Correspondence Archive.
4. Johann is a Germanisation of the Italian name Giovanni.
5. Filipuzzi, 1994, p. 92.
6. Rubini, 2008.
7. Filipuzzi, 1994, p. 93.
8. Letter from Carl Jacobsen to Johann Odorico, 11 December 1885. Carl Jacobsen's Correspondence Archive.
9. Alonso, 1906, p. 603.
10. *Nestved Tidende*, 2 March 1905, front page.
11. The lotus motif in Gallery 4 symbolises Upper Egypt (South, Nile River valley), although it was later discovered that the symbol for Upper Egypt was a form of lily. Papyrus, which features in Kampmann's mosaic and terrazzo floor in Gallery 1, is a symbol of Lower Egypt (North, Nile Delta). Thanks to curator and Egyptologist Tine Bagh at the Glyptotek for her expertise on the Egyptian plants depicted in the mosaics at the museum.
12. The rose in question is probably modelled on the dog rose (*Rosa canina*), which is widespread in Denmark. Thanks to Professor Emeritus Niels Jacobsen from the University of Copenhagen's Department of Plant and Environmental Sciences for the identification of the plant motifs discussed in this article.
13. Common corncockle, *Agrostemma githago*.
14. The motif is probably based on the common thistle, *Cirsium vulgare*.
15. "Kong Victor Emmanuels Besøg imorges paa Glyptoteket", 1922.
16. Ibid.
17. "Un tappeto policromo dall'anima lapidea, fresco d'estate e facile da pulire", cited by Colledani, 2021, pp. 28–29.
18. "Ce biel mestèr il teracèr! Dret il voli plet il zenoli, simpri tal svuaç a smuelâ teraç. E a lavòr finît un pràt flurît". Ibid.

Bibliography

Publications

Benzon, Gorm: *Gamle danske gulve*. Copenhagen: Kreditforeningen Danmark, 1988.

Caillarec, Clare, and Fabienne Martin-Adam: *Odorico, 100 ans de mosaïques*. Rennes: Musée de Bretagne, Apogée, 2009.

Dirckinck-Holmfeld, Kim, Elisabeth Gehl and Marie Louise Kampmann Soldbro: *Hack Kampmann del 2: En individualist i en brydningstid*. Nykøbing Sj.: Bogværket, 2017.

Friborg, Flemming, and Anne Marie Nielsen (eds.): *Ny Carlsberg Glyptotek i tiden*. Copenhagen: Ny Carlsberg Glyptotek, 2006.

Gehl, Elisabeth, and Marie Louise Kampmann Soldbro: *Hack Kampmann del 1: De unge år belyst gennem tegninger, akvareller og breve*. Nykøbing Sj.: Bogværket, 2015.

Gelfer-Jørgensen, Mirjam: *Kunstarternes forbrødring: Skønvirke – en kalejdoskopisk periode*. Copenhagen: Strandberg Publishing, 2020.

Glamann, Kristof: *Øl og Marmor – Carl Jacobsen på Ny Carlsberg*. Copenhagen: Gyldendal, 1995.

Olsen, Axel, Carl Hansen and Peter Andersen: *Jord- og Betonarbejdernes Fagorganisations 50 Aars Stiftelsesfest den 3. April 1934 – Optegnelser og Billeder fra 50 Aars Organisations-Virksomhed af de københavnske Jord- og Betonarbejdere*. Copenhagen: Andreassens Bogtrykkeri, 1934.

Articles

Alonso: "Kampmanns og Jacobsens nye Glyptotek", *Hver 8. Dag*, No. 38, Year 12 (17 June 1906).

Colledani, Gianni: "Terrazzi alla veneziana, un'arte tutta made in Friuli", *Friuli Nel Mondo*, November–December 2021, pp. 28–29.

Dagens Nyheder, Kalundborg, 21 June 1922, front page.

Felix: "Det ny Glyptotek – En pragtfuld Nybygning", *Nestved Tidende – Sydsjællands Folkeblad*, 2 March 1905, front page.

Filipuzzi, Angelo: "Gli Odorico ed i Carnera di Copenhagen", in: Gianni Colledani and Tullio Perfetti (eds.): *Dal sasso al mosaico – storia dei terrazzieri e mosaicisti di Sequals*. Sequals: Comune di Sequals, 1994, pp. 89–98.

"Kong Victor Emmanuels Besøg imorges paa Glyptoteket", *Berlingske Politiske og Avertissementstidende, Aften*, 23 June 1922, front page.

"Vore Egne Italienere – Kolonien i København", *Dagens Nyheder*, Kalundborg, 21 June 1922, pp. 5–6.

Other Sources

Comune di Sequals: http://www.comune.sequals.pn.it/index.php?id=6274

"Da Gian Domenico Facchina alla Scuola dei Mosaicisti del Friuli". *Nella Patria del Friuli –Luoghi, Storia, Leggende*, television series broadcast 21 September 2022.

Destination Rennes: "Retracing the History of Odorico Mosaics": https://www.tourisme-rennes.com/en/discover-rennes/history-rennes/retracing-the-history-of-odorico-mosaics/

Kampmann, Hack: Drawings for the construction of the Glyptoteket (1906). The Glyptotek Archive.

Rubini, Irene: *Il lungo cammino dei Terrazzieri e Mosaicisti Friulani in Europa*. DVD documentary, Municipality of Arba, 2008.

Kiste i form af et hus   Coffin in the shape of a house
Sedment, ca. 2700 f.Kr.   Sedment, c. 2700 B.C.

Timeline

1847 J.C. Jacobsen founds the Carlsberg brewery in Valby.

1880 Carl and Ottilia Jacobsen move to Gammel Bakkegård, the old main house on the farm where the New Carlsberg brewery was later to be built.

1882 Carl Jacobsen founds the New Carlsberg brewery and he and Ottilia start extending their private residence to exhibit their art collection. The collection is open to the public on specified days.

1883 Architect Vilhelm Dahlerup exhibits his proposal for a sepulchral monument for the Italian king Victor Emmanuel II at Charlottenborg.

1884 After a fire at Christiansborg Palace Carl and Ottilia Jacobsen offer to donate their art collection to the people of Denmark on condition that Copenhagen City Council provide a building plot, and the council and state share the cost of building a museum to house the collection.

1886 Vilhelm Dahlerup submits his first proposal for a building to exhibit the collection.

1888 Carl and Ottilia Jacobsen donate their collection of French and Danish art to the people of Denmark by deed of gift.

1889 Copenhagen City Council provides a building plot on Vestre Boulevard (now H.C. Andersen's Boulevard). Carl Jacobsen finds the location "somewhat remote" and later wrote: "Being next door to what I considered the plebian Tivoli also held little appeal."

1890 Vilhelm Dahlerup starts to plan the Glyptotek building. Osvald Rosendahl Langballe serves as resident architect during its construction.

Due to the expense, Dahlerup's original proposal of four wings and a dome is reduced to three wings without a dome.

1892 Construction of Vilhelm Dahlerup's building begins.

1897 Despite not being entirely finished, the first building of the Glyptotek is inaugurated by Carl Jacobsen. The marble and granite on the walls of the main staircase are installed the following year.

1899 Carl and Ottilia Jacobsen donate their collection of antiquities and the Egyptian part of their art collection to the Glyptotek. Copenhagen City Council insists that an architectural competition is held for the extension to house it.

1900 Hack Kampmann wins the competition to build an extension to the Glyptotek.

1901 The construction of Hack Kampmann's building begins.

1904 Vilhelm Dahlerup designs a domed cover for the courtyard between the original three-winged building and Hack Kampmann's new building. The construction of the Winter Garden begins the same year.

1906 Carl Jacobsen inaugurates the Winter Garden and Hack Kampmann's extension to the Glyptotek.

1908 Inauguration of the Glyptotek's museum garden. The garden is a collaboration between Hack Kampmann and the City of Copenhagen's head gardener, Valdemar Fabricius Hansen.

1909 The use of electricity is extended and a new heating system installed.

1911 Architect Osvald Rosendahl Langballe converts the first floor of Vilhelm Dahlerup's building, and a stair tower is built in the courtyard between Vilhelm Dahlerup and Hack Kampmann's buildings.

1919-1921 Architect Carl Harild designs an extension to Hack Kampmann's building in the eastern courtyard. The extension is demolished in connection with the 1996 extension of the museum.

1923-1925 Carl Harild designs a new administration and library wing in the western courtyard of Hack Kampmann's building.

1927-1929 The upper floor of Vilhelm Dahlerup's building is converted and the roof covered with copper.

1949 A central heating system is installed. As a result, the museum is no longer partially closed during the winter.

1954-1958 Architects Viggo Sten Møller and Vilhelm Wohlert convert and restore the ground and first floors of Vilhelm Dahlerup's building.

1967 The glass roof of the Central Hall is replaced.

1977 The main entrance to the museum facing Dante's Square is rebuilt with a new revolving door.

1982 The Glyptotek is certified as a listed building.

1992 The architecture firm Dissing+Weitling extend the library. The Glyptotek invites selected architects to submit entries for a new building in the eastern courtyard of Hack Kampmann's building. Danish architect Henning Larsen wins the competition.

1994 Construction of the new extension begins.

1996 Inauguration of the new building designed by Henning Larsen.

2004-2006 The architecture firm Dissing+Weitling convert the basement below Vilhelm Dahlerup's building with improved visitor facilities and accessibility.

2022- The ongoing future-proofing of all three buildings is initiated.

Vilhelm Dahlerup
(1836–1907)

Vilhelm Dahlerup was one of the most productive architects in 19th-century Denmark, particularly in Copenhagen during the rapid development of the city in the second half of the 1800s. He started studying at the Royal Danish Academy of Fine Arts' school of architecture in 1854. After intensive training in drawing at Aarhus Cathedral School, in 1853 he applied to the art academy to study painting. He switched to architecture just one year into his studies, graduating in 1858. He started working as an architect under J.H. Nebelong (1817–1871) during his education and remained on his staff until starting his own architecture firm in the 1860s.

Like most Danish architects of the period Dahlerup found inspiration in historical architecture. His buildings were initially Gothic in style, but a study trip to Germany, France, Spain and Italy led to a shift in focus to the Italian High Renaissance, something clearly seen on the façade of the Glyptotek. He travelled extensively in Europe and to the US during his career.

Dahlerup had worked for both public and private clients before being hired by the brewer Carl Jacobsen to design the New Carlsberg brewery complex in Valby (1880–1883), where his buildings later included the brewery's landmark double gateway and tower (1892), its engine house with a winding chimney (1898–1899) and the famous Carlsberg Elephant Tower (1900–1901). He came to the brewery with prior experience of the period's new industrial architecture. He had previously worked on Copenhagen Harbour, which developed apace during the second half of the 19th century. Dahlerup designed the harbour authority's administration offices at Nordre Toldbod (1868 with architect Frederik Bøttger) now a listed building. He also designed the new Frihavnen harbour, building warehouses where he experimented with new techniques and materials such as reinforced

Osvald Rosendahl Langballe (1859–1930)

concrete at the same time as the Glyptotek was under construction. In the Dahlerup Warehouse (1895), for example, he used the same Monier arch system as at the Glyptotek.

In addition to designing industrial buildings and complexes, Dahlerup also won architectural competitions to design landmark public buildings in Copenhagen such as the Royal Danish Theatre (1872–1874 with architect Ove Petersen (1830–1892)) and the National Gallery (1889–1896 with architect Georg E.W. Møller). He also designed Queen Louise Bridge (1885) and from 1868 he was Tivoli's architect. As with many historicist architects, posterity was a harsh judge of Vilhelm Dahlerup's work, which was described as "a frivolous masquerade of different styles". Yet several of Dahlerup's buildings also point to the future by demonstrating his interest in new materials and construction methods. His buildings gave Copenhagen the metropolitan character of Vienna, Berlin, Paris and London.

Osvald Rosendahl Langballe was a carpenter's apprentice certified by Copenhagen Technical College before applying to the Royal Danish Academy of Fine Arts' school of architecture in 1876 where he graduated in 1882. During his time as a student he worked for Ferdinand Meldahl, also on Frederik's Church in Copenhagen from 1879 to 1881. He then worked for Ludvig Fenger (1833–1905) before being hired by Vilhelm Dahlerup in 1892. He was the on-site architect for the first three-wing building of the Glyptotek inaugurated in 1897, and was also in charge of the construction of the Winter Garden from 1905 to 1906. After Dahlerup's death he became the Glyptotek's architectural advisor. Projects in his own name include St Anne's School and Amager School (1902–1903) in Copenhagen, as well as state schools and factory buildings in the city. With their wealth of detail, use of genuine materials and quality of craftmanship his buildings demonstrate the contemporary dominance of Danish National Romanticism.

Hack Kampmann
(1856–1920)

Hack Kampmann was one of Denmark's leading architects when he started to work on the Glyptotek for the brewer Carl Jacobsen. He studied at the Royal Danish Academy of Fine Arts' school of architecture in Copenhagen from 1873 to 1878, where his professor was the architect Hans J. Holm (1835–1916). It was through Holm that Kampmann became interested in historical Danish buildings, an interest that can clearly be traced in his architecture. He returned to the academy in 1908, where alongside running his own architectural firm he was a professor until 1918. He started a new class at the academy focussing on traditional Danish building culture, including village churches and cottages. His teaching at the academy had a major impact on the development of Danish architecture in the 20th century.

Hack Kampmann became widely known in Denmark when he designed the Viborg Archive, completed in 1891. The following year he was appointed Royal Inspector of Listed State Buildings in Northern Jutland, a position he held until 1920. It was during his period of office that he made some of his most famous and distinctive buildings, many of them in Aarhus. His work in the city included the first building of the National Library (1902), later the Danish National Business Archive and now the city court. He also designed Aarhus Theatre (1900), Aarhus Custom House (1897), Marselisborg Palace (1902) and his family home Villa Kampen (1902). Most of these are now listed buildings.

Even though he spent a lot of time in Jutland at the end of the 19th century, he also had assignments in Copenhagen, including working for Carl and Ottilia Jacobsen. He designed their new villa at the Carlsberg brewery complex in Valby in 1890 after the demolition of their previous home, an old farm called Bakkegården. In the years that followed he also designed an extension to the villa to house the first Glyptotek (1895).

One of Hack Kampmann's last assignments in 1918 was a new police headquarters in Copenhagen. He died before he could complete the building. This was left to his son Hans Jørgen Kampmann and fellow architects Anton Frederiksen, Holger Jacobsen and Aage Rafn. The new headquarters were inaugurated in 1924.

Hack Kampmann had a major influence on the role of Danish National Romanticism and later Neo-Classicism in Danish architecture. His work is characterised by clear forms and an extensive use of decorative elements, usually references to the function of the building or symbols such as the use of hops in a floor mosaic at the Glyptotek to symbolise Carl Jacobsen's brewing business.

Carl Harild (1868–1932)

Valdemar Fabricius Hansen (1866–1953)

Carl Harild was one of Hack Kampmann's key members of staff during the construction of the Glyptotek, and from 1919 – the year before Kampmann's death – the Glyptotek's architect. From the beginning of the 1920s he also worked at the Carlsberg brewery complex in Valby, designing new buildings and extending others. His most famous works here were the mineral-water factory (1920–1927) and the boiler house (1925–1926) which combined traditional craftmanship with new techniques and materials.

Harild completed his apprenticeship as a mason in 1886, and from 1888 to 1896 attended classes at the Royal Danish Academy of Fine Arts' school of architecture. As well as being the on-site architect at the Glyptotek, he was part of the team behind Aarhus Theatre (1897–1900) and Aarhus Custom House (1895–1897). Harild's buildings were heavily influenced by the time he spent working for Kampmann. His first buildings were rich in decorative detail, whereas later buildings were dominated by the simple lines of classicism. One of Harild's main architectural achievements is Egelund House (1915–1917) where the main building is Danish manorial baroque in style and the remaining buildings are inspired by the contemporary Arts & Crafts movement.

The museum garden at the Glyptotek is the result of a collaboration between Hack Kampmann, landscape architect Edvard Glæsel and Valdemar Fabricius Hansen, the City of Copenhagen's head gardener. After completing his apprenticeship as a gardener, Valdemar Fabricius Hansen worked in Germany for several years before continuing his education at the Royal Veterinary and Agricultural College in Copenhagen where he graduated in 1896. From 1901–1907 he was a self-employed landscape gardener in Frederiksberg before being hired as a departmental gardener by the City of Copenhagen in 1907. He was the city's head gardener from 1919 to 1936. In addition to the museum garden at the Glyptotek his landscaping projects included Lersø Park (1910–1913), Christianshavn Ramparts (1916–1927), the grounds of National Gallery of Denmark (1916–1920), Classen Park (1925–1926), Enghave Park (1927–1929) and Nørrebro Park (1933–1934).

He also landscaped private gardens, for example the garden of a villa at 40 Bakkekammen in Holbæk designed by Ivar Bentsen and Marius Pedersen (1917).

Henning Larsen
(1925–2013)

Henning Larsen is widely held to be one of Denmark's most outstanding architects. When his firm won the competition to build an extension to the Glyptotek (1994–1996) in 1992 it was one of the leading contemporary architecture firms in the country with a back catalogue including cultural institutions, schools and office blocks.

After graduating from high school in 1943 Henning Larsen became a carpenter's apprentice. He received his technical certificate from Copenhagen Technical School in 1948, then applied to the Royal Danish Academy of Fine Arts' school of architecture, where he qualified as an architect in 1952. During his time at the academy he studied in London and Boston and worked for the Danish architect Arne Jacobsen (1902–1971). In 1959 he founded the firm that was to become Henning Larsen Architects. Today the firm – now called Henning Larsen – has become an international name with assignments worldwide. Henning Larsen also founded the gallery and journal *Skala* with articles on the latest international architecture and design written by some of Denmark's leading architects.

Among the firm's most acclaimed work are the Danish Embassy (1986–1988) and Ministry of Foreign Affairs (1982–1984) in Riyadh. The latter's blend of traditional Middle Eastern and contemporary Western architecture made the firm an international name. Also worthy of mention are Copenhagen Business School (1985–1989), the apartment complex Dalgas Have (1989–1991), Gentofte Library (1984–1985) and Copenhagen Opera House (2004). With architecture characterised by a strong eye for detail on many scales Henning Larsen's firm has won numerous competitions in Denmark and abroad.

In 1992 the Glyptotek announced a competition to design a new building in the east courtyard of Hack Kampmann's building. Henning Larsen was one of four architecture firms invited to submit proposals. The proposal by Henning Larsen Architects was the only one without physical contact between the extension and Kampmann's building. Instead, the new building was surrounded by atriums on all sides, creating an autonomous monolithic block with a skylit passage functioning as a stairwell.

Henning Larsen's architecture has a clear sense of the contemporary zeitgeist expressed in a distinct, personal style balancing functionality, technology and aesthetic form. Whilst different in style his buildings have stood the test of time. One of their hallmark features has always been incorporating natural light as an architectural element in new and original ways. This can also be seen in Larsen's extension to the Glyptotek, one of the most photographed features of the museum's architecture.

The Authors

Ida Carnera (b. 1991). Architect from the Royal Danish Academy – Architecture, Design, Conservation. Has specialised in urban development with a range of Danish architecture firms. She is the great-grandchild of the Italians Ida Odorico Carnera and Andrea Carnera who feature in the article she has co-written and whose mosaic company in Copenhagen her grandfather and his two brothers ran for many years. In 2011 she went to Italy to study language and culture. Her connection to Friuli is kept alive by spending holidays in the ancestral family home in the village of Sequals.

Jesper Christiansen (b. 1955). Visual artist from the Royal Danish Academy of Fine Arts where he studied from 1981–1988 and was professor from 2002–2008. His solo exhibitions include *Jesper Christiansen at Ordrupgaard*, Ordrupgaard 2023, *The Four Seasons*, Odsherred Art Museum, Skovgaard Museum and La Maison du Danemark, Paris 2022, *Forbillede*, GL STRAND 2018, *Go Back*, Brandts, Odense 2013 and *Time Passes for Virginia Woolf*, Galerie Mikael Andersen 2012. His work has also featured in group shows including *At the Table: People, Food & Nature Morte*, Fuglsang and Skagen Museum 2017 and *Veranda*, GL STRAND 2007.

Vibeke Cristofoli (b. 1930). Studied at the Royal Danish Academy of Music and was married to the late opera conductor Francesco Cristofoli, whose father Giovanni Cristofoli emigrated to Denmark from Sequals with his father and four brothers, all mosaicists. She has worked at the mosaic studio Arte Musiva in Milan and studied at Scuola Mosaicisti del Friuli in Spilimbergo. One of her two daughters lives in the family's old house in the village of Sequals.

Claus Grønne (b. 1957). MPhil in classical archaeology from the University of Copenhagen in 1986. Formerly employed by the Glyptotek and since 2014 archivist at New Carlsberg Foundation responsible for the digitalisation projects *Carl Jacobsen's Correspondence Archive* and *Sources in Danish Art History*. His specialised fields are Roman art and the history of the Glyptotek and New Carlsberg Foundation.

Gertrud Hvidberg-Hansen (b. 1968). MA in art history and French from Aarhus University. Director of the Glyptotek since 2020 where she has been responsible for developing research on the museum's architecture and its dissemination. She also has a key role in coordinating the planned renovation and restoration of the Glyptotek's listed buildings. She is the former director of Faaborg Museum, where she published books and articles on the museum's architecture including *I Skøn forening – Faaborg Museum 1915*, (2015). She has also contributed to a range of research projects and publications focussing on Danish and European art in the 19th and 20th centuries from a transdisciplinary perspective.

Sophia Kalkau (b. 1960). Visual artist from the Royal Danish Academy of Fine Arts and MA in art theory. She has held solo exhibitions at Kunsten Museum of Modern Art Aalborg (*Stoffet og Ægget*, 2019), Maison du Danemark, Paris (*Part of the Mill*, 2009), Kunsthallen Brandts, Odense (*Dog and Die*, 2008), the Glyptotek, Copenhagen (*Fra Hexa til Vasen*, 2007). She has received awards and accolades including the Carl Nielsen and Anne Marie Carl-Nielsen Honorary Award (2010), the Eckersberg Medal (2008) and the Astrid Noack Grant (2004).

Birgitte Kleis (b. 1963). Architect from the Royal Danish Academy – Architecture, Design, Conservation. As well as running the company arkitekturformidling.dk, she is a member of the editorial staff at the BYG-ERFA Foundation and former editor of the Danish journal *Arkitekten*. She has written articles and books on architecture focussing on the conservation and renovation of built cultural heritage. She has also written books on social housing, including *Bakkehusene* (with Jannie Rosenberg Bendsen, Strandberg Publishing 2022), *Tingbjerg – vision og virkelighed* (with Jannie Rosenberg Bendsen and Mogens A. Morgen, Strandberg Publishing 2020) and

Bellahøj – Fortællinger om en bebyggelse (with Jannie Rosenberg Bendsen and Mogens A. Morgen, Strandberg Publishing 2015).

Peter Thule Kristensen (b. 1966) is professor of architecture and the history of interiors at the Royal Danish Academy – Architecture, Design, Conservation and an associate of the Centre for Privacy Studies at the University of Copenhagen. He graduated as an architect from the Royal Danish Academy in 1994, where he took his PhD (2014). He also holds a MPhil from Aarhus University (2014). He is the author of monographs on Danish architects such as Lauritz de Thurah, Gottlieb Bindesbøll, Vilhelm Klein and Svenn Eske Kristensen.

Kristina Lindholdt (b. 1990). MSc in Conservation specialising in monumental art and architectural paint research. Conservator at Københavns Konservator and teaching assistant at the Royal Danish Academy – Architecture, Design, Conservation.

Kasper Lægring (b. 1980) holds an MPhil in art history and a PhD in architecture from Aarhus University where he is currently a New Carlsberg Foundation scholar. He was awarded the University of Copenhagen's Gold Medal for his work on Berlin museums and monuments and is the recipient of numerous grants and scholarships, including from the Fulbright Program and the Danish Arts Foundation. He has published extensively in peer-reviewed journals, is a reviewer for the journal *Arkitekten*, and has contributed to anthologies including *A Cultural History of the Avant-Garde in the Nordic Countries* (Brill 2022) and *The Contested Territory of Architectural Theory* (Routledge 2022).

Mogens A. Morgen (b. 1959). Architect from the Royal Danish Academy – Architecture, Design, Conservation. Professor in architectural heritage at Aarhus School of Architecture. Former partner at Korshagen Architects and head of department at the Danish Agency for Culture and Palaces responsible for building preservation and the restoration and modernisation of the Finn Juhl Chamber at the UN's' headquarters in New York. He is the author of numerous books, head of the NORDMAK Nordic Master Programme in Architectural Heritage programme and president of ICOMOS Denmark.

Jakob Ingemann Parby (b. 1973). PhD and curator at the Museum of Copenhagen with a long list of exhibitions, books and articles on urban history, museology, public infrastructure, literature, migration and identity to his name. Head curator of the Museum of Copenhagen's permanent exhibition which opened in 2020, and head of several research projects on urban history, most recently *Sound, Language and the Making of Urban Space* (2020–2024). Author of *Den grænseløse by*, the 6th volume in the series *København og historien* on the development of Copenhagen from 1850 to 1920 (Gads Forlag 2022).

Anne Jonstrup Simonsen (b. 1973). MSc in Conservation specialising in architectural paint research and the restoration of art and architecture. Since 2002 director of Københavns Konservator, a company specialising in the investigation, analysis and restoration of historical interiors.

Martin Søberg (b. 1978). MPhil in art history, PhD in architecture and senior lecturer at the Royal Danish Academy – Architecture, Design, Conservation. His research on the history and theory of architecture focusses on artistic processes in architecture and the relationship between concept and creation. Martin Søberg is the editor of several books on architecture and art and author of the monograph Kay *Fisker: Works and Ideas in Danish Modern Architecture* (2021). He is the president of the Danish Association of Art Critics.

Eva Tind (b. 1974). Novelist and architect from the Royal Danish Academy – Architecture, Design, Conservation. Author of novels including *Astas skygge* (Gyldendal 2016), *Ophav* (Gyldendal 2019), *Kvinden der samlede verden* (Gyldendal 2021) and most recently *Citronbjerget* (Gyldendal 2023).

Sif Itona Westerberg (b. 1985). Visual artist from the Royal Danish Academy of Fine Arts. She has held solo exhibitions at ARoS (DK), Tranen (DK) and Gether Contemporary (DK). Her work has also featured in group shows at ARKEN Museum of Modern Art (DK), Malmö Konstmuseum (SE), Gianni Manhattan (AT), Den Frie Centre of Contemporary Art (DK), Museum of Religious Art (DK), Bornholm Art Museum (DK), Oluf Høst Museum (DK), Cassandra Cassandra (CA), PERMM Museum of Contemporary Art (RU) and Latvian Centre for Contemporary Art (LV).

Name Index

**The Architecture
of the Glyptotek**

© Ny Carlsberg Glyptotek,
Strandberg Publishing,
the authors and artists

Published in connection
with the exhibition

*Behind the Façade – Discover
the Architecture of the Glyptotek*
Ny Carlsberg Glyptotek
17 May – 19 November 2023

Idea and concept: Gertrud
    Hvidberg-Hansen
Project management: Kasper
    Riisholt
Editors: Jannie Rosenberg Bendsen
    and Anna Manly
Image editors: Jannie Rosenberg
    Bendsen and Anna Manly
Publisher's editor: Dorte Einarsson
Translation: Jane Rowley
Graphic design: Studio Atlant
Cover photo: Anders Sune Berg
Font: Berthe og Proto Grotesk
Paper: 130g Munken Lynx
Image processing, printing and
    binding: Narayana Press
Print run: 1.400
Printed in Denmark 2023
1st edition, 1st print run
ISBN: 978-87-94102-92-6

The articles by Kasper Lægring,
Jakob Ingemann Parby, Martin
Søberg and Peter Thule Kristensen
have all been peer reviewed.

PEER
REVIEWED

The certification means that an
independent peer of at least PhD
level has made a written assessment
approving the article's academic
standard and the originality of the
contribution it makes to its field.

Published by:

Ny Carlsberg Glyptotek
Dantes Plads 7
DK-1556 Copenhagen V
www.glyptoteket.dk

Strandberg Publishing
Gammel Mønt 14
DK-1117 Copenhagen K
www.strandbergpublishing.dk

The publication and the exhibition
are supported by:

AUGUSTINUS FONDEN
STIFTET 25. MARTS 1942

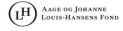

AAGE OG JOHANNE
LOUIS-HANSENS FOND

NY
CARLSBERG
FONDET
NEW CARLSBERG FOUNDATION

KNUD HØJGAARDS FOND

DREYERSFOND

Illustrations:

All photography by Anders Sune
Berg with the exception of:

Archivio Ente Friuli nel Mondo: 301.
Archivio Scuola Mosaicisti del
    Friuli: 302–303, 320.
Collection Artedia/Bridgeman
    Images: 304.
Carlsberg Archive: 43(t), 54, 59.
Carl Jacobsen's Correspondence
    Archive: 44(l), 47(l), 50(r), 57.
Copenhagen City Archives: 44(r),
    48(t), 163–165, 169(b).
Danish Art Library: 43(b), 45, 53,
    58, 74, 94, 133, 136–137, 139–142,
    149–152, 199–200, 206, 274–275,
    280, 307.
Frederik Riise, Museum of
    Copenhagen: 198.
Henning Larsen: 107(t).
Illustration from Andreas Bruun,
    *Jens Vilhem Dahlerups Liv og
    Virksomhed*, 1907: 194.
Illustration from Carl Jacobsen,
    *Ny Carlsberg Glyptoteks
    Tilblivelse*, 1906: 41.
Illustration from *Hver 8. Dag*, 1906:
    308, 336.
J. Henschel, Museum of
    Copenhagen: 159.
Jeanne Kornum/Scanpix: 338.
Johan Gottlieb Julius Aagaard,
    Museum of Copenhagen: 305.
Københavns Konservator: 273, 277,
    279, 282, 286(l), 287.
Ny Carlsberg Glyptotek: 42, 46,
    49–50, 56, 60(t), 70, 72, 82, 95,
    144–148, 221–224, 226–228,
    230–236, 238, 283, 316–317.
Oluf W. Jørgensen, Museum of
    Copenhagen: 160.
Oluf W. Jørgensen (Chr. Neuhaus
    Eftf.), Museum of Copenhagen:
    201.
Peter Elfelt, Museum of
    Copenhagen: 172.
Pierpaolo Mittica: 300.
Ritzau Scanpix/akg-images: 134.
Ritzau Scanpix/akg-images/
    brandstaetter images: 196.
Royal Danish Library: 17, 47(r), 48(b),
    51, 52, 334.
Royal Danish Library, photo: Holger
    Damgaard: 285.
Unknown photographer, Museum
    of Copenhagen: 162, 167–168,
    170.
Unknown photographer, Niels
    Ludvig Mariboe's Collection,
    Museum of Copenhagen: 161(b).
© Unknown photographer/VISDA
    2023: 276.